Bad Night

Colors by Val Staf

CRIMINAL VOL. 4: BAD NIGHT. Contains material originally published in magazine form as CRIMINAL Vol 2 #4-7. First printing 2009. ISBN# 978-0-7851-3228-8
Published by MARVEL PUBLISHING. INC., a subsidiary of MARVEL ENTERTAINMENT INC. OFFICE OF PUBLICATION: 417 5th Avenue, New York, NY 10016.

Printed in Canada.

10 9 8 7 6 5 4 3 2 1

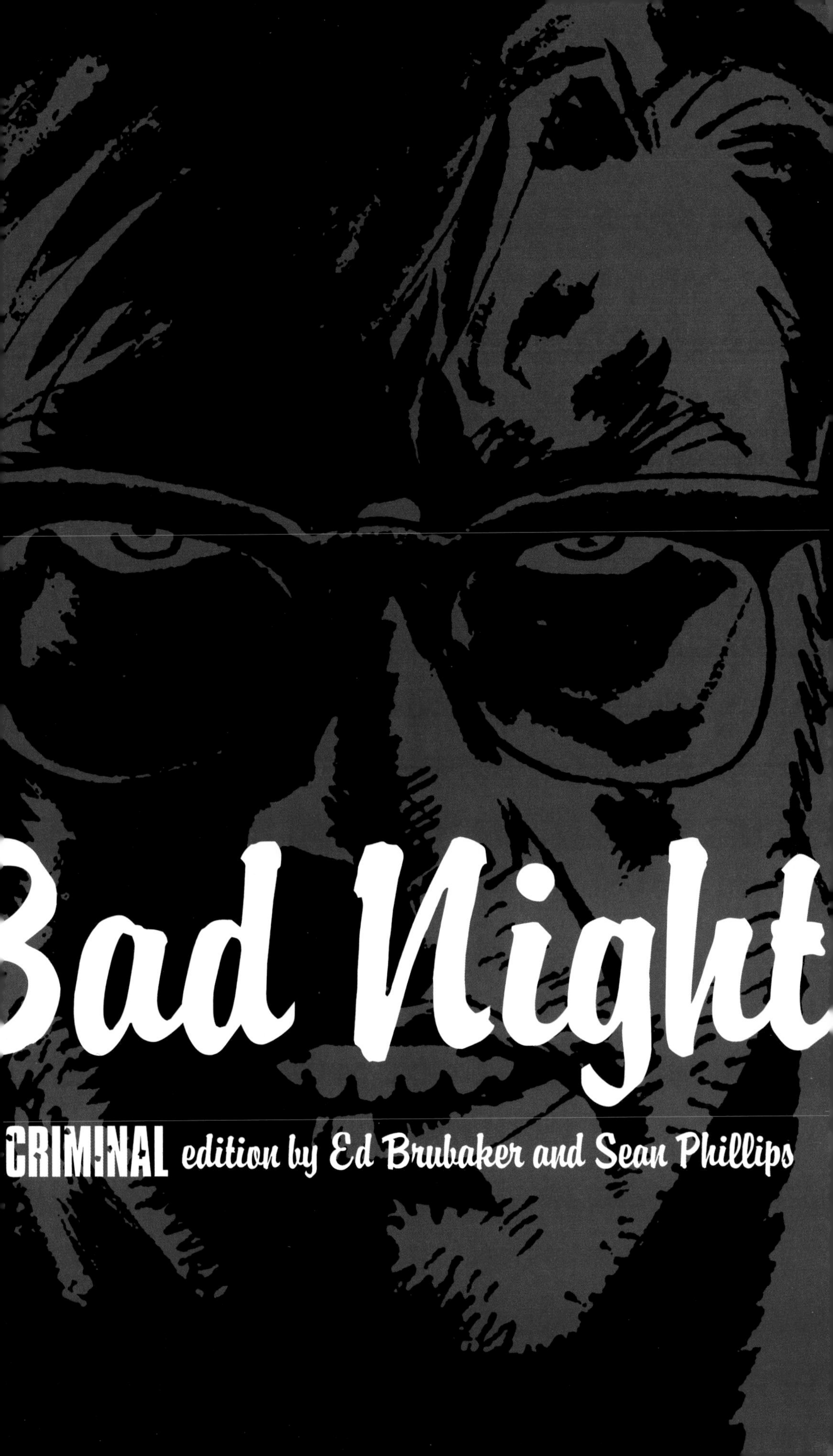

Bad Night

CRIMINAL edition by Ed Brubaker and Sean Phillips

Introduction

I fess up.

I came late to comics.

Call it a word blindness or just a total immersion in mystery.

Ed Brubaker changed that and magnificently so.

He has converted me into an avid, if not indeed rabid addict of the medium.

The man is a genius.

I say that without reservation.

I think I've maybe used that term twice in me whole life.

He deserves it, doubly so.

They want someone to write the next Batman and do the impossible, make it as compelling and dark

without Heath Ledger, call Ed.

Call him now!

He is a comics mastermind.

When Tom Cruise and Sam Raimi are trying to procure his '**Sleeper**'.............you know this guy has

some serious talent.

Check out

Criminal

Sleeper

Incognito

And behold.

Imagination writ mega.

Hunter S. Thompson would have loved this guy.

Ralph Steadman must surely hate his guts.

Bad Night spins a delicious deadly story of lies, murder and .....ah.....to tell more would be a sin.

Remember Jacob K's life in the forthcoming book, torn asunder by one chance meeting on............you

guessed it, a very bad night.

as won numerous awards

Best Writer Eisner twice

an Eisner for the **Criminal** monthly series.

ous kudos.

the wanna-be's who'd sell their dark soul to even be nominated.

like any real true artist, he has soul.

tioned off his 2 year Captain America Notebook to raise funds for a fellow artist's medical bills.

w that's class.

ne time cartoonist, and a writer since the early 90's, he has been translated round the world.

ugh his primary work now is in comics, he has also written screenplays.

ere the hell does he get the time?

d still produce the meisterwork that is Bad Night.

cover alone should adorn every bookcase in the land.

at truly adds to the magic of Ed is the sheer wondrous artistry of Sean Phillips. Ed works with him

DeNiro and Scorsese, two artists in perfect harmony.

rely, in truth, envy other writers, they do their gig and good luck with that.

vy the hell out of Ed.

d Bad Night and you'll see why.

n Bruen

of the most acclaimed voices in modern crime fiction, Ken Bruen was a finalist for the Edgar, and the Private

Writers of America presented him with the Shamus Award for the Best Novel for THE GUARDS. His novel

NDON BOULEVARD is currently in development as a film, to be adapted by William Monahan (the Departed).

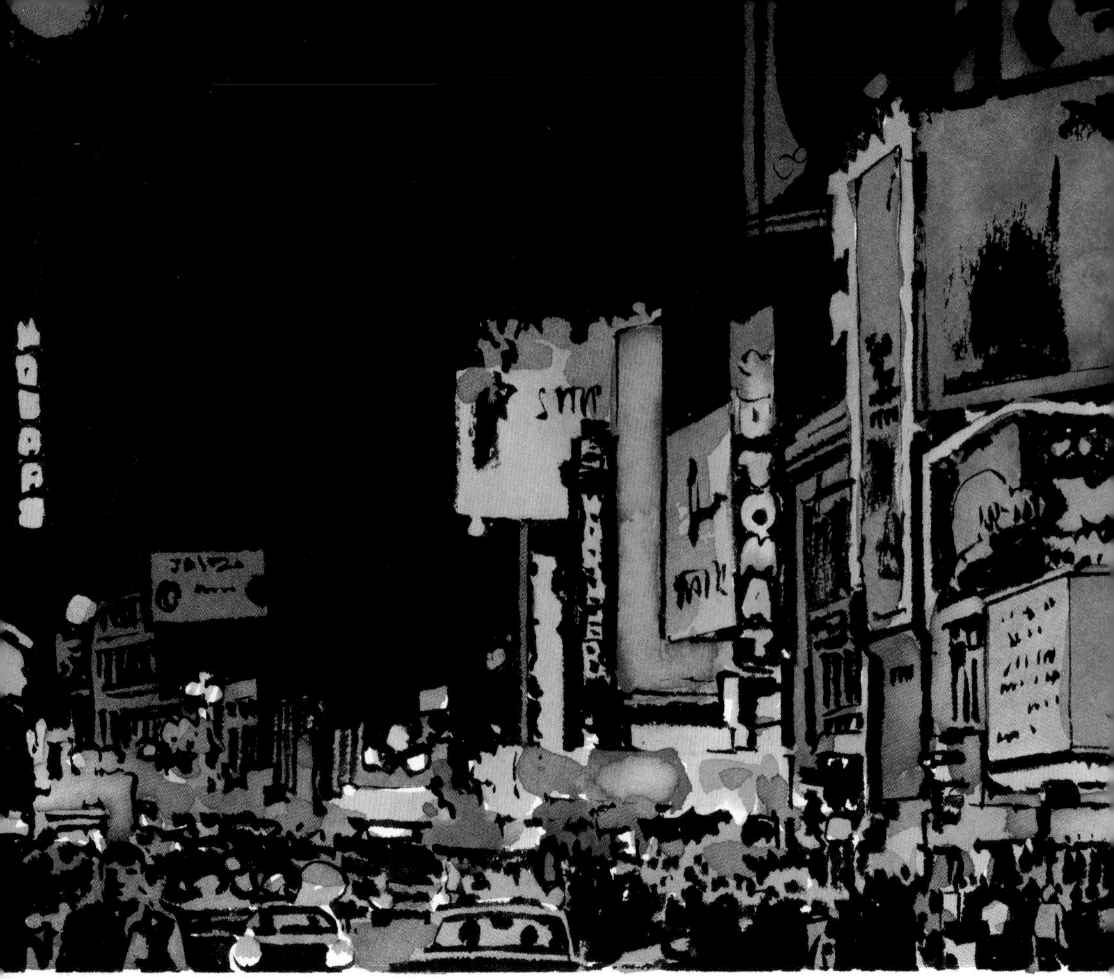

For Melanie.
Well, they're all for you, really,
but this one more than most.

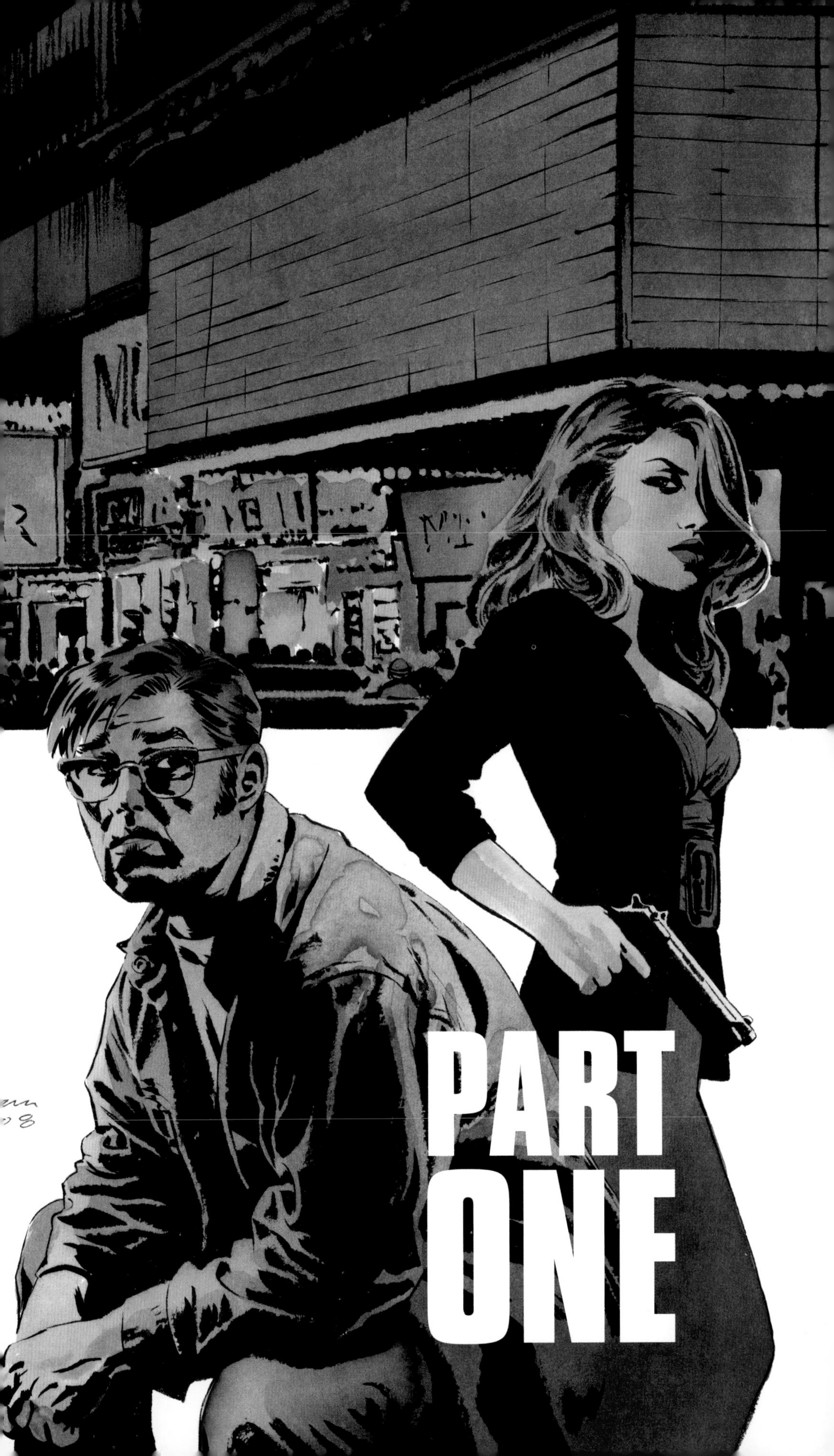
PART
ONE

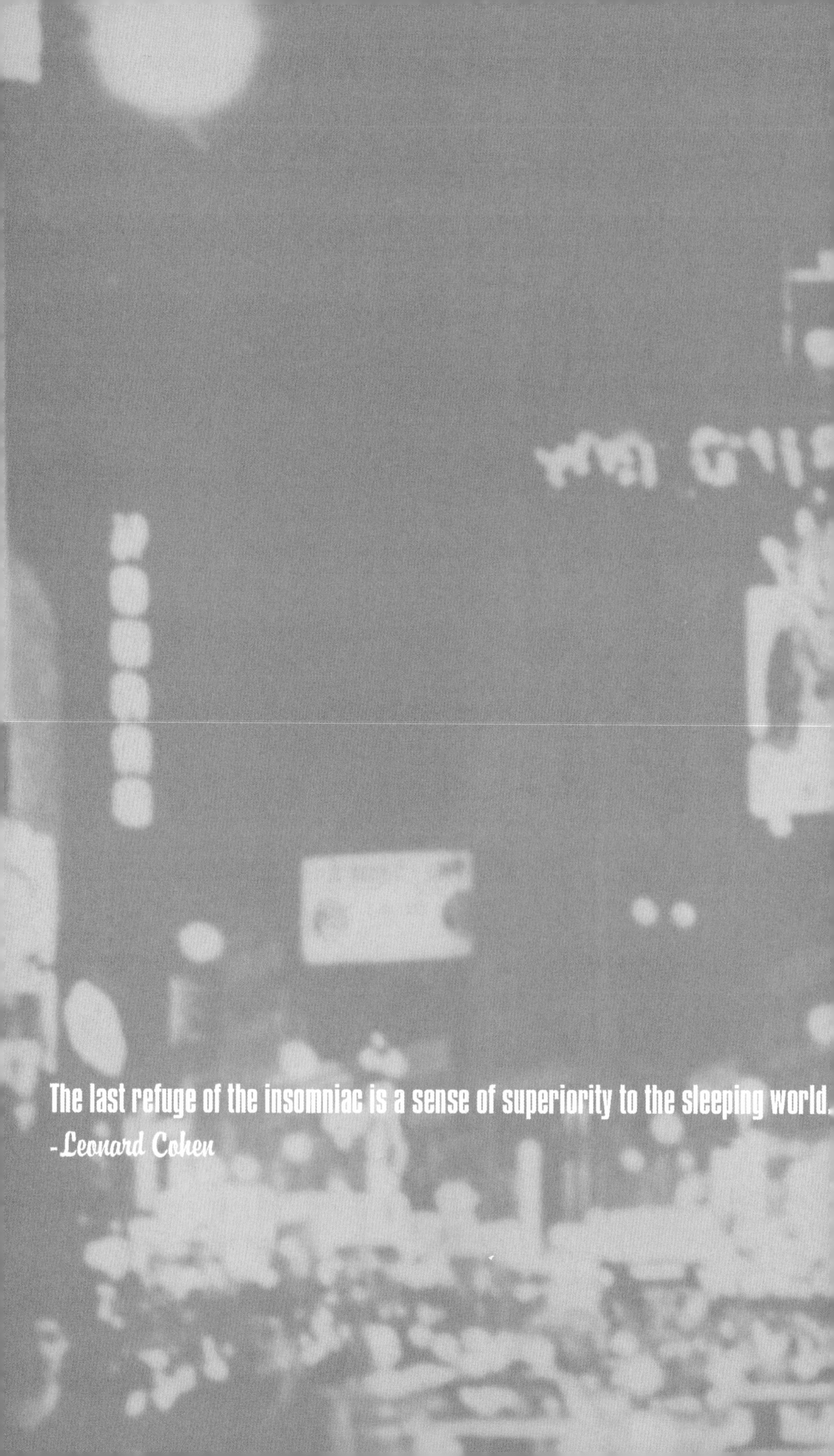

The last refuge of the insomniac is a sense of superiority to the sleeping world.

-*Leonard Cohen*

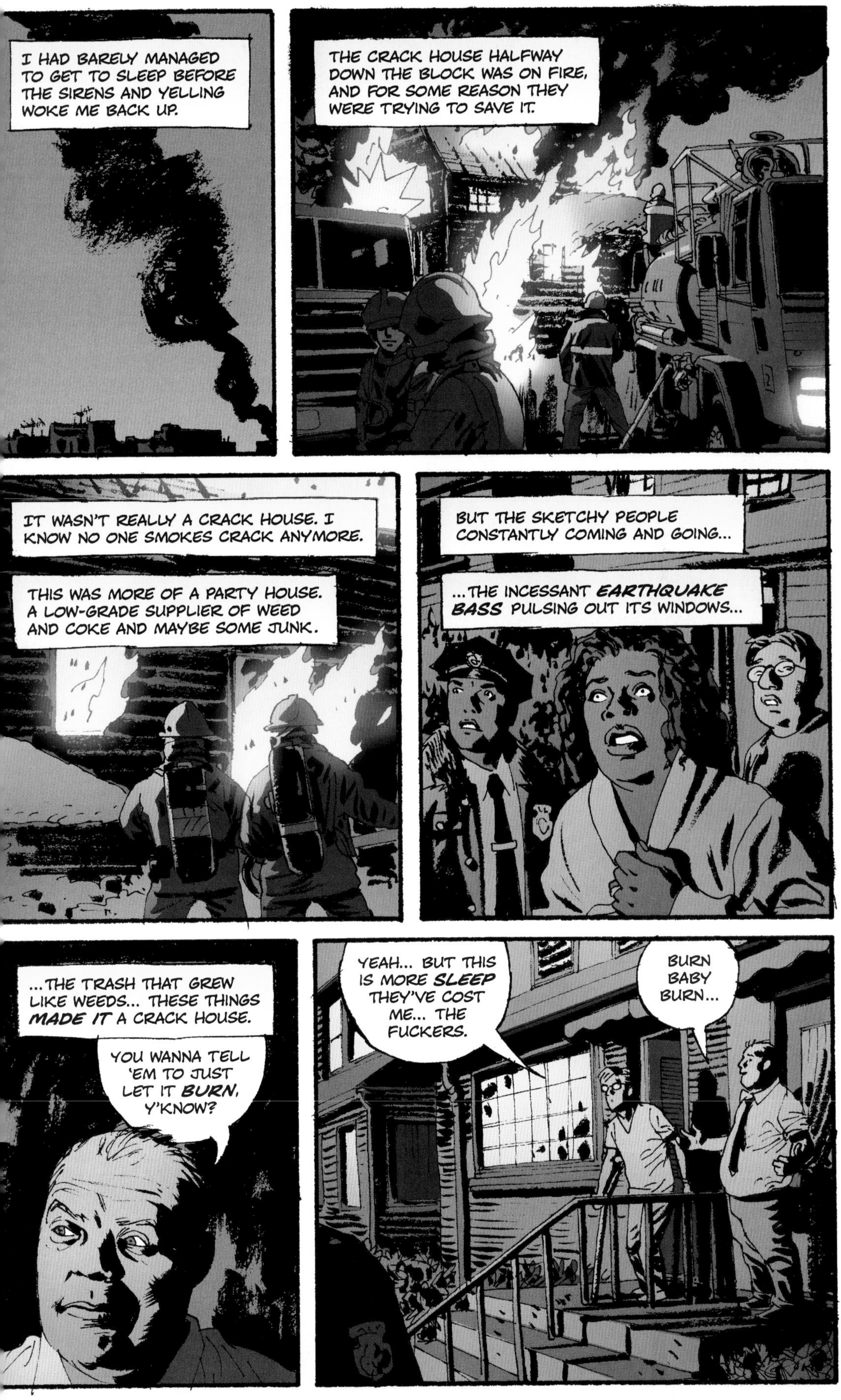
I HAD BARELY MANAGED TO GET TO SLEEP BEFORE THE SIRENS AND YELLING WOKE ME BACK UP.
THE CRACK HOUSE HALFWAY DOWN THE BLOCK WAS ON FIRE, AND FOR SOME REASON THEY WERE TRYING TO SAVE IT.
IT WASN'T REALLY A CRACK HOUSE. I KNOW NO ONE SMOKES CRACK ANYMORE.
THIS WAS MORE OF A PARTY HOUSE. A LOW-GRADE SUPPLIER OF WEED AND COKE AND MAYBE SOME JUNK.
BUT THE SKETCHY PEOPLE CONSTANTLY COMING AND GOING...
...THE INCESSANT EARTHQUAKE BASS PULSING OUT ITS WINDOWS...
...THE TRASH THAT GREW LIKE WEEDS... THESE THINGS MADE IT A CRACK HOUSE.
YOU WANNA TELL 'EM TO JUST LET IT BURN, Y'KNOW?
YEAH... BUT THIS IS MORE SLEEP THEY'VE COST ME... THE FUCKERS.
BURN BABY BURN...

I'M USUALLY GOOD FOR AT LEAST FOUR HOURS SLEEP A NIGHT, AT SOME POINT BETWEEN SIX A.M. AND NOON.

IF I GET THAT, I'M OKAY. I CAN FOCUS.

DAYS WHERE I DON'T, DAYS LIKE THIS ONE... I CALL THOSE LOST DAYS.

I'M BEYOND TIRED, BUT MY MIND WON'T SHUT UP.

...AND THEN... BUT... WAIT, WHAT WAS...?

WORK IS A WASTE ON THESE DAYS, BUT I DO IT ANYWAY, OUT OF HABIT.

OKAY, FRANK... IT'S JUST YOU AN' ME...

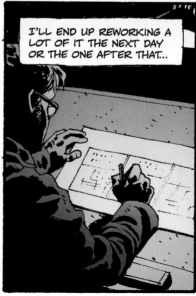

I'LL END UP REWORKING A LOT OF IT THE NEXT DAY OR THE ONE AFTER THAT...

...BUT AT LEAST I HAVE THE ILLUSION OF PROGRESS.

...ED TELL ME OR HOW LONG...

I'M AFRAID I DON'T UNDERSTAND?

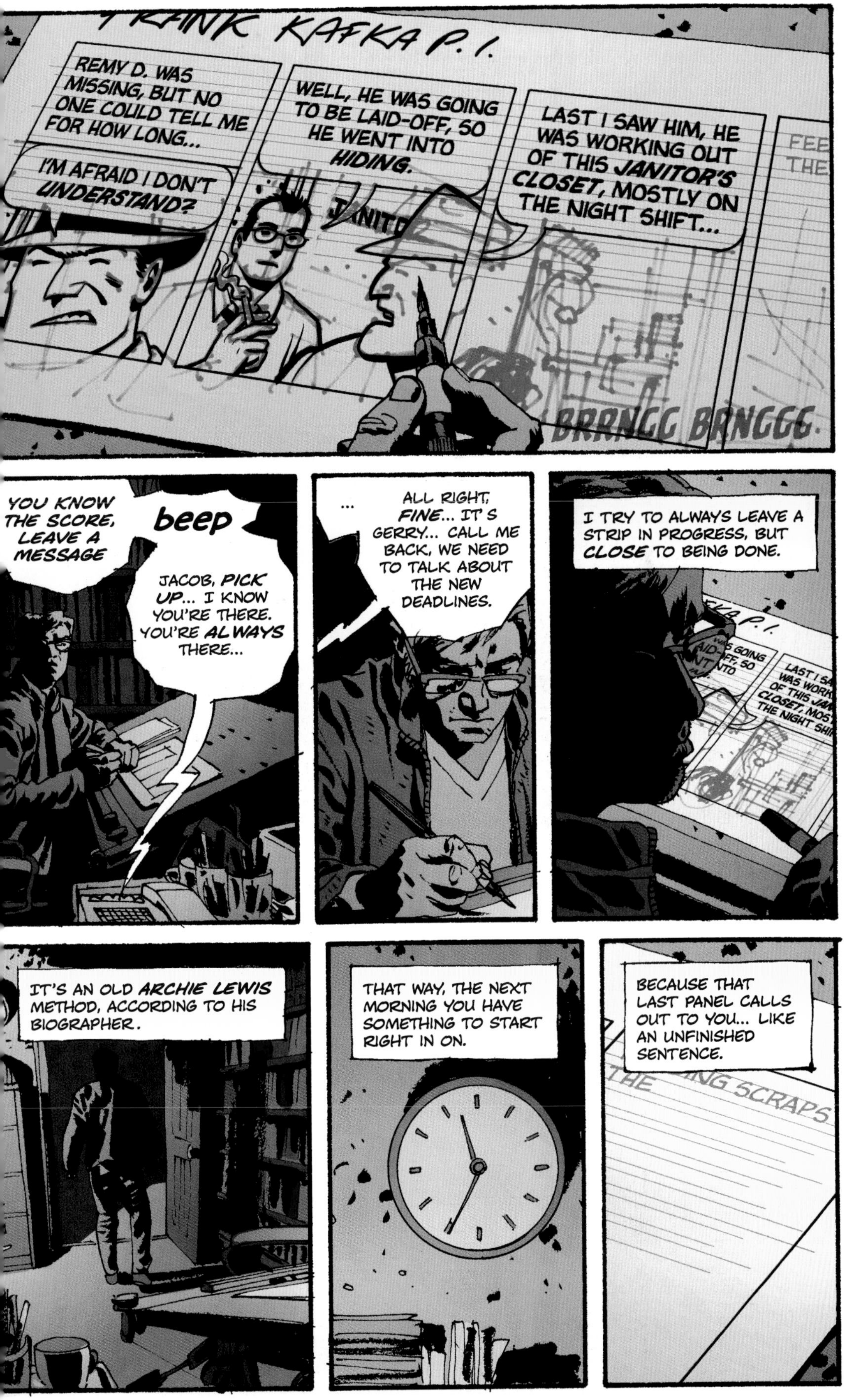

FRANK KAFKA P.I.
REMY D. WAS MISSING, BUT NO ONE COULD TELL ME FOR HOW LONG...
I'M AFRAID I DON'T UNDERSTAND?
WELL, HE WAS GOING TO BE LAID-OFF, SO HE WENT INTO HIDING.
LAST I SAW HIM, HE WAS WORKING OUT OF THIS JANITOR'S CLOSET, MOSTLY ON THE NIGHT SHIFT...
BRRNGG BRNGGG.
YOU KNOW THE SCORE, LEAVE A MESSAGE
beep
JACOB, PICK UP... I KNOW YOU'RE THERE. YOU'RE ALWAYS THERE...
... ALL RIGHT, FINE... IT'S GERRY... CALL ME BACK, WE NEED TO TALK ABOUT THE NEW DEADLINES.
I TRY TO ALWAYS LEAVE A STRIP IN PROGRESS, BUT CLOSE TO BEING DONE.
IT'S AN OLD ARCHIE LEWIS METHOD, ACCORDING TO HIS BIOGRAPHER.
THAT WAY, THE NEXT MORNING YOU HAVE SOMETHING TO START RIGHT IN ON.
BECAUSE THAT LAST PANEL CALLS OUT TO YOU... LIKE AN UNFINISHED SENTENCE.

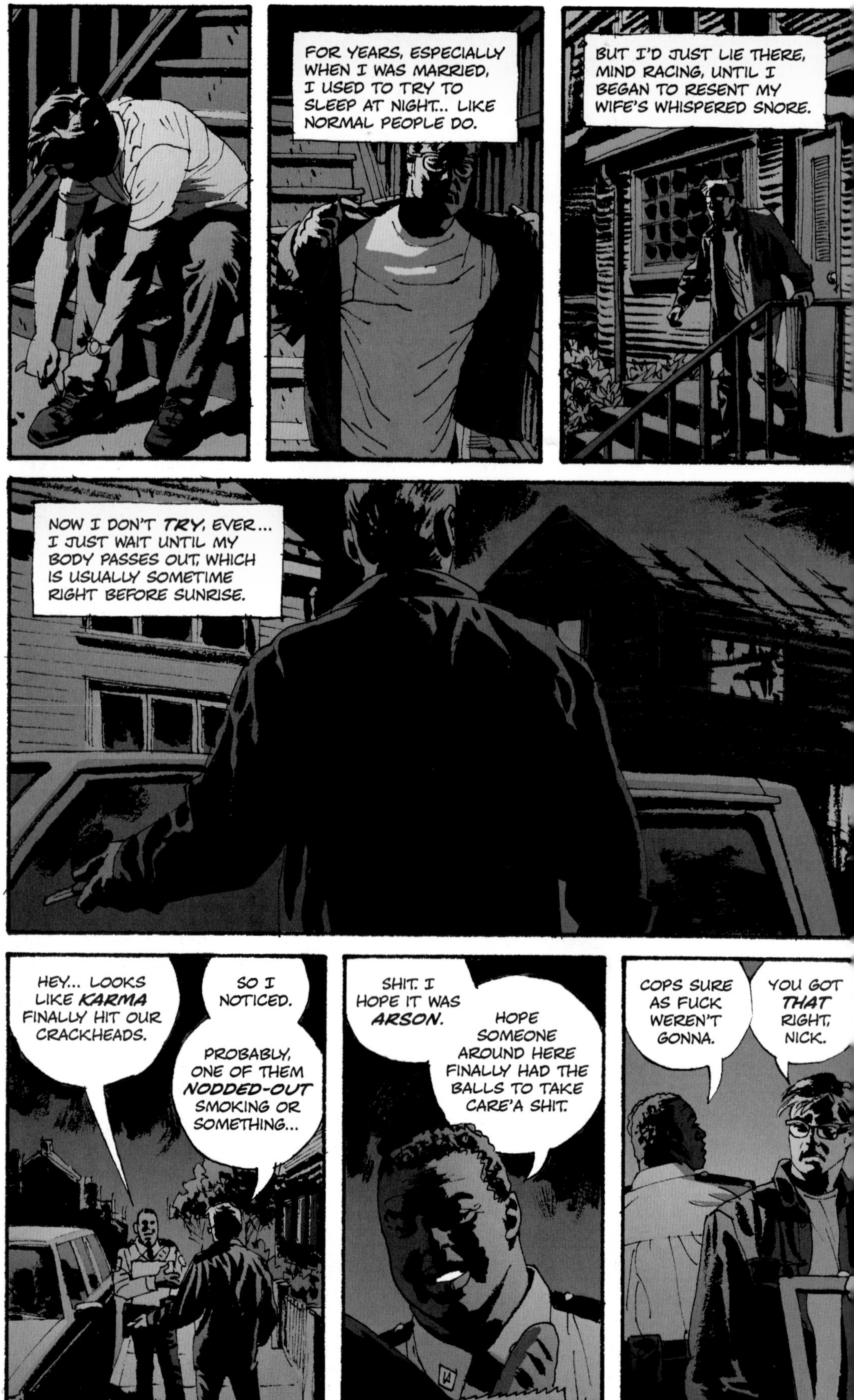
FOR YEARS, ESPECIALLY WHEN I WAS MARRIED, I USED TO TRY TO SLEEP AT NIGHT... LIKE NORMAL PEOPLE DO.
BUT I'D JUST LIE THERE, MIND RACING, UNTIL I BEGAN TO RESENT MY WIFE'S WHISPERED SNORE.
NOW I DON'T TRY, EVER... I JUST WAIT UNTIL MY BODY PASSES OUT, WHICH IS USUALLY SOMETIME RIGHT BEFORE SUNRISE.
HEY... LOOKS LIKE KARMA FINALLY HIT OUR CRACKHEADS.
SO I NOTICED.
PROBABLY, ONE OF THEM NODDED-OUT SMOKING OR SOMETHING...
SHIT. I HOPE IT WAS ARSON.
HOPE SOMEONE AROUND HERE FINALLY HAD THE BALLS TO TAKE CARE'A SHIT.
COPS SURE AS FUCK WEREN'T GONNA.
YOU GOT THAT RIGHT, NICK.

I'M NOT ONE OF THOSE "I JUST LOVE THE CITY AT NIGHT" KIND OF PEOPLE.

I GO OUT INTO IT BECAUSE I HAVE TO. IT'S PART OF THE *NOT-SLEEPING SICKNESS*, I GUESS.

AS A BONUS, MY PHYSICAL THERAPIST SAYS THE WALKING AROUND I DO IS HELPING.

IT'S GOTTEN ME OFF THE CRUTCHES, FOR THE MOST PART.

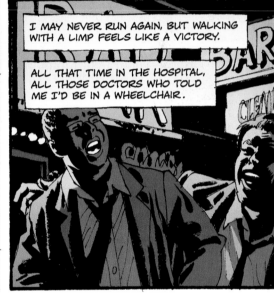

I MAY NEVER RUN AGAIN, BUT WALKING WITH A LIMP FEELS LIKE A VICTORY.

ALL THAT TIME IN THE HOSPITAL, ALL THOSE DOCTORS WHO TOLD ME I'D BE IN A WHEELCHAIR.

THE CITY FELT DIFFERENT TO ME WHEN I GOT OUT, AND EVEN NOW, IT STILL DOES.

THEY'RE THE SAME STREETS I'VE KNOWN MY WHOLE LIFE... THE SAME NOISE, THE SAME JUNKIES AND BUMS AND LUNATICS...

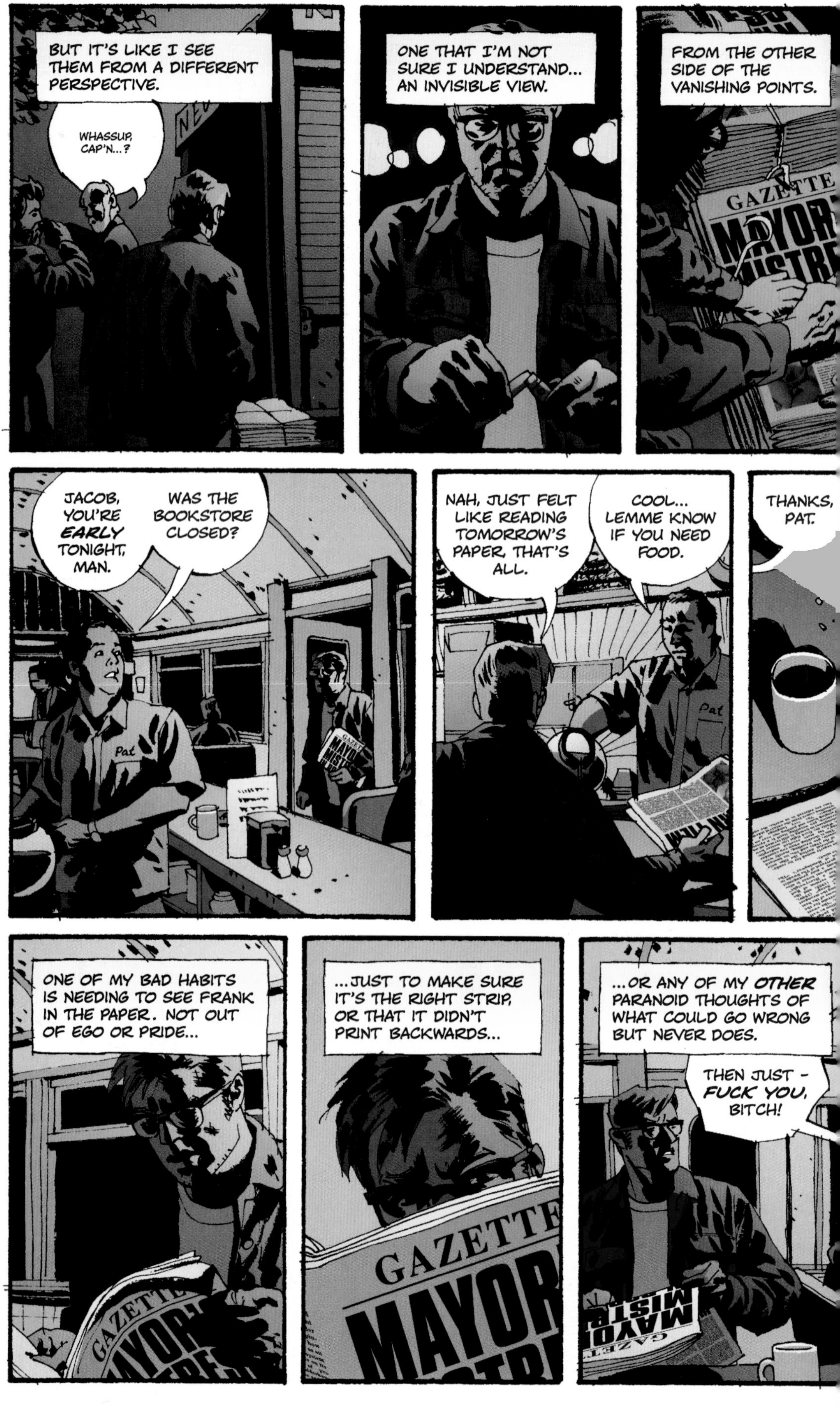
BUT IT'S LIKE I SEE THEM FROM A DIFFERENT PERSPECTIVE.
WHASSUP, CAP'N...?
ONE THAT I'M NOT SURE I UNDERSTAND... AN INVISIBLE VIEW.
FROM THE OTHER SIDE OF THE VANISHING POINTS.
GAZETTE
JACOB, YOU'RE EARLY TONIGHT, MAN.
WAS THE BOOKSTORE CLOSED?
Pat
NAH, JUST FELT LIKE READING TOMORROW'S PAPER, THAT'S ALL.
COOL... LEMME KNOW IF YOU NEED FOOD.
Pat
THANKS, PAT.
ONE OF MY BAD HABITS IS NEEDING TO SEE FRANK IN THE PAPER. NOT OUT OF EGO OR PRIDE...
...JUST TO MAKE SURE IT'S THE RIGHT STRIP, OR THAT IT DIDN'T PRINT BACKWARDS...
GAZETTE
MAYOR
...OR ANY OF MY OTHER PARANOID THOUGHTS OF WHAT COULD GO WRONG BUT NEVER DOES.
THEN JUST - FUCK YOU, BITCH!

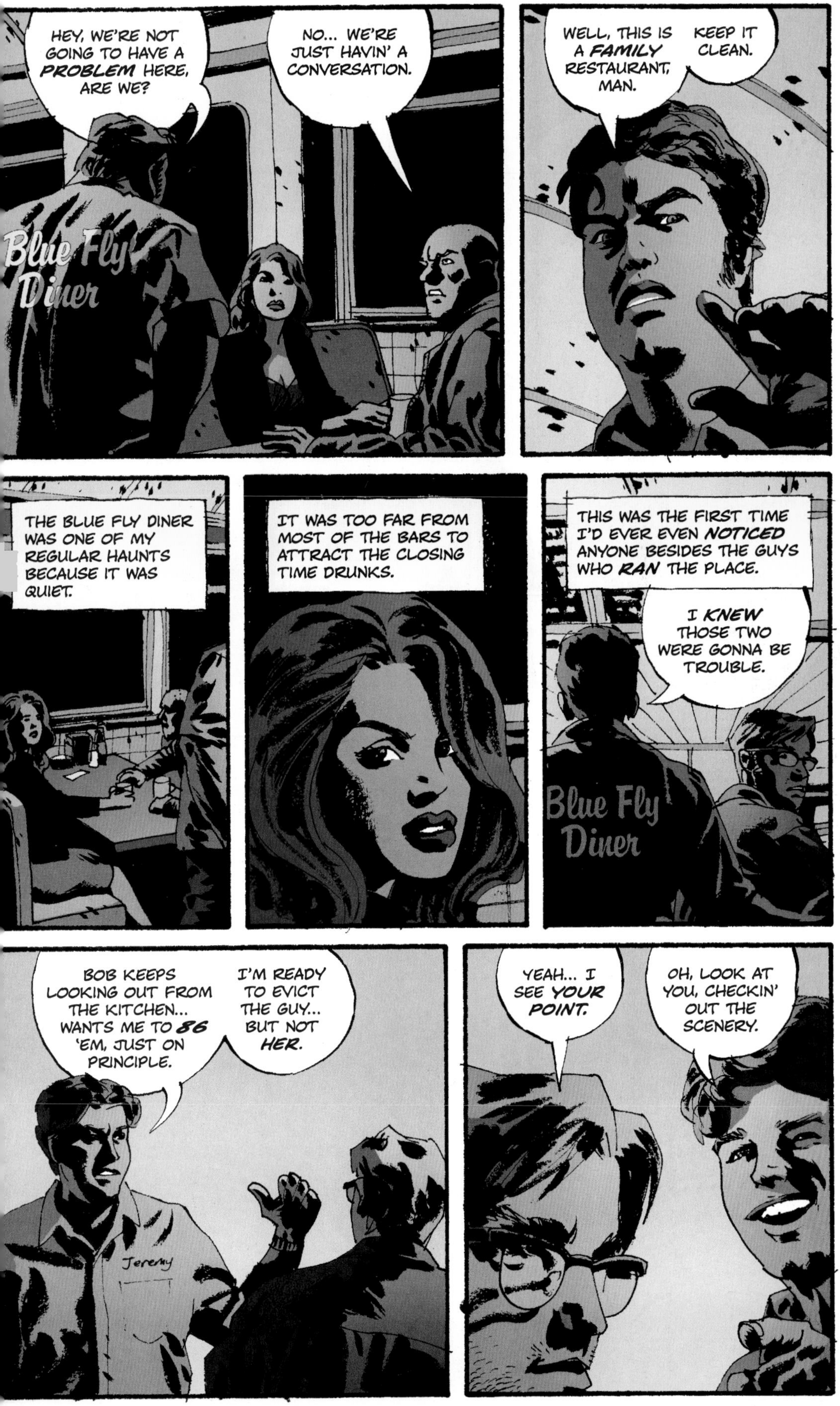
HEY, WE'RE NOT GOING TO HAVE A PROBLEM HERE, ARE WE?
NO... WE'RE JUST HAVIN' A CONVERSATION.
Blue Fly Diner
WELL, THIS IS A FAMILY RESTAURANT, MAN.
KEEP IT CLEAN.
THE BLUE FLY DINER WAS ONE OF MY REGULAR HAUNTS BECAUSE IT WAS QUIET.
IT WAS TOO FAR FROM MOST OF THE BARS TO ATTRACT THE CLOSING TIME DRUNKS.
THIS WAS THE FIRST TIME I'D EVER EVEN NOTICED ANYONE BESIDES THE GUYS WHO RAN THE PLACE.
I KNEW THOSE TWO WERE GONNA BE TROUBLE.
Blue Fly Diner
BOB KEEPS LOOKING OUT FROM THE KITCHEN... WANTS ME TO 86 'EM, JUST ON PRINCIPLE.
I'M READY TO EVICT THE GUY... BUT NOT HER.
Jeremy
YEAH... I SEE YOUR POINT.
OH, LOOK AT YOU, CHECKIN' OUT THE SCENERY.

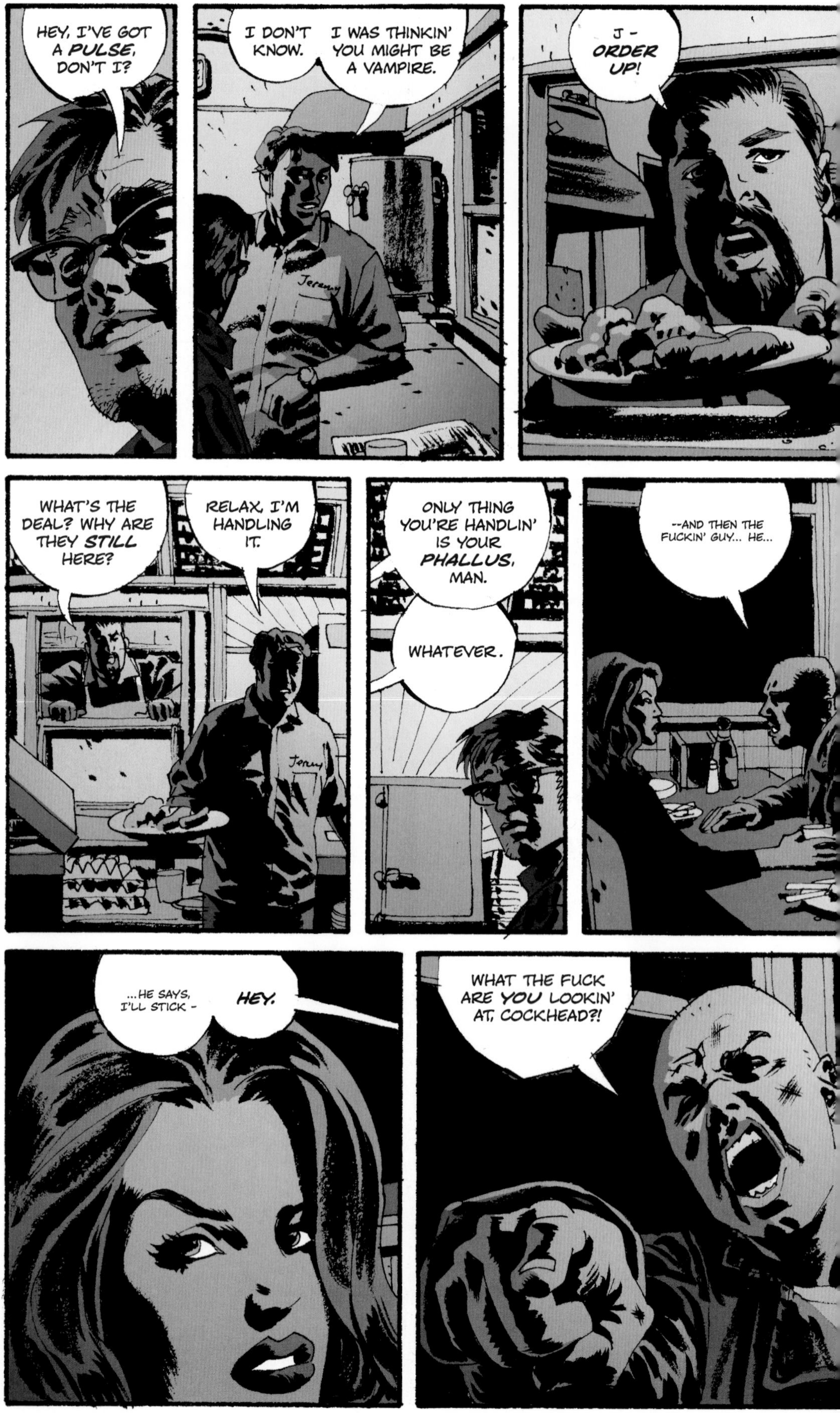
HEY, I'VE GOT A PULSE, DON'T I?
I DON'T KNOW.
I WAS THINKIN' YOU MIGHT BE A VAMPIRE.
J - ORDER UP!
WHAT'S THE DEAL? WHY ARE THEY STILL HERE?
RELAX, I'M HANDLING IT.
ONLY THING YOU'RE HANDLIN' IS YOUR PHALLUS, MAN.
WHATEVER.
--AND THEN THE FUCKIN' GUY... HE...
...HE SAYS, I'LL STICK -
HEY.
WHAT THE FUCK ARE YOU LOOKIN' AT, COCKHEAD?!

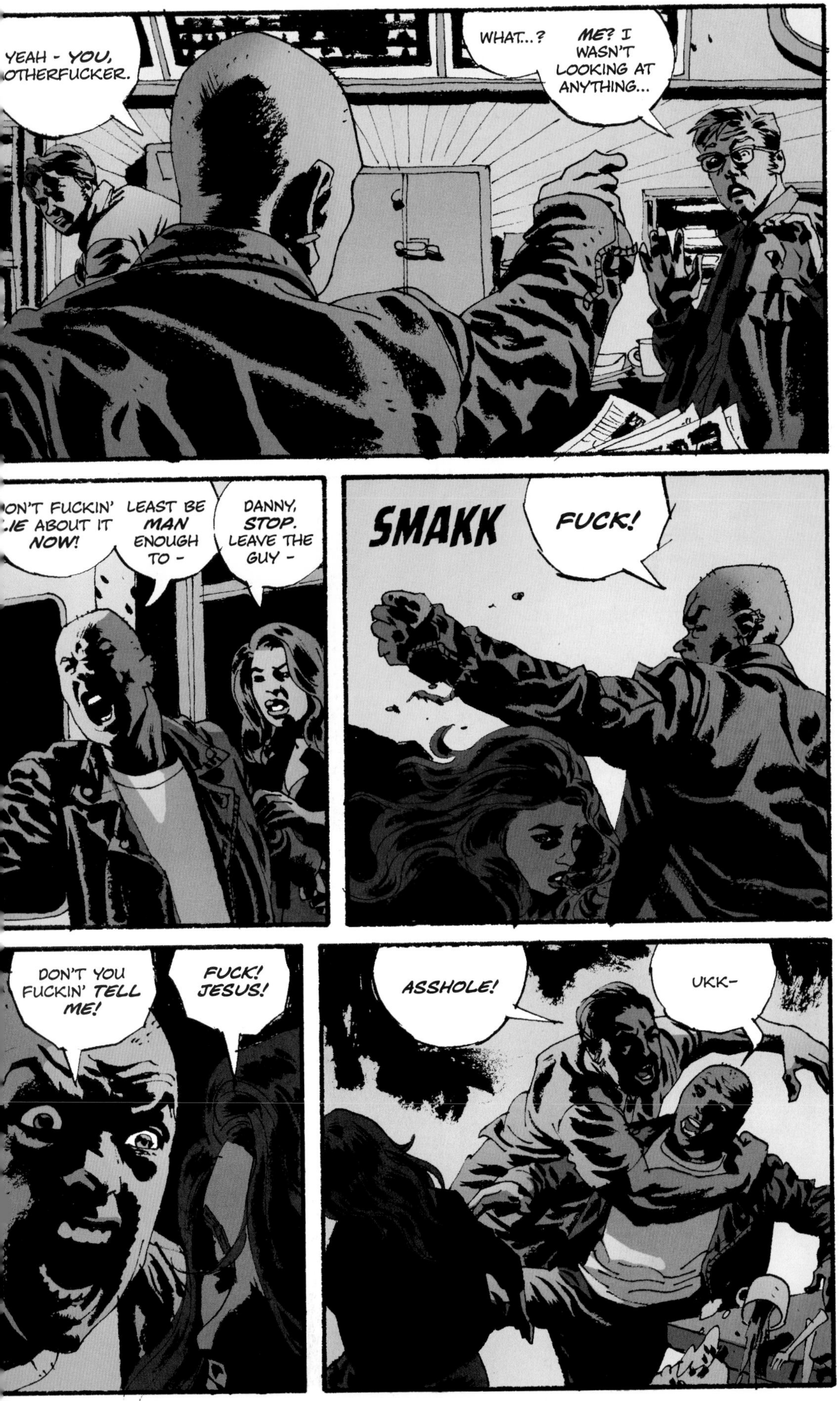
YEAH - YOU, OTHERFUCKER.
WHAT...?
ME? I WASN'T LOOKING AT ANYTHING...
ON'T FUCKIN' IE ABOUT IT NOW!
LEAST BE MAN ENOUGH TO -
DANNY, STOP. LEAVE THE GUY -
SMAKK
FUCK!
DON'T YOU FUCKIN' TELL ME!
FUCK! JESUS!
ASSHOLE!
UKK-

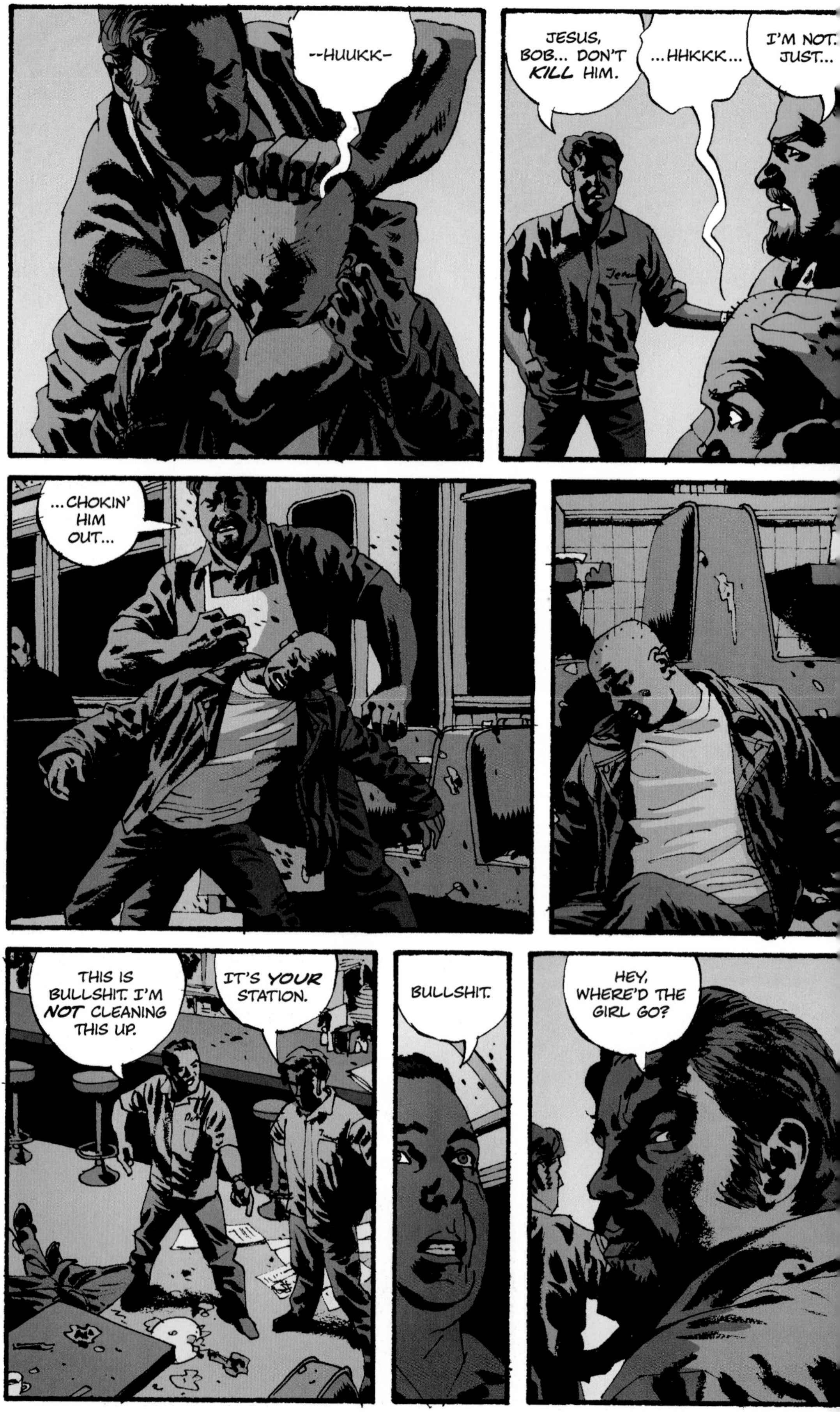
--HUUKK-
JESUS, BOB... DON'T KILL HIM.
...HHKKK...
I'M NOT. JUST...
...CHOKIN' HIM OUT...
THIS IS BULLSHIT. I'M NOT CLEANING THIS UP.
IT'S YOUR STATION.
BULLSHIT.
HEY, WHERE'D THE GIRL GO?

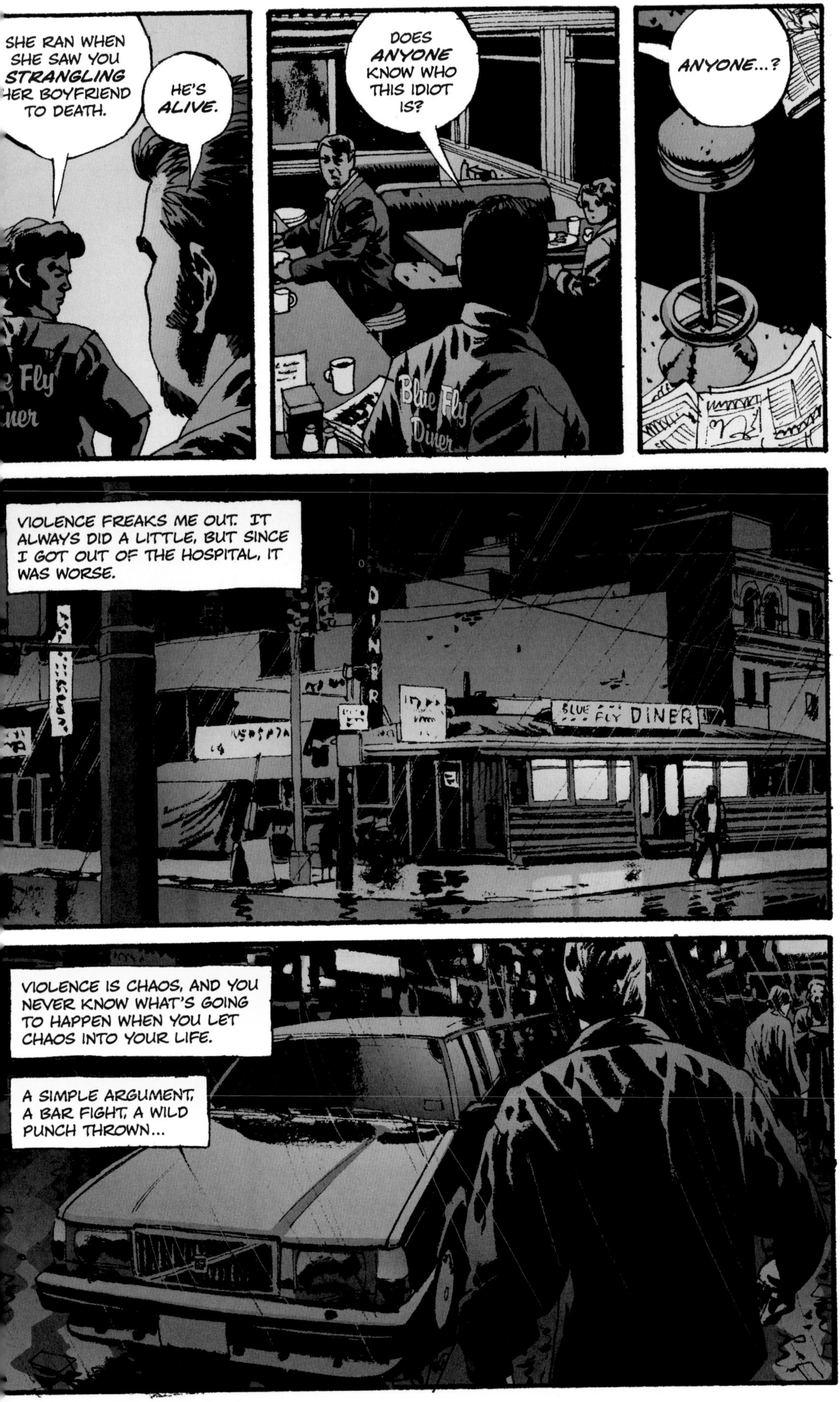
SHE RAN WHEN SHE SAW YOU STRANGLING HER BOYFRIEND TO DEATH.
HE'S ALIVE.
Blue Fly Diner
DOES ANYONE KNOW WHO THIS IDIOT IS?
Blue Fly Diner
ANYONE...?
VIOLENCE FREAKS ME OUT. IT ALWAYS DID A LITTLE, BUT SINCE I GOT OUT OF THE HOSPITAL, IT WAS WORSE.
DINER
BLUE FLY DINER
VIOLENCE IS CHAOS, AND YOU NEVER KNOW WHAT'S GOING TO HAPPEN WHEN YOU LET CHAOS INTO YOUR LIFE.
A SIMPLE ARGUMENT, A BAR FIGHT, A WILD PUNCH THROWN...

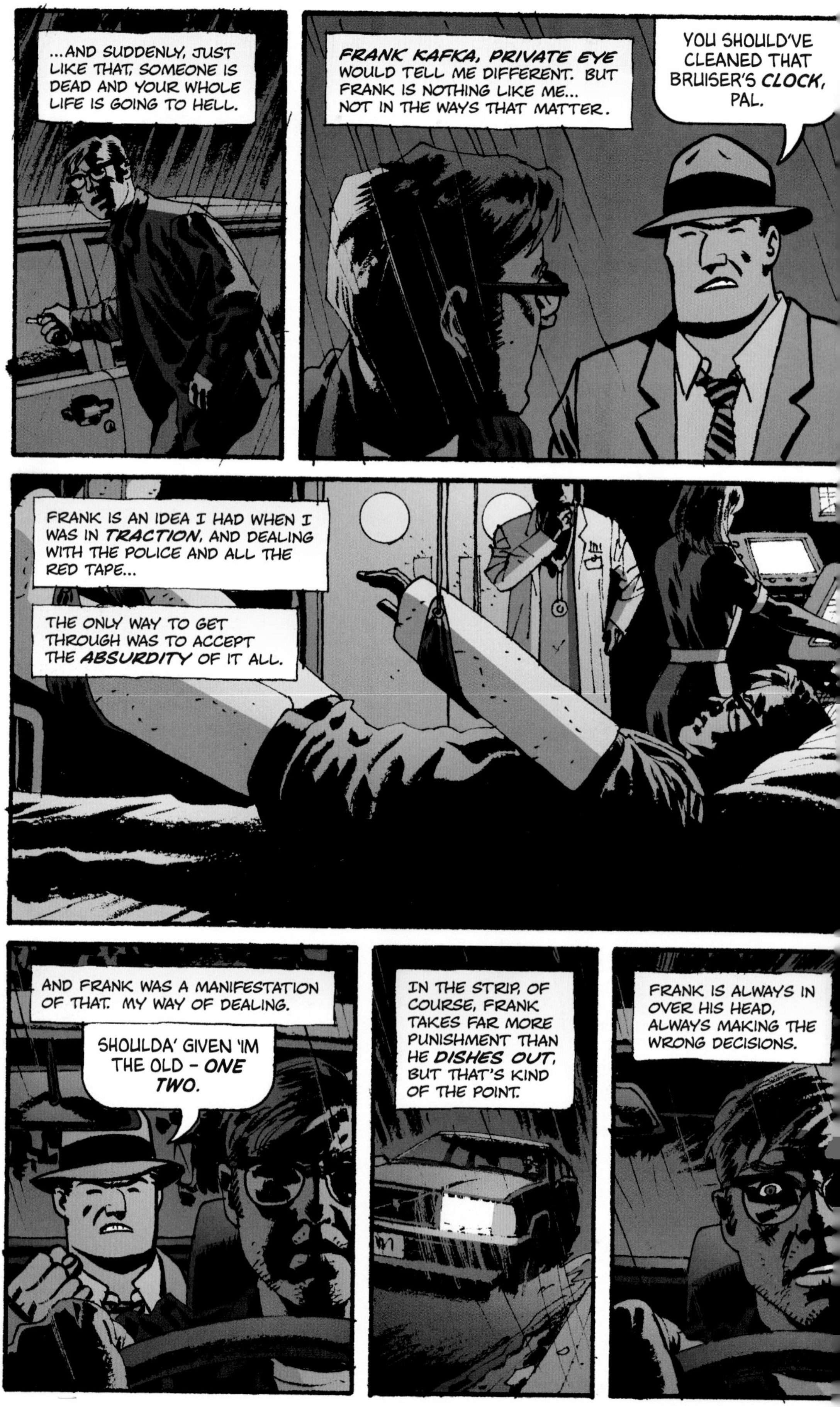

...AND SUDDENLY, JUST LIKE THAT, SOMEONE IS DEAD AND YOUR WHOLE LIFE IS GOING TO HELL.
FRANK KAFKA, PRIVATE EYE WOULD TELL ME DIFFERENT. BUT FRANK IS NOTHING LIKE ME... NOT IN THE WAYS THAT MATTER.
YOU SHOULD'VE CLEANED THAT BRUISER'S CLOCK, PAL.
FRANK IS AN IDEA I HAD WHEN I WAS IN TRACTION, AND DEALING WITH THE POLICE AND ALL THE RED TAPE...
THE ONLY WAY TO GET THROUGH WAS TO ACCEPT THE ABSURDITY OF IT ALL.
AND FRANK WAS A MANIFESTATION OF THAT. MY WAY OF DEALING.
SHOULDA' GIVEN 'IM THE OLD - ONE TWO.
IN THE STRIP, OF COURSE, FRANK TAKES FAR MORE PUNISHMENT THAN HE DISHES OUT, BUT THAT'S KIND OF THE POINT.
FRANK IS ALWAYS IN OVER HIS HEAD, ALWAYS MAKING THE WRONG DECISIONS.

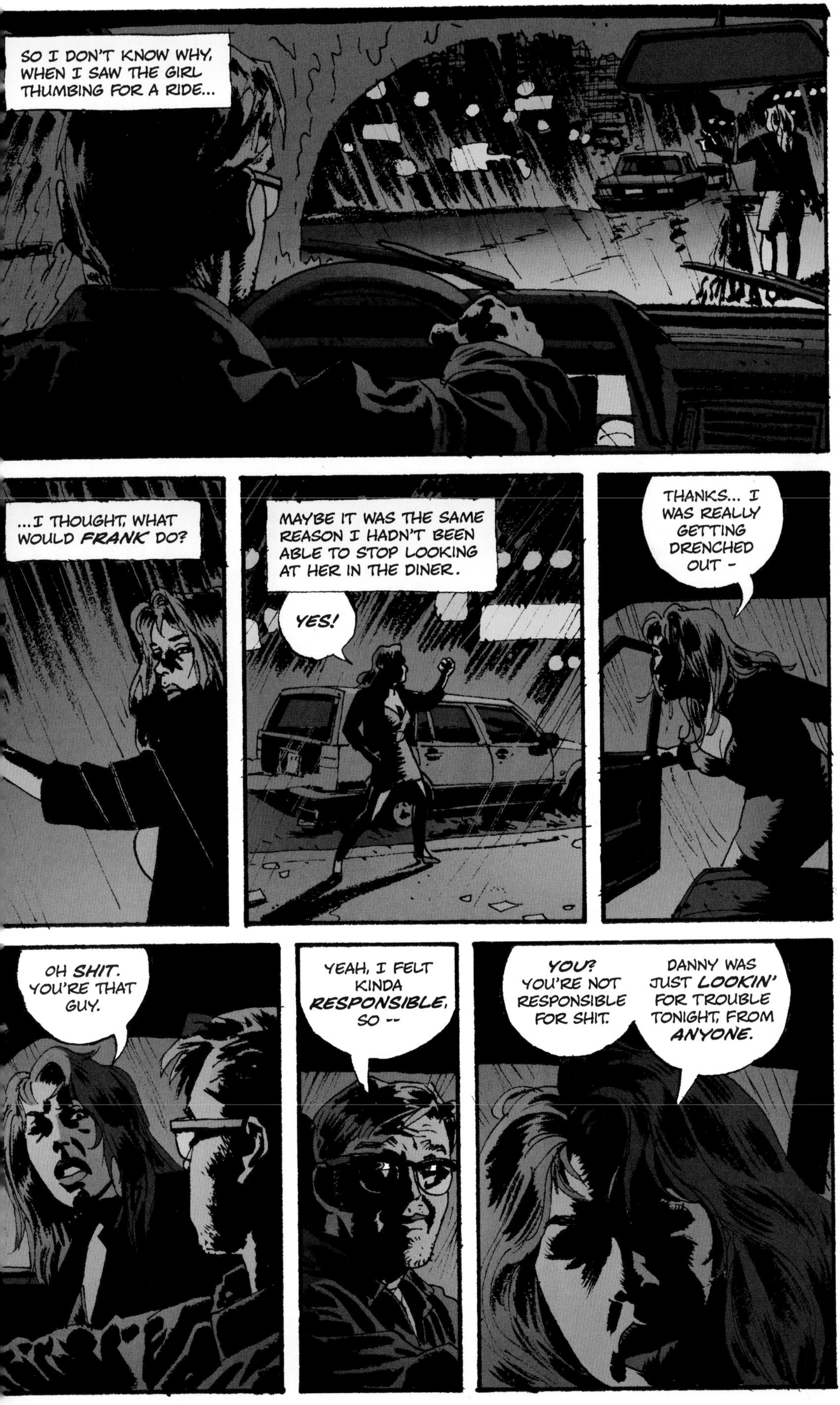
SO I DON'T KNOW WHY, WHEN I SAW THE GIRL THUMBING FOR A RIDE...
...I THOUGHT, WHAT WOULD *FRANK* DO?
MAYBE IT WAS THE SAME REASON I HADN'T BEEN ABLE TO STOP LOOKING AT HER IN THE DINER.
YES!
THANKS... I WAS REALLY GETTING DRENCHED OUT -
OH *SHIT*. YOU'RE THAT GUY.
YEAH, I FELT KINDA *RESPONSIBLE*, SO --
YOU? YOU'RE NOT RESPONSIBLE FOR SHIT.
DANNY WAS JUST *LOOKIN'* FOR TROUBLE TONIGHT, FROM *ANYONE*.

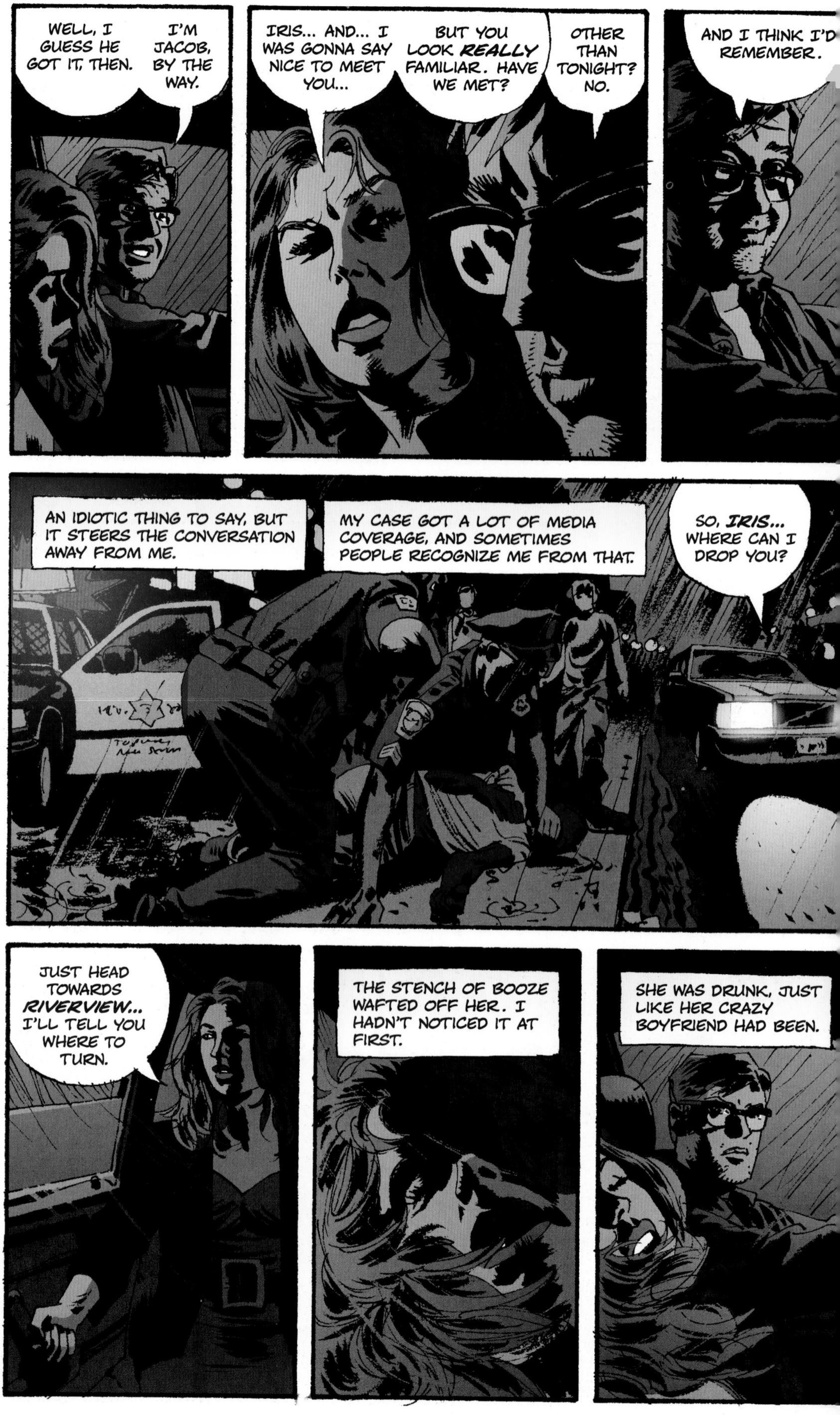
WELL, I GUESS HE GOT IT, THEN.
I'M JACOB, BY THE WAY.
IRIS... AND... I WAS GONNA SAY NICE TO MEET YOU...
BUT YOU LOOK *REALLY* FAMILIAR. HAVE WE MET?
OTHER THAN TONIGHT? NO.
AND I THINK I'D REMEMBER.
AN IDIOTIC THING TO SAY, BUT IT STEERS THE CONVERSATION AWAY FROM ME.
MY CASE GOT A LOT OF MEDIA COVERAGE, AND SOMETIMES PEOPLE RECOGNIZE ME FROM THAT.
SO, *IRIS*... WHERE CAN I DROP YOU?
JUST HEAD TOWARDS *RIVERVIEW*... I'LL TELL YOU WHERE TO TURN.
THE STENCH OF BOOZE WAFTED OFF HER. I HADN'T NOTICED IT AT FIRST.
SHE WAS DRUNK, JUST LIKE HER CRAZY BOYFRIEND HAD BEEN.

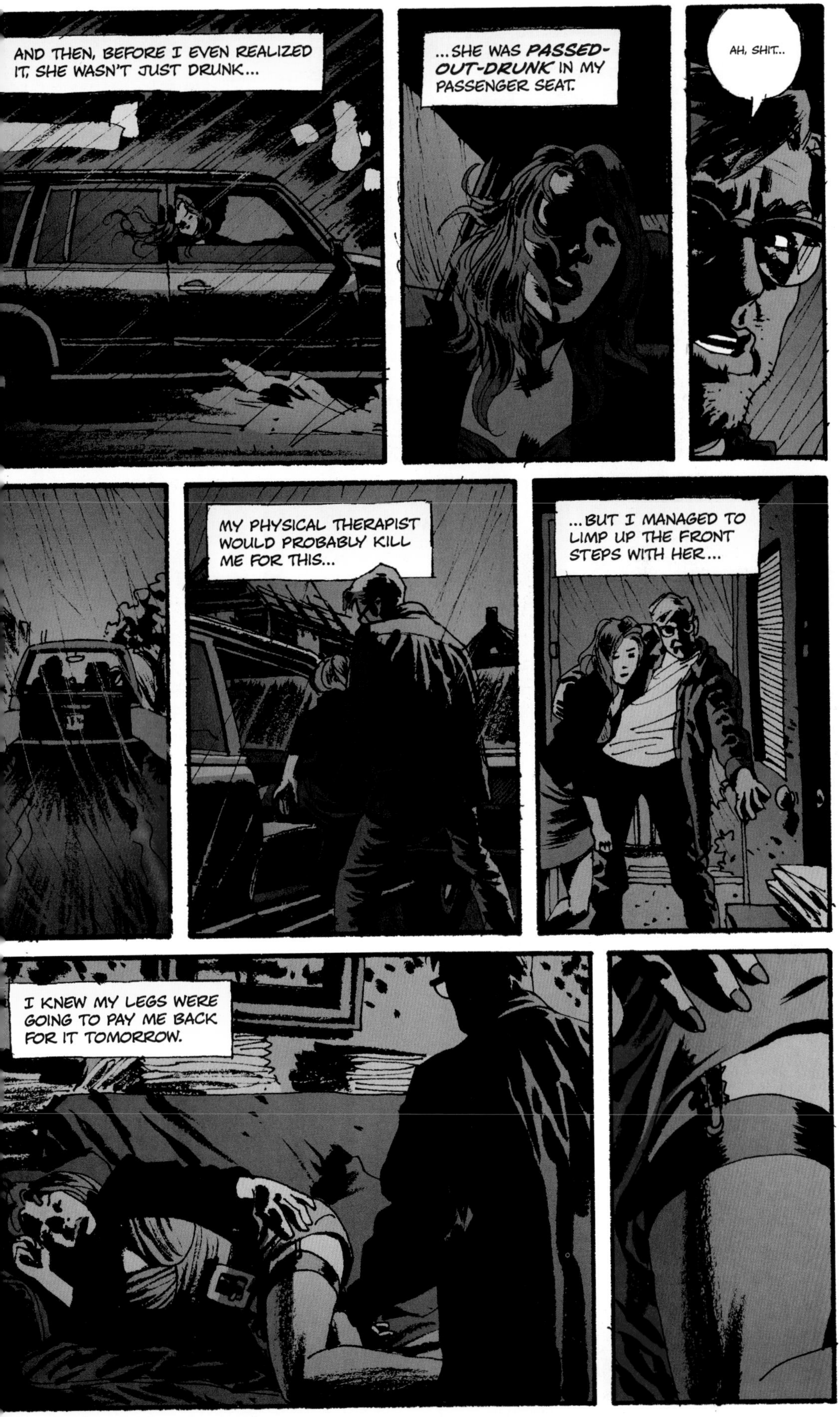

AND THEN, BEFORE I EVEN REALIZED IT, SHE WASN'T JUST DRUNK...
...SHE WAS PASSED-OUT-DRUNK IN MY PASSENGER SEAT.
AH, SHIT...
MY PHYSICAL THERAPIST WOULD PROBABLY KILL ME FOR THIS...
...BUT I MANAGED TO LIMP UP THE FRONT STEPS WITH HER...
I KNEW MY LEGS WERE GOING TO PAY ME BACK FOR IT TOMORROW.

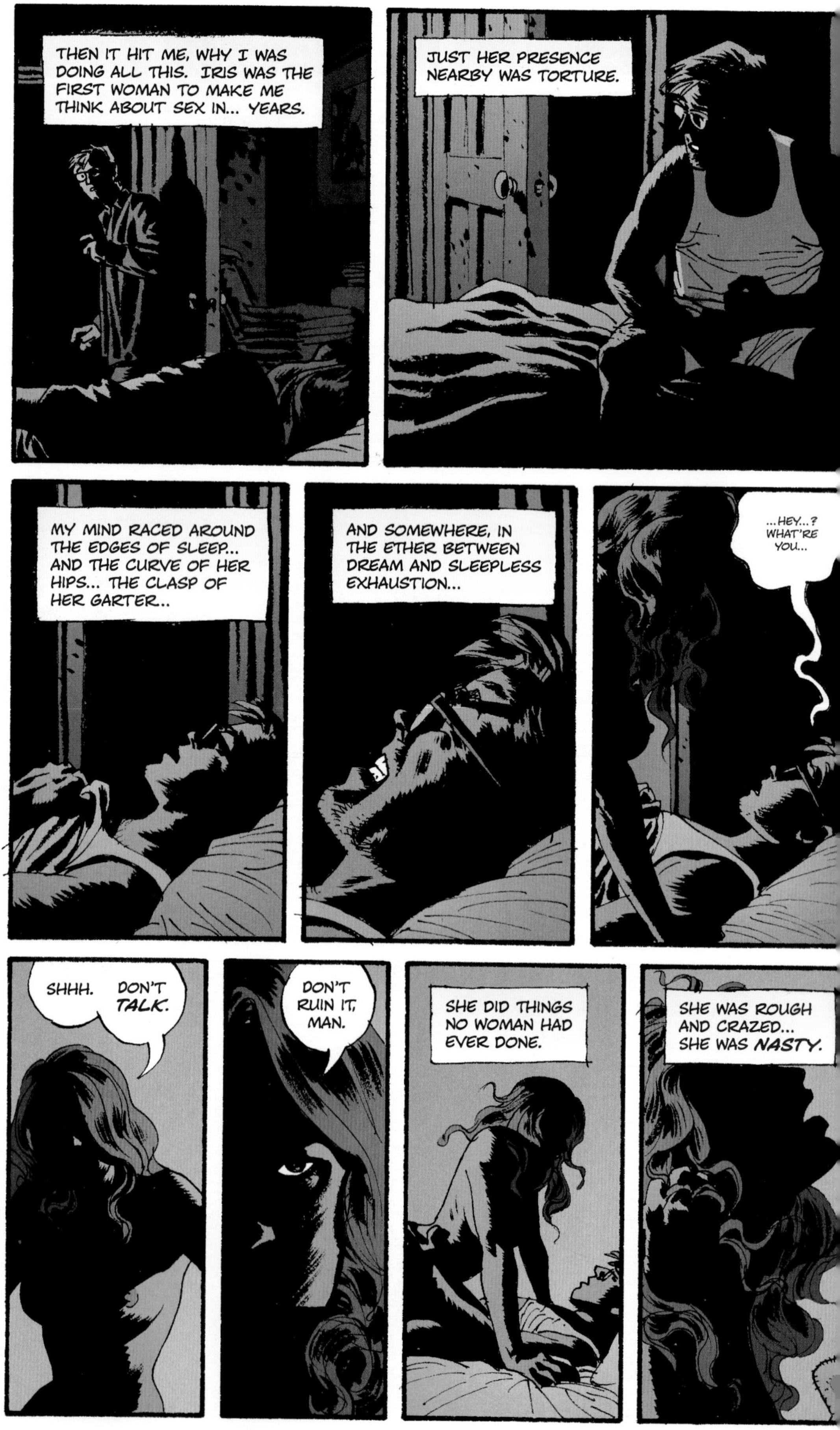
THEN IT HIT ME, WHY I WAS DOING ALL THIS. IRIS WAS THE FIRST WOMAN TO MAKE ME THINK ABOUT SEX IN... YEARS.
JUST HER PRESENCE NEARBY WAS TORTURE.
MY MIND RACED AROUND THE EDGES OF SLEEP... AND THE CURVE OF HER HIPS... THE CLASP OF HER GARTER..
AND SOMEWHERE, IN THE ETHER BETWEEN DREAM AND SLEEPLESS EXHAUSTION...
...HEY...? WHAT'RE YOU...
SHHH. DON'T *TALK*.
DON'T RUIN IT, MAN.
SHE DID THINGS NO WOMAN HAD EVER DONE.
SHE WAS ROUGH AND CRAZED... SHE WAS *NASTY*.

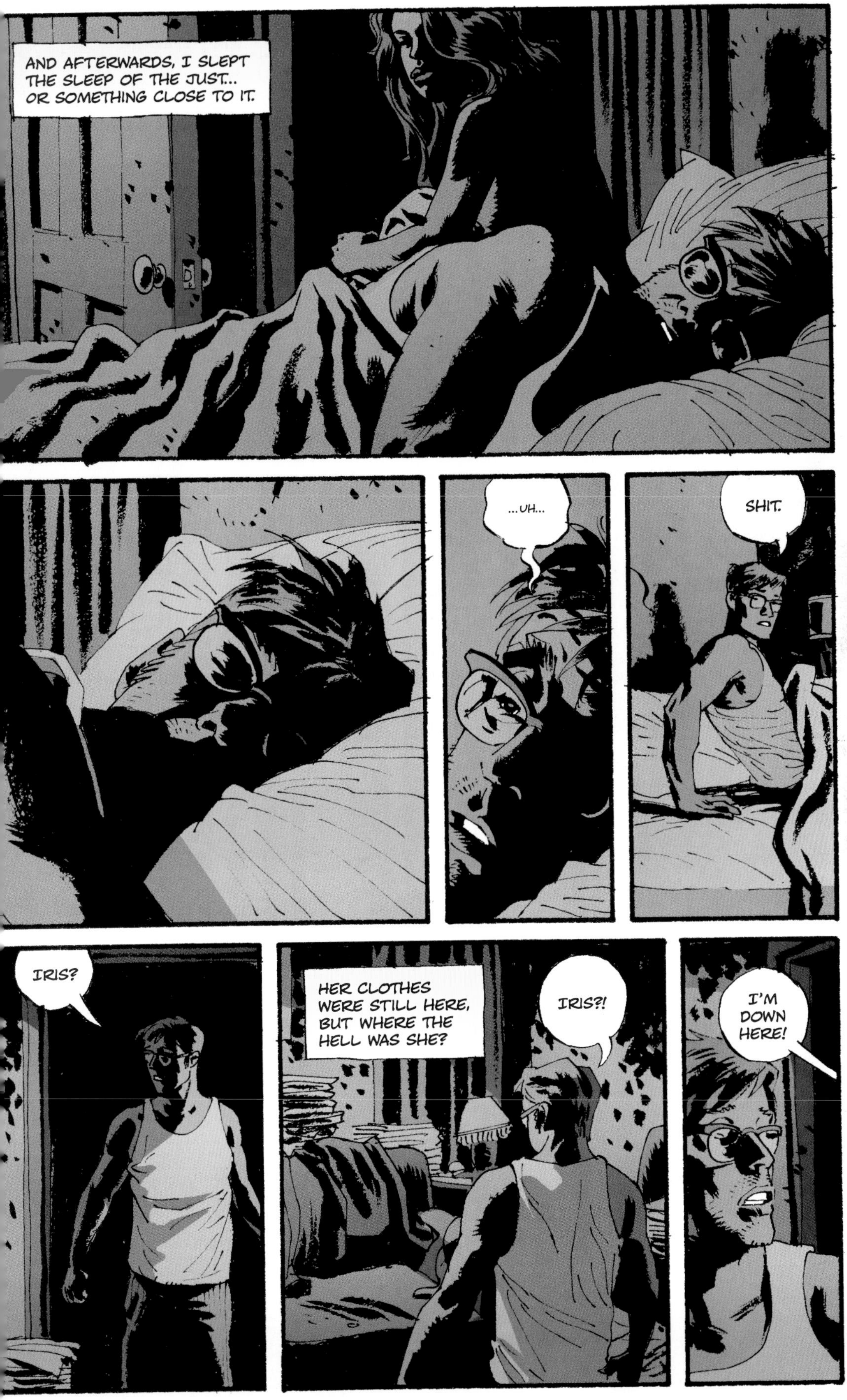
AND AFTERWARDS, I SLEPT THE SLEEP OF THE JUST... OR SOMETHING CLOSE TO IT.
...UH...
SHIT.
IRIS?
HER CLOTHES WERE STILL HERE, BUT WHERE THE HELL WAS SHE?
IRIS?!
I'M DOWN HERE!

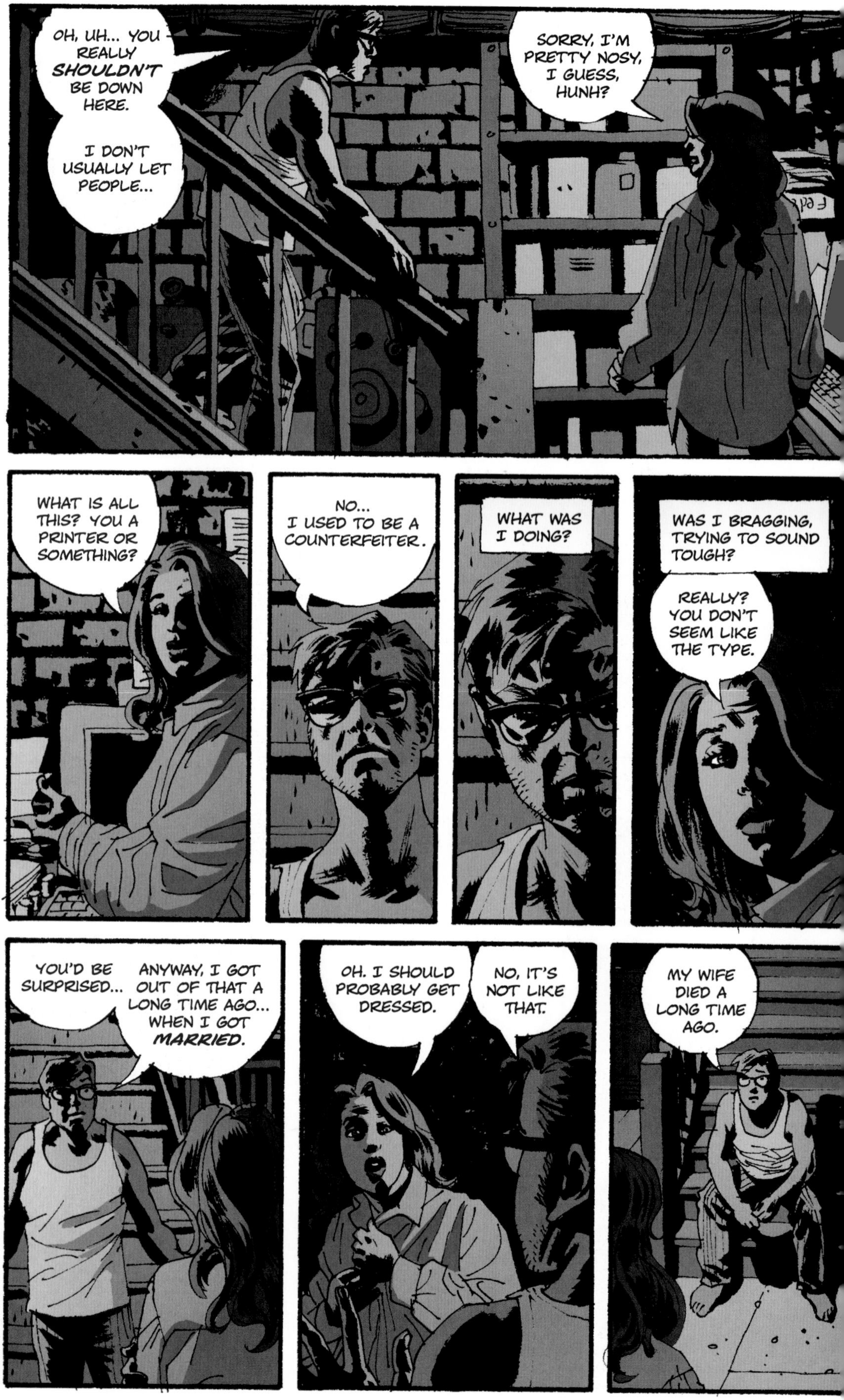
OH, UH... YOU REALLY SHOULDN'T BE DOWN HERE.
I DON'T USUALLY LET PEOPLE...
SORRY, I'M PRETTY NOSY, I GUESS, HUNH?
WHAT IS ALL THIS? YOU A PRINTER OR SOMETHING?
NO... I USED TO BE A COUNTERFEITER.
WHAT WAS I DOING?
WAS I BRAGGING, TRYING TO SOUND TOUGH?
REALLY? YOU DON'T SEEM LIKE THE TYPE.
YOU'D BE SURPRISED...
ANYWAY, I GOT OUT OF THAT A LONG TIME AGO... WHEN I GOT MARRIED.
OH. I SHOULD PROBABLY GET DRESSED.
NO, IT'S NOT LIKE THAT.
MY WIFE DIED A LONG TIME AGO.

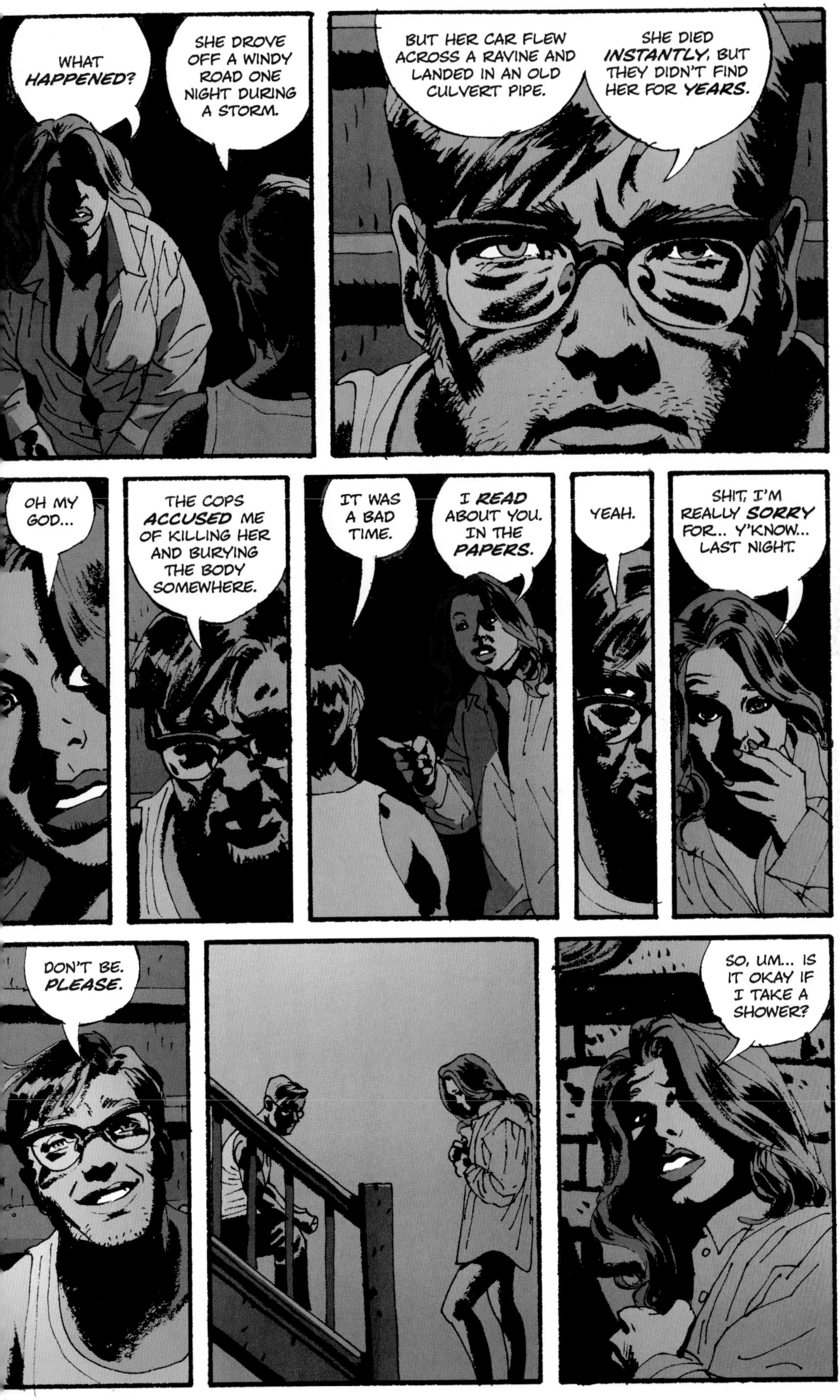
WHAT HAPPENED?
SHE DROVE OFF A WINDY ROAD ONE NIGHT DURING A STORM.
BUT HER CAR FLEW ACROSS A RAVINE AND LANDED IN AN OLD CULVERT PIPE.
SHE DIED INSTANTLY, BUT THEY DIDN'T FIND HER FOR YEARS.
OH MY GOD...
THE COPS ACCUSED ME OF KILLING HER AND BURYING THE BODY SOMEWHERE.
IT WAS A BAD TIME.
I READ ABOUT YOU. IN THE PAPERS.
YEAH.
SHIT, I'M REALLY SORRY FOR... Y'KNOW... LAST NIGHT.
DON'T BE. PLEASE.
SO, UM... IS IT OKAY IF I TAKE A SHOWER?

WHILE SHE CLEANED UP...

... I HOBBLED DOWN TO THE STORE TO GET SOME COFFEE AND PASTRIES.

I CAN STILL SEE MYSELF.. LIMPING HOME WITH A BIG DUMB GRIN...

...LIKE AN IDIOT.

IRIS? HELLO...?

WHAT'D YOU EXPECT, JACOB?

THINK A DAME LIKE *THAT* IS GONNA STICK AROUND FOR *YOU*?

FUCKING HELL...

BETTER MAKE SURE THAT TWIST IS THE *ONLY THING* THAT'S GONE, TOO.

SHE LOOKED LIKE THE TYPE TO HAVE *STICKY FINGERS*.

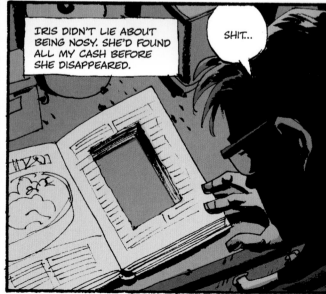

IRIS DIDN'T LIE ABOUT BEING NOSY. SHE'D FOUND ALL MY CASH BEFORE SHE DISAPPEARED.

SHIT...

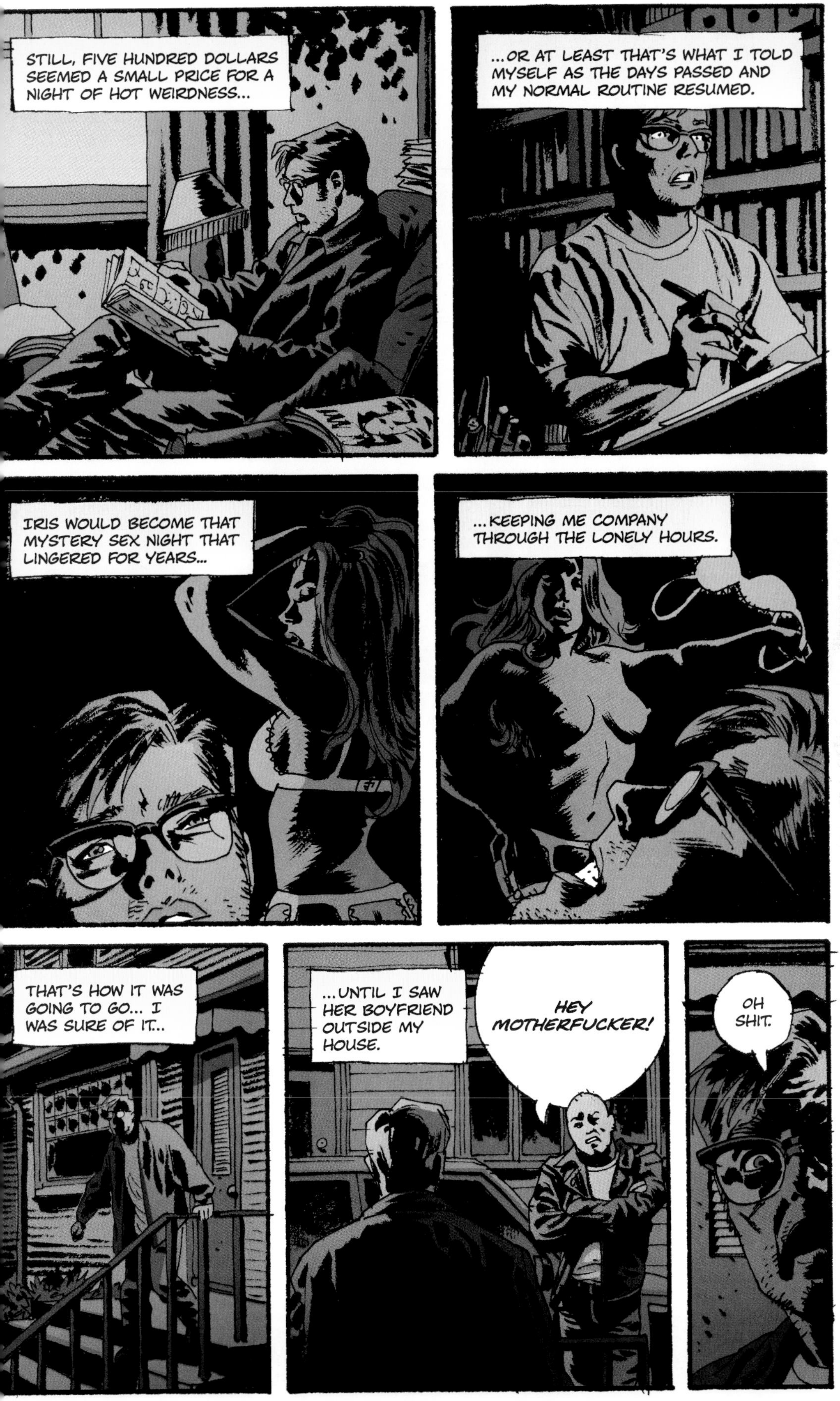
STILL, FIVE HUNDRED DOLLARS SEEMED A SMALL PRICE FOR A NIGHT OF HOT WEIRDNESS...
...OR AT LEAST THAT'S WHAT I TOLD MYSELF AS THE DAYS PASSED AND MY NORMAL ROUTINE RESUMED.
IRIS WOULD BECOME THAT MYSTERY SEX NIGHT THAT LINGERED FOR YEARS...
...KEEPING ME COMPANY THROUGH THE LONELY HOURS.
THAT'S HOW IT WAS GOING TO GO... I WAS SURE OF IT...
...UNTIL I SAW HER BOYFRIEND OUTSIDE MY HOUSE.
HEY MOTHERFUCKER!
OH SHIT.

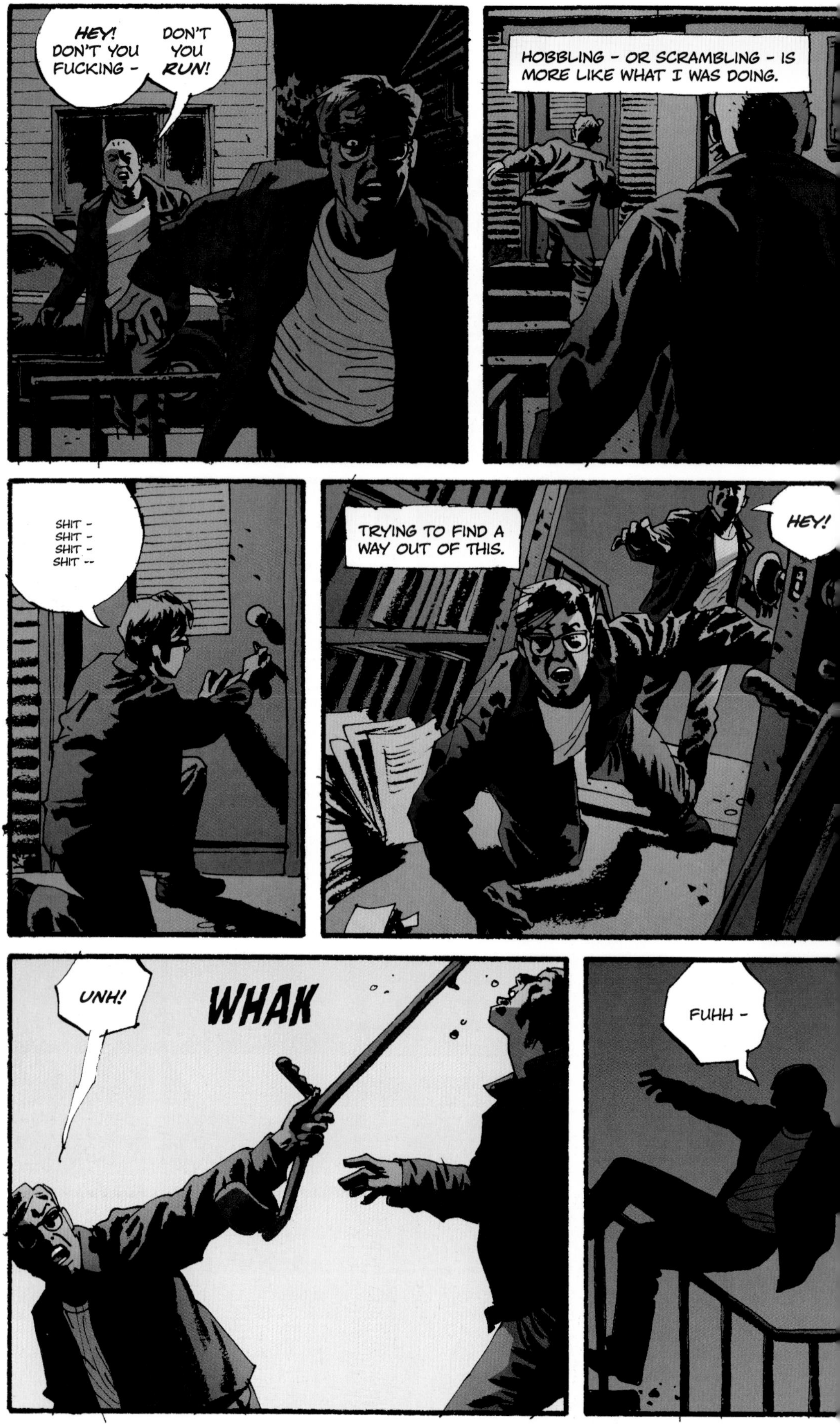
HEY! DON'T YOU FUCKING -
DON'T YOU RUN!
HOBBLING - OR SCRAMBLING - IS MORE LIKE WHAT I WAS DOING.
SHIT - SHIT - SHIT - SHIT --
TRYING TO FIND A WAY OUT OF THIS.
HEY!
UNH!
WHAK
FUHH -

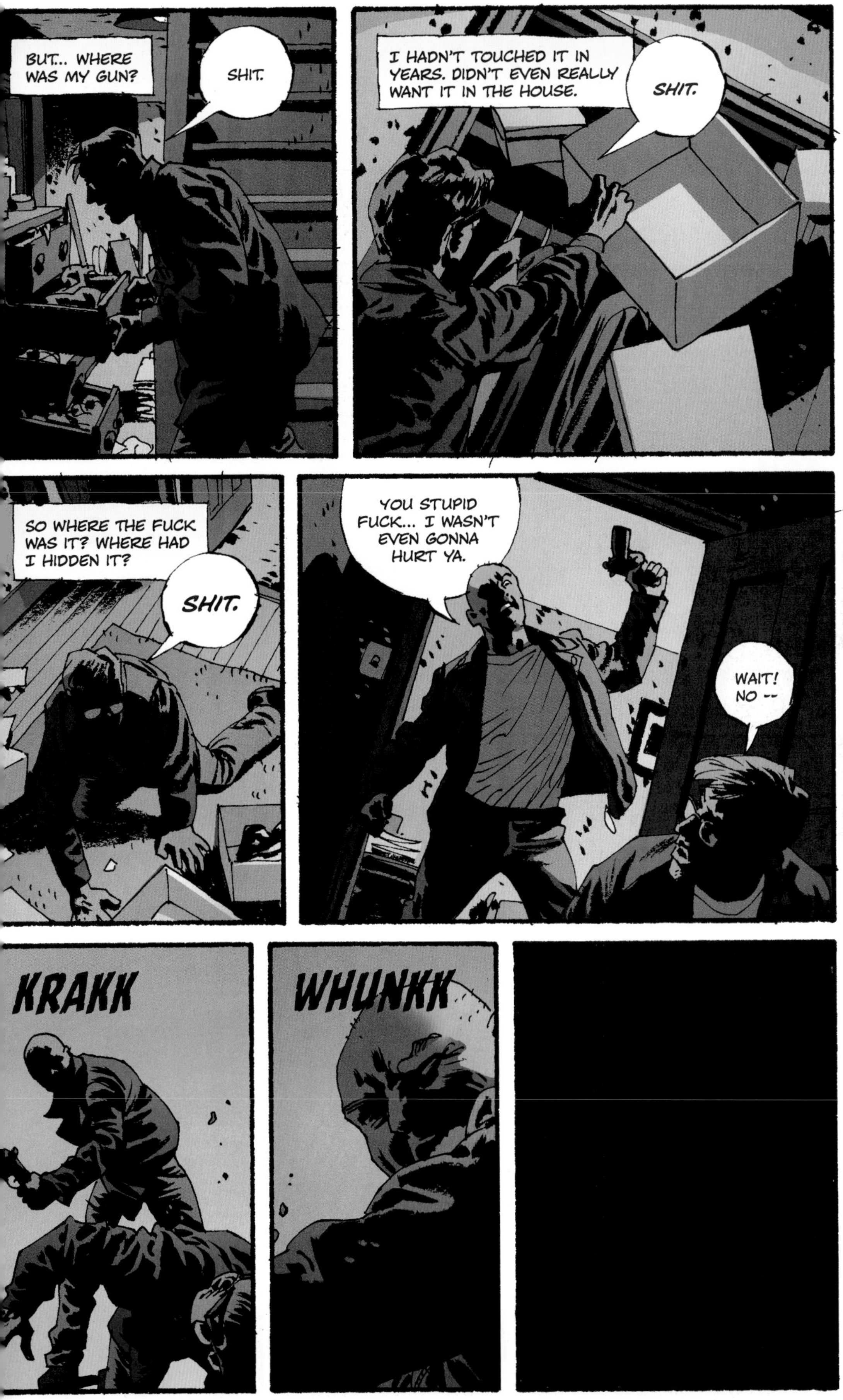
BUT... WHERE WAS MY GUN?
SHIT.
I HADN'T TOUCHED IT IN YEARS. DIDN'T EVEN REALLY WANT IT IN THE HOUSE.
SHIT.
SO WHERE THE FUCK WAS IT? WHERE HAD I HIDDEN IT?
SHIT.
YOU STUPID FUCK... I WASN'T EVEN GONNA HURT YA.
WAIT! NO --
KRAKK
WHUNKK

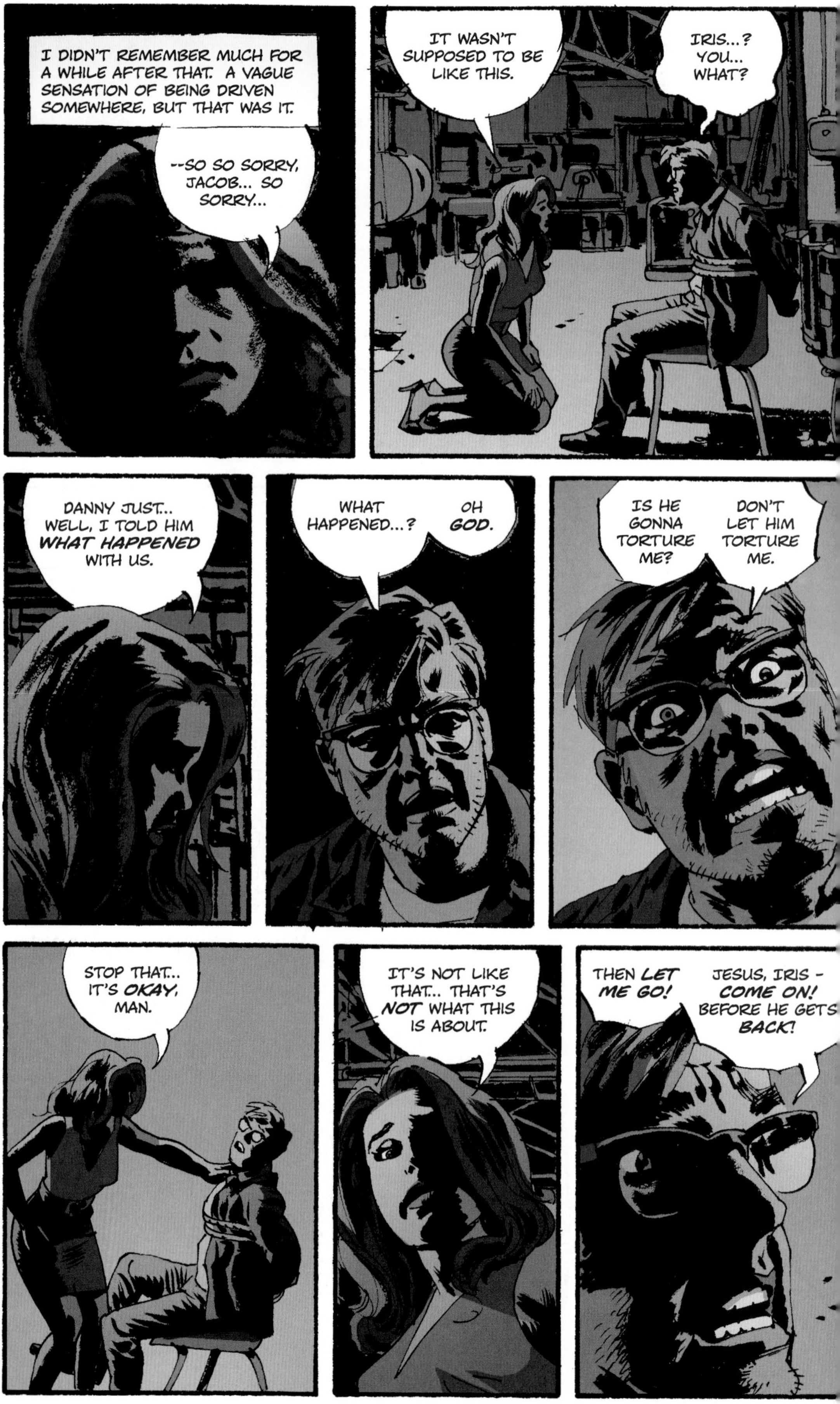
I DIDN'T REMEMBER MUCH FOR A WHILE AFTER THAT. A VAGUE SENSATION OF BEING DRIVEN SOMEWHERE, BUT THAT WAS IT.
--SO SO SORRY, JACOB... SO SORRY...
IT WASN'T SUPPOSED TO BE LIKE THIS.
IRIS...? YOU... WHAT?
DANNY JUST.. WELL, I TOLD HIM WHAT HAPPENED WITH US.
WHAT HAPPENED...?
OH GOD.
IS HE GONNA TORTURE ME?
DON'T LET HIM TORTURE ME.
STOP THAT... IT'S OKAY, MAN.
IT'S NOT LIKE THAT... THAT'S NOT WHAT THIS IS ABOUT.
THEN LET ME GO!
JESUS, IRIS - COME ON! BEFORE HE GETS BACK!

I CAN'T... WE NEED YOUR HELP.

IT'S IMPORTANT.

MY HELP? WHAT... WHAT CAN I DO?

I DON'T - I'M JUST... JUST A GUY...

NOT THE WAY I HEAR IT, DUDE...

IRIS HERE SAYS YOU USED TO BE SOME KINDA BADASS COUNTERFEITER AN' SHIT...

AND THEN I KNEW I WAS *SUNK*... THAT MY STUPID CHOICES, MY STUPID BRAGGING...

MY GENERAL STUPIDITY... HAD BROUGHT THIS ON. I HAD DONE THIS TO MYSELF.

OKAY... WHAT DO YOU WANT?

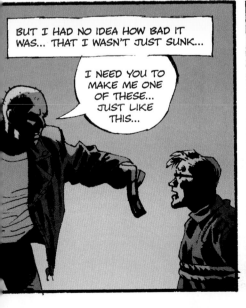

BUT I HAD NO IDEA HOW BAD IT WAS... THAT I WASN'T JUST SUNK...

I NEED YOU TO MAKE ME ONE OF THESE... JUST LIKE THIS...

...I WAS DROWNING.

FBI

SPECIAL AGENT

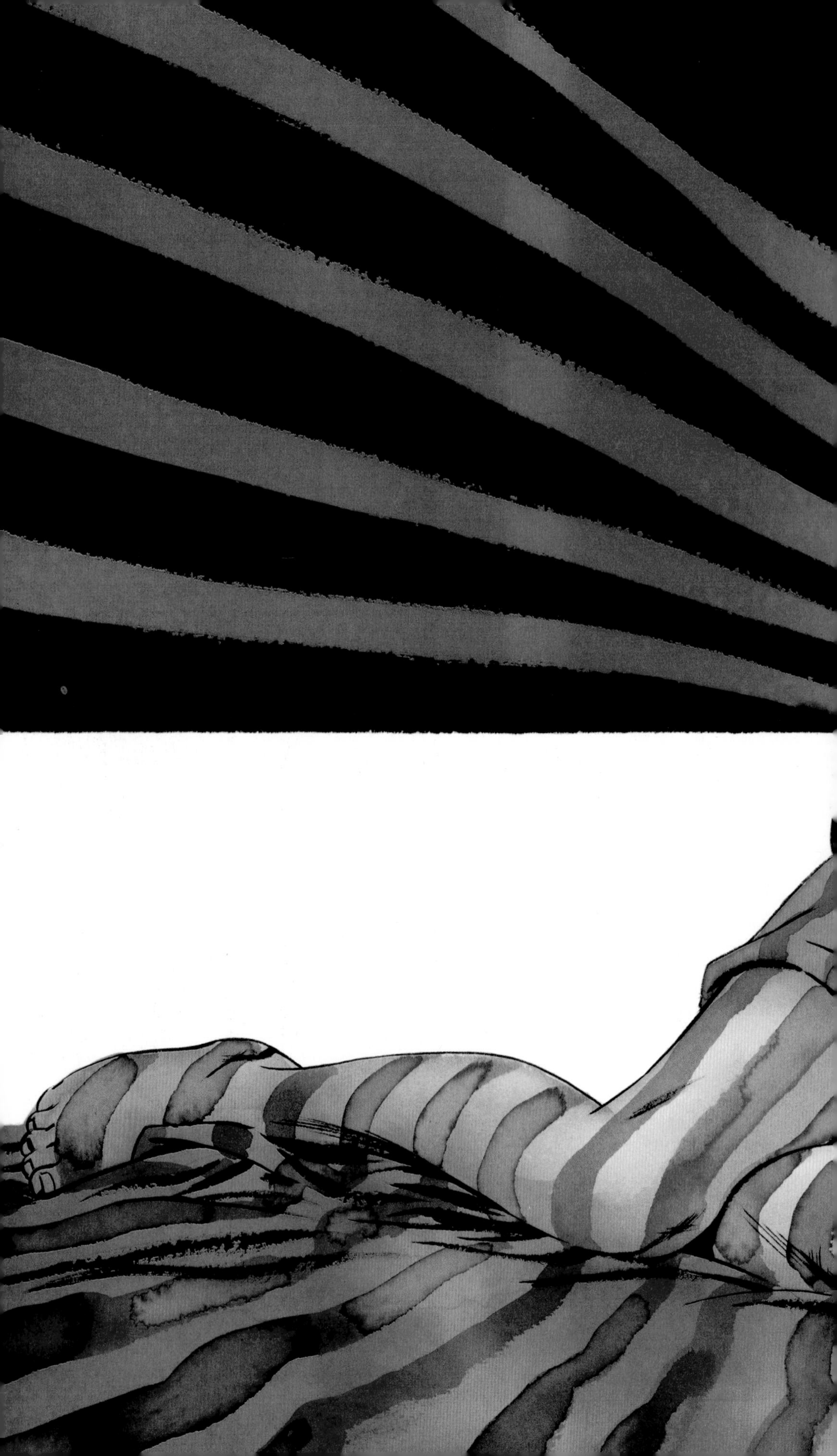

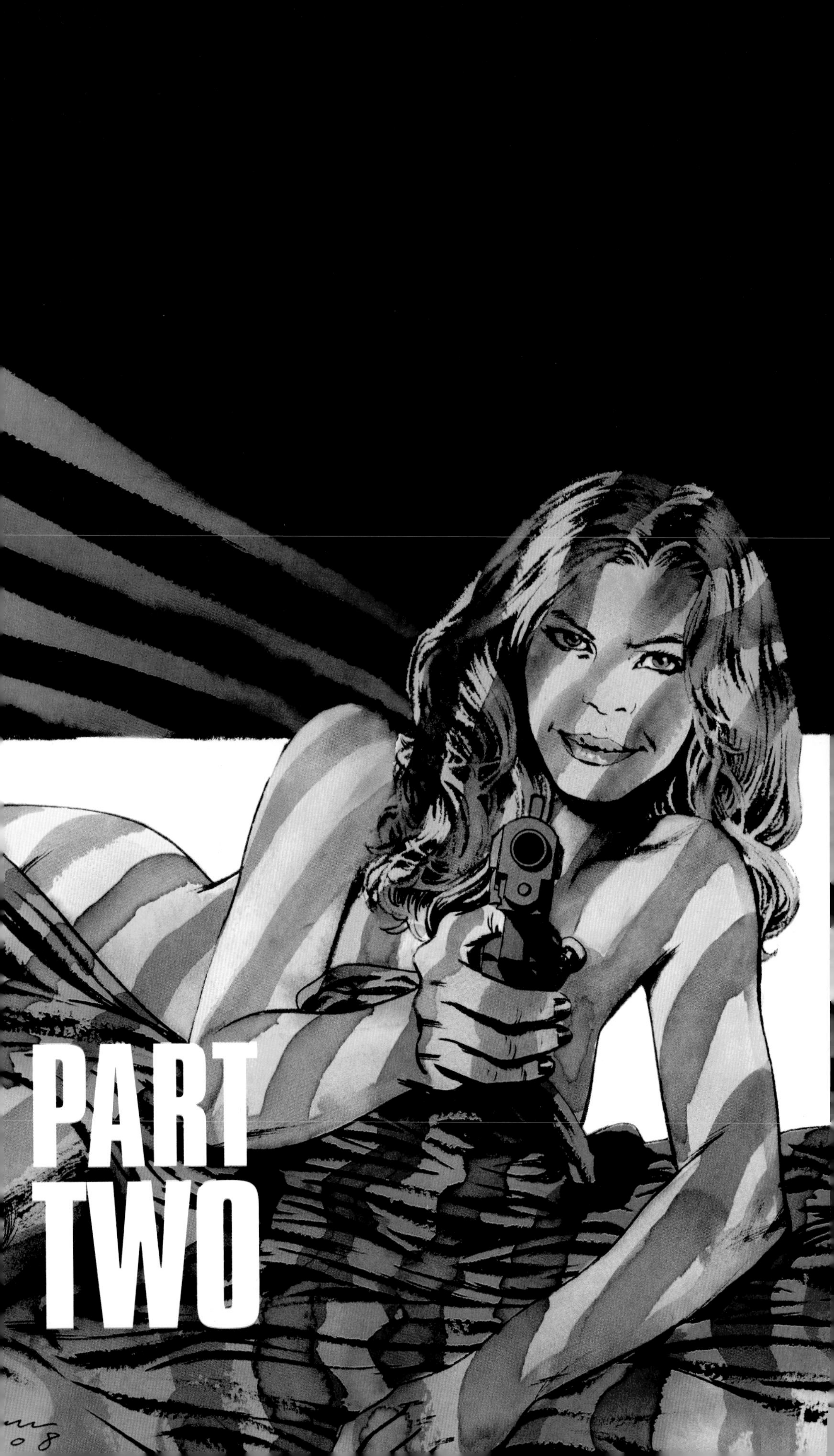
PART
TWO

Sometimes I lie awake at night and I ask, 'Why me?' Then a voice answers, 'Nothing personal, your name just happened to come up.'
-Charlie Brown (from Peanuts by Charles M. Schulz)

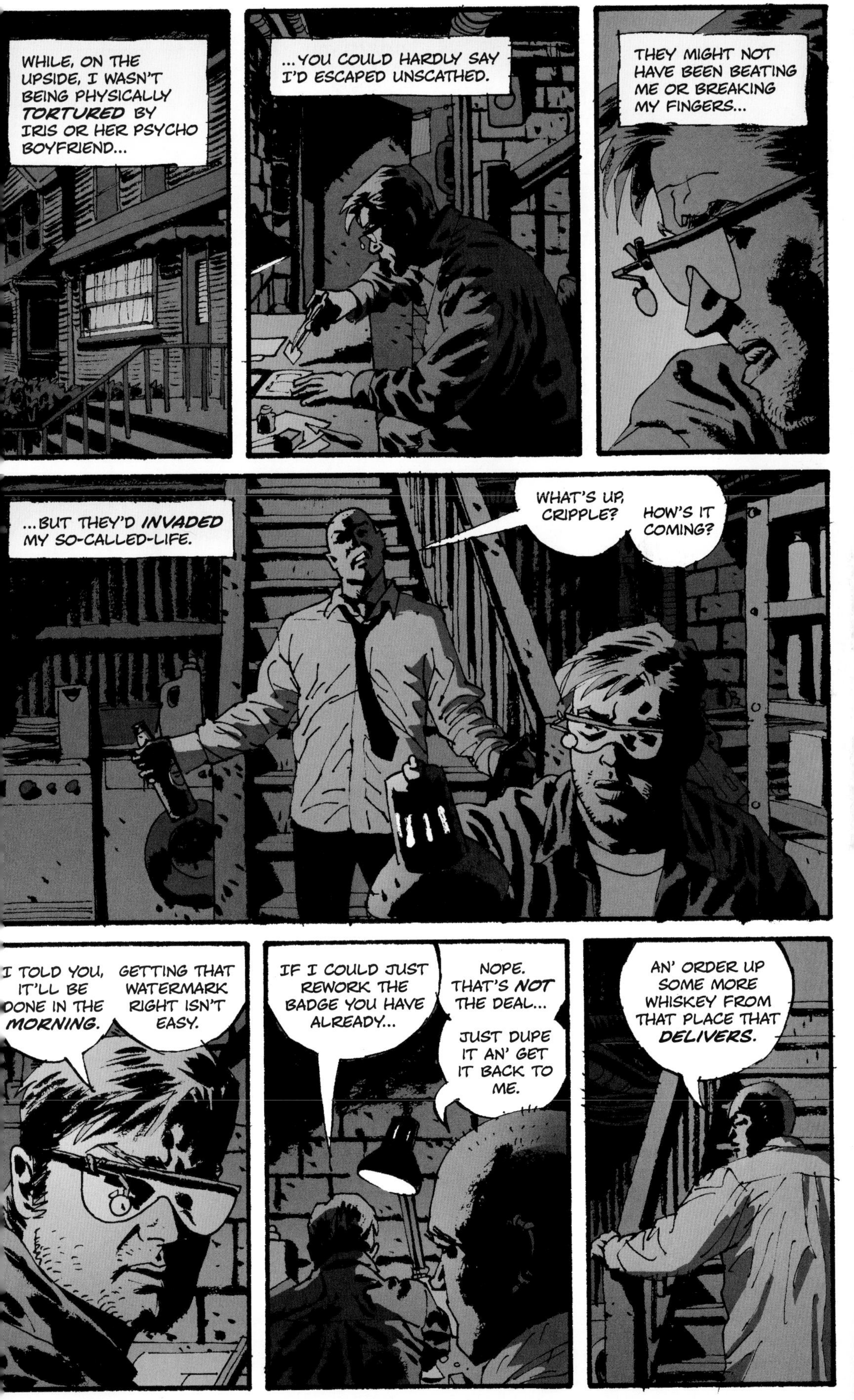

WHILE, ON THE UPSIDE, I WASN'T BEING PHYSICALLY TORTURED BY IRIS OR HER PSYCHO BOYFRIEND...
...YOU COULD HARDLY SAY I'D ESCAPED UNSCATHED.
THEY MIGHT NOT HAVE BEEN BEATING ME OR BREAKING MY FINGERS...
...BUT THEY'D INVADED MY SO-CALLED-LIFE.
WHAT'S UP, CRIPPLE?
HOW'S IT COMING?
I TOLD YOU, IT'LL BE DONE IN THE MORNING.
GETTING THAT WATERMARK RIGHT ISN'T EASY.
IF I COULD JUST REWORK THE BADGE YOU HAVE ALREADY...
NOPE. THAT'S NOT THE DEAL...
JUST DUPE IT AN' GET IT BACK TO ME.
AN' ORDER UP SOME MORE WHISKEY FROM THAT PLACE THAT DELIVERS.

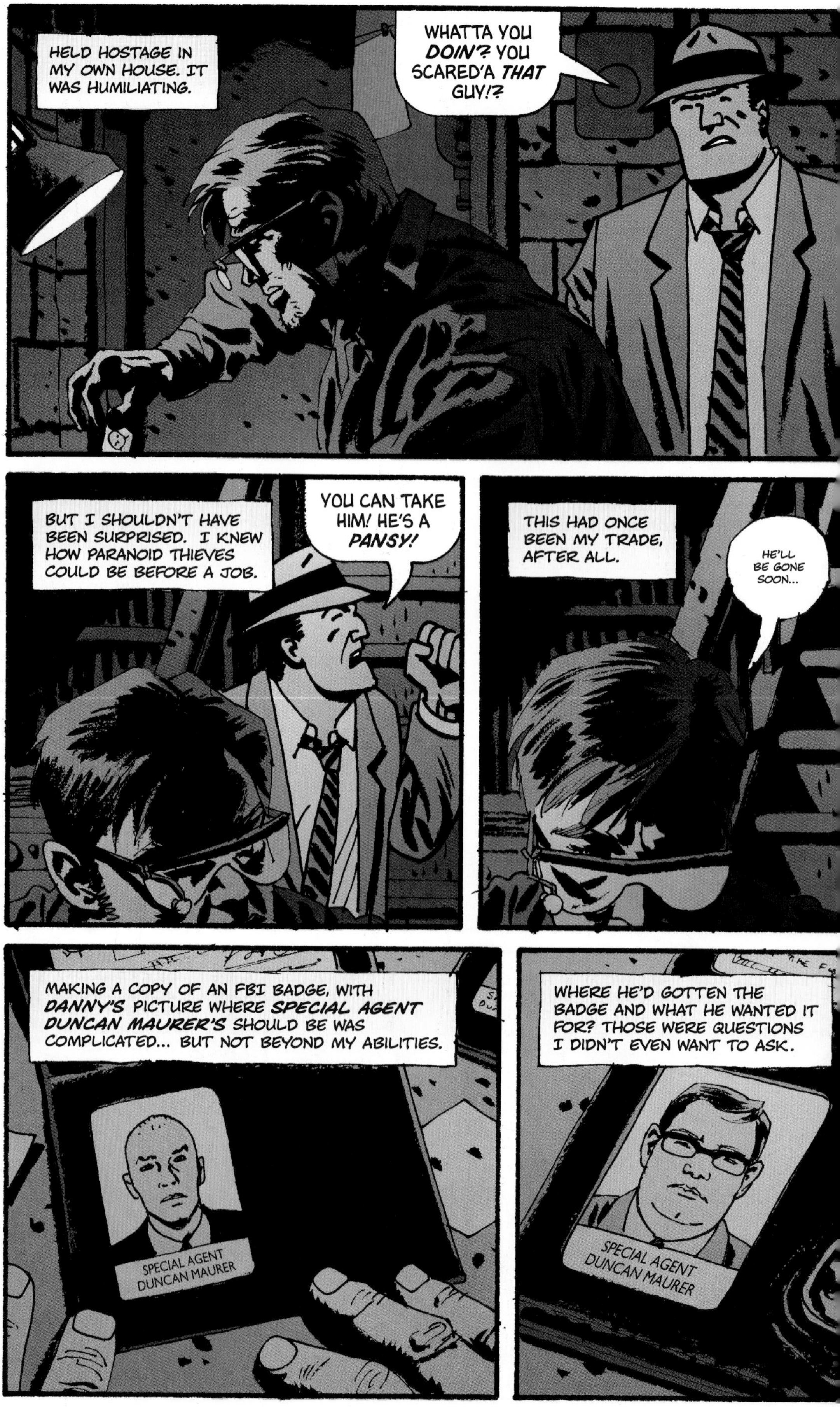
HELD HOSTAGE IN MY OWN HOUSE. IT WAS HUMILIATING.
WHATTA YOU DOIN'? YOU SCARED'A THAT GUY!?
BUT I SHOULDN'T HAVE BEEN SURPRISED. I KNEW HOW PARANOID THIEVES COULD BE BEFORE A JOB.
YOU CAN TAKE HIM! HE'S A PANSY!
THIS HAD ONCE BEEN MY TRADE, AFTER ALL.
HE'LL BE GONE SOON...
MAKING A COPY OF AN FBI BADGE, WITH DANNY'S PICTURE WHERE SPECIAL AGENT DUNCAN MAURER'S SHOULD BE WAS COMPLICATED... BUT NOT BEYOND MY ABILITIES.
SPECIAL AGENT DUNCAN MAURER
WHERE HE'D GOTTEN THE BADGE AND WHAT HE WANTED IT FOR? THOSE WERE QUESTIONS I DIDN'T EVEN WANT TO ASK.
SPECIAL AGENT DUNCAN MAURER

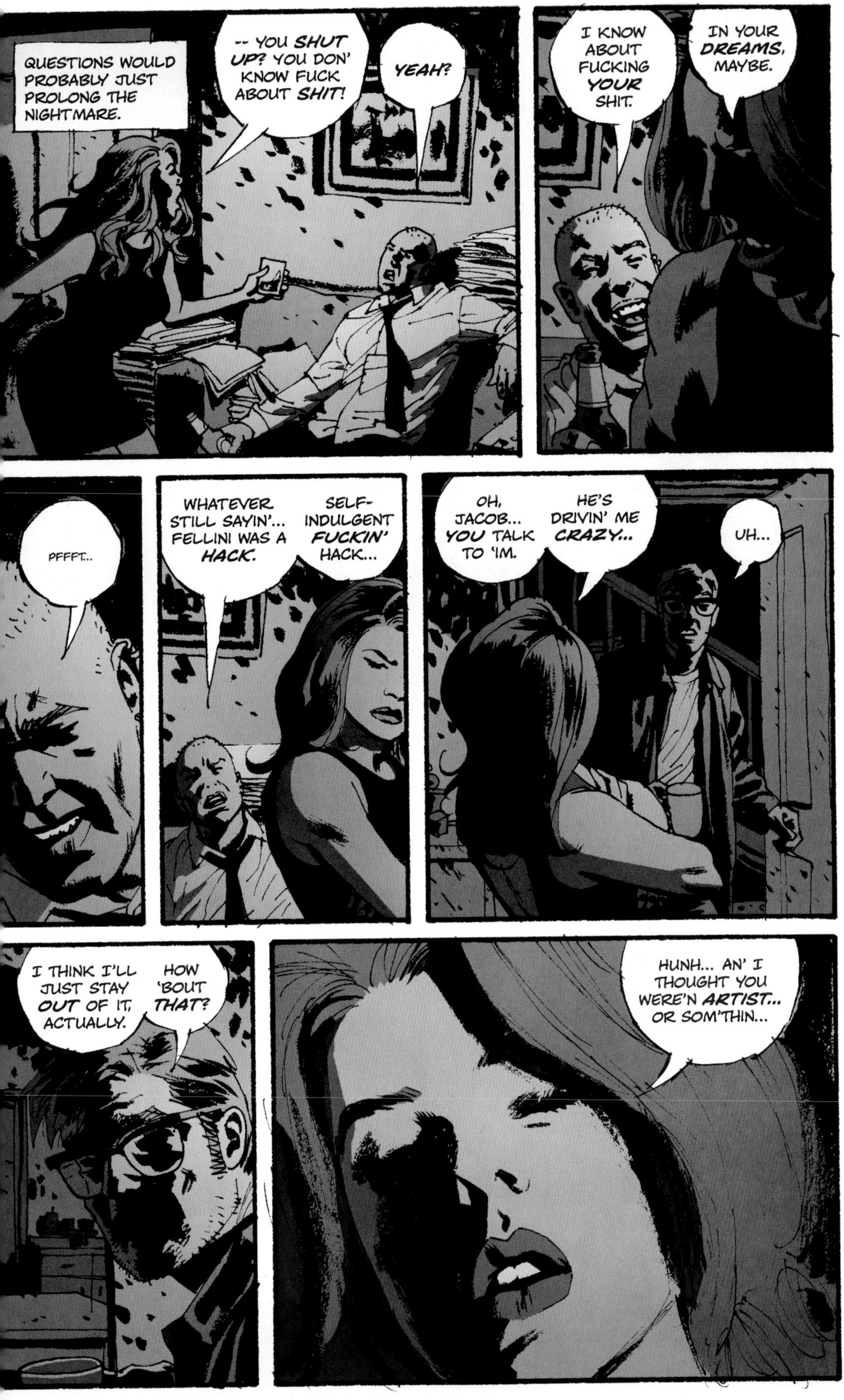
QUESTIONS WOULD PROBABLY JUST PROLONG THE NIGHTMARE.
-- YOU SHUT UP? YOU DON' KNOW FUCK ABOUT SHIT!
YEAH?
I KNOW ABOUT FUCKING YOUR SHIT.
IN YOUR DREAMS, MAYBE.
PFFFT...
WHATEVER STILL SAYIN'... FELLINI WAS A HACK.
SELF-INDULGENT FUCKIN' HACK...
OH, JACOB... YOU TALK TO 'IM.
HE'S DRIVIN' ME CRAZY...
UH...
I THINK I'LL JUST STAY OUT OF IT, ACTUALLY.
HOW 'BOUT THAT?
HUNH... AN' I THOUGHT YOU WERE'N ARTIST... OR SOM'THIN...

IRIS WAS PRETENDING WE WERE ALL OLD FRIENDS. LIKE IT WAS A BIG SLUMBER PARTY.

MY GUESS WAS THAT SHE COULDN'T ACCEPT WHAT SHE'D REALLY DONE.

HOW *BADLY* SHE'D SOLD ME OUT.

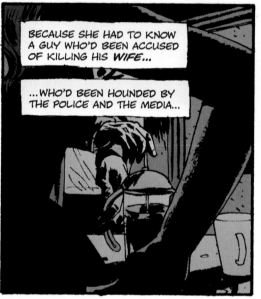

BECAUSE SHE HAD TO KNOW A GUY WHO'D BEEN ACCUSED OF KILLING HIS *WIFE*...

...WHO'D BEEN HOUNDED BY THE POLICE AND THE MEDIA...

NO WAY WAS THAT GUY GOING TO CALL THE COPS TO SHOW THEM THE FBI BADGE HE WAS FORGING...

...OR TELL THEM ABOUT THE *THIEVES* FORCING HIM BACK INTO A LIFE OF CRIME.

GOD! YOU'RE NOT EVEN LISTENIN' TO ME!

'CAUSE YER *DRUNK* AN' TALKIN' SHIT.

IT WAS *MURRAY* WHO SAID THAT, NOT EVAN.

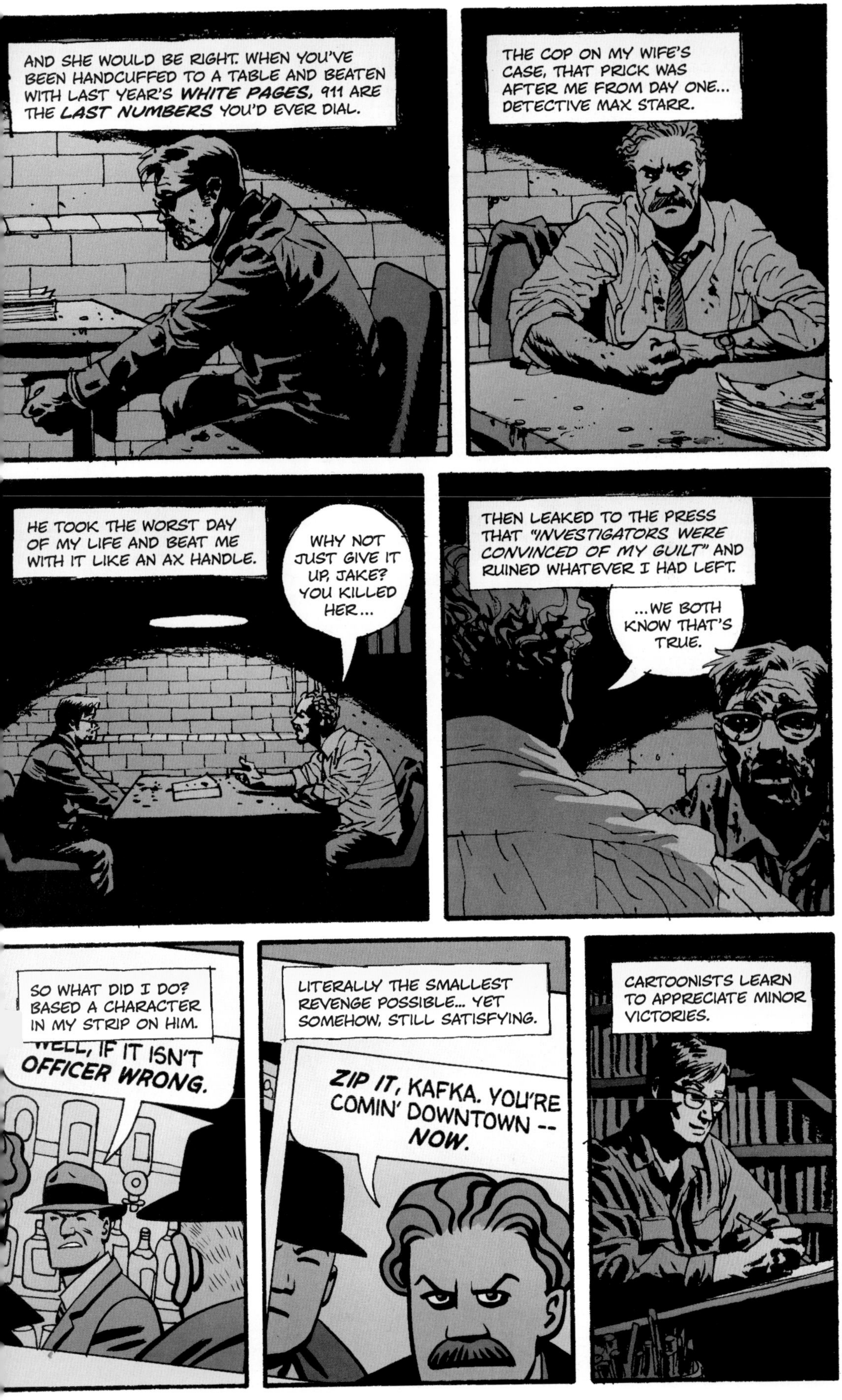
AND SHE WOULD BE RIGHT. WHEN YOU'VE BEEN HANDCUFFED TO A TABLE AND BEATEN WITH LAST YEAR'S WHITE PAGES, 911 ARE THE LAST NUMBERS YOU'D EVER DIAL.
THE COP ON MY WIFE'S CASE, THAT PRICK WAS AFTER ME FROM DAY ONE... DETECTIVE MAX STARR.
HE TOOK THE WORST DAY OF MY LIFE AND BEAT ME WITH IT LIKE AN AX HANDLE.
WHY NOT JUST GIVE IT UP, JAKE? YOU KILLED HER...
THEN LEAKED TO THE PRESS THAT "INVESTIGATORS WERE CONVINCED OF MY GUILT" AND RUINED WHATEVER I HAD LEFT.
...WE BOTH KNOW THAT'S TRUE.
SO WHAT DID I DO? BASED A CHARACTER IN MY STRIP ON HIM.
IF IT ISN'T OFFICER WRONG.
LITERALLY THE SMALLEST REVENGE POSSIBLE... YET SOMEHOW, STILL SATISFYING.
ZIP IT, KAFKA. YOU'RE COMIN' DOWNTOWN -- NOW.
CARTOONISTS LEARN TO APPRECIATE MINOR VICTORIES.

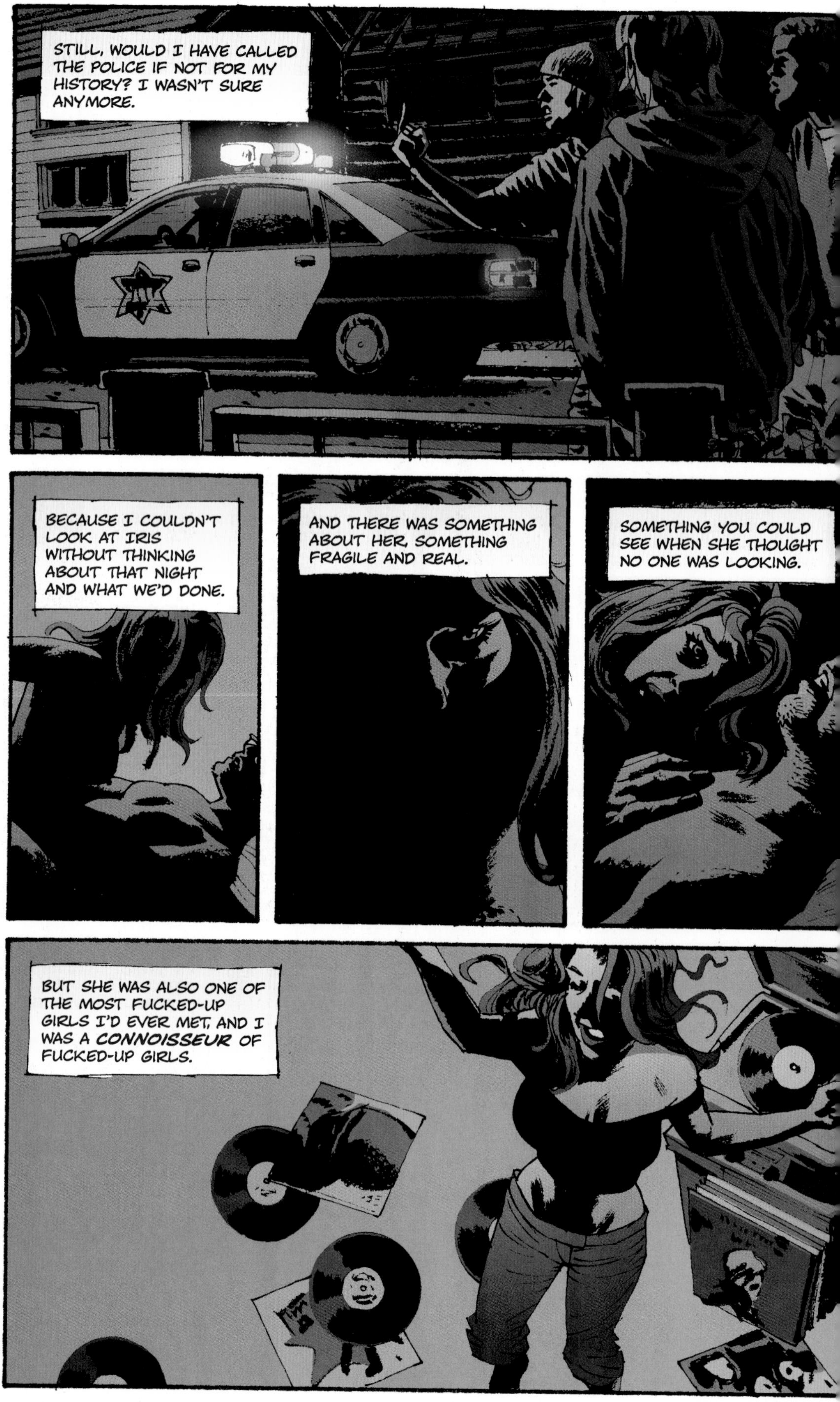
STILL, WOULD I HAVE CALLED THE POLICE IF NOT FOR MY HISTORY? I WASN'T SURE ANYMORE.
BECAUSE I COULDN'T LOOK AT IRIS WITHOUT THINKING ABOUT THAT NIGHT AND WHAT WE'D DONE.
AND THERE WAS SOMETHING ABOUT HER, SOMETHING FRAGILE AND REAL.
SOMETHING YOU COULD SEE WHEN SHE THOUGHT NO ONE WAS LOOKING.
BUT SHE WAS ALSO ONE OF THE MOST FUCKED-UP GIRLS I'D EVER MET, AND I WAS A *CONNOISSEUR* OF FUCKED-UP GIRLS.

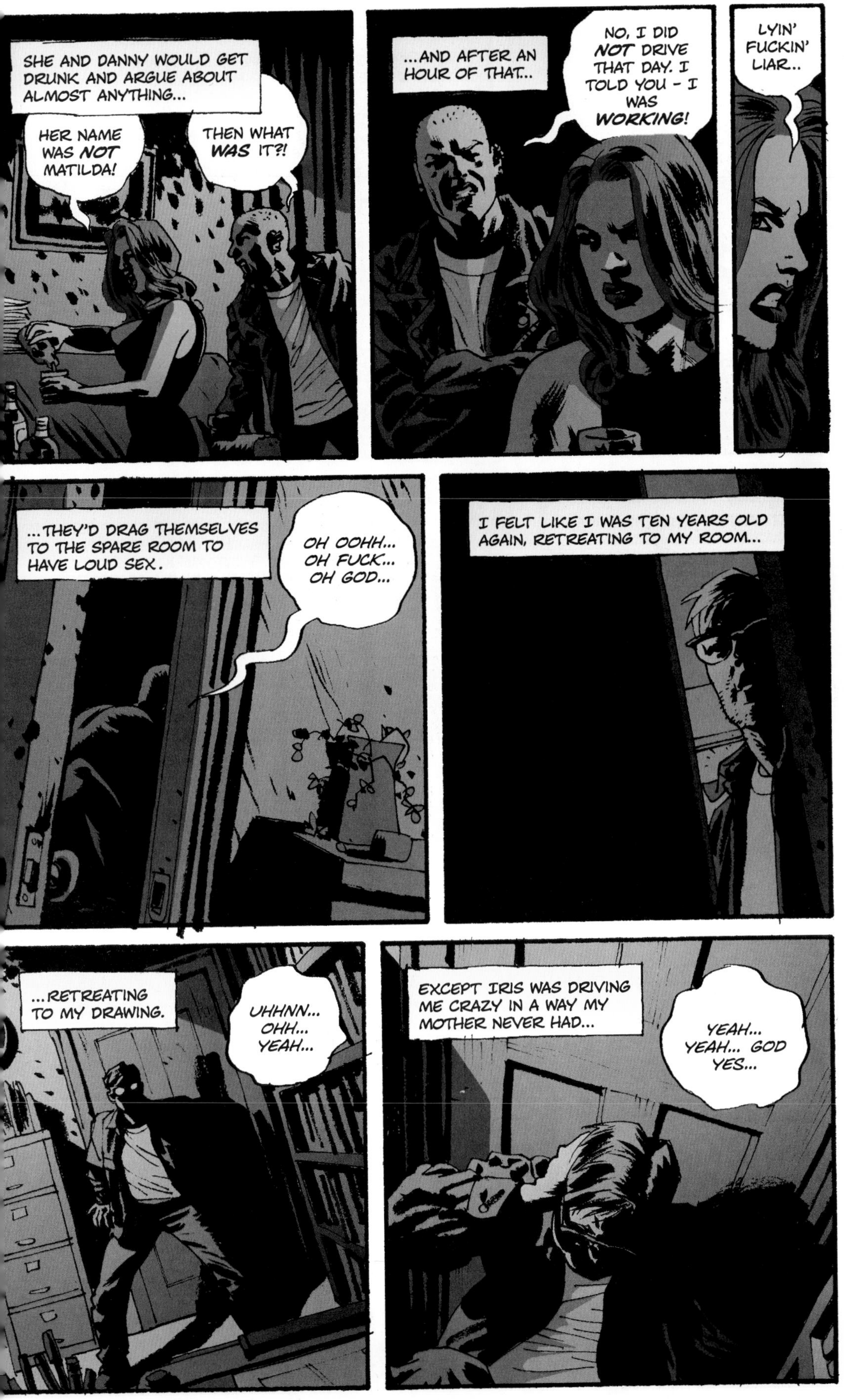
SHE AND DANNY WOULD GET DRUNK AND ARGUE ABOUT ALMOST ANYTHING...
HER NAME WAS NOT MATILDA!
THEN WHAT WAS IT?!
...AND AFTER AN HOUR OF THAT...
NO, I DID NOT DRIVE THAT DAY. I TOLD YOU - I WAS WORKING!
LYIN' FUCKIN' LIAR...
...THEY'D DRAG THEMSELVES TO THE SPARE ROOM TO HAVE LOUD SEX.
OH OOHH... OH FUCK... OH GOD...
I FELT LIKE I WAS TEN YEARS OLD AGAIN, RETREATING TO MY ROOM...
...RETREATING TO MY DRAWING.
UHHNN... OHH... YEAH...
EXCEPT IRIS WAS DRIVING ME CRAZY IN A WAY MY MOTHER NEVER HAD...
YEAH... YEAH... GOD YES...

...AND WORK WAS NOT GOING WELL.

REMY D. HAD WORKED THE NIGHT-SHIFT, AND SO WOULD I...

...THAT'S WHERE THE SECRET WOULD BE FOUND, I WAS SURE.

ALTHOUGH I COULDN'T *REALLY* BLAME THAT ON HER. THE STRIP HAD NEVER COME EASILY, BECAUSE OF MY CONTRACT.

ORKING OUT S *JANITOR'S* ET, MOSTLY ON NIGHT SHIFT...

SO THEY WOULDN'T ATTACK HIM.

SEBASTIAN HYDE, MY WIFE'S UNCLE, HAD LEANED ON SOMEONE AT THE PAPER TO GET ME MY DEAL.

HE DID IT OUT OF GUILT, BECAUSE HE HAD HIS MAN CHESTER *CRIPPLE ME* WHEN EVERYONE THOUGHT I WAS A MURDERER.

ONCE THAT TURNED OUT TO BE A BIG MISTAKE, HYDE ASKED ME WHAT I WANTED TO DO WITH WHAT WAS *LEFT* OF MY LIFE.

SO, *FRANK KAFKA, PRIVATE EYE* CAN NEVER BE CANCELED, AND I HAVE TOTAL ARTISTIC FREEDOM.

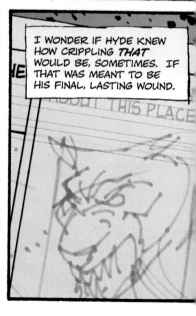

I WONDER IF HYDE KNEW HOW CRIPPLING *THAT* WOULD BE, SOMETIMES. IF THAT WAS MEANT TO BE HIS FINAL, LASTING WOUND.

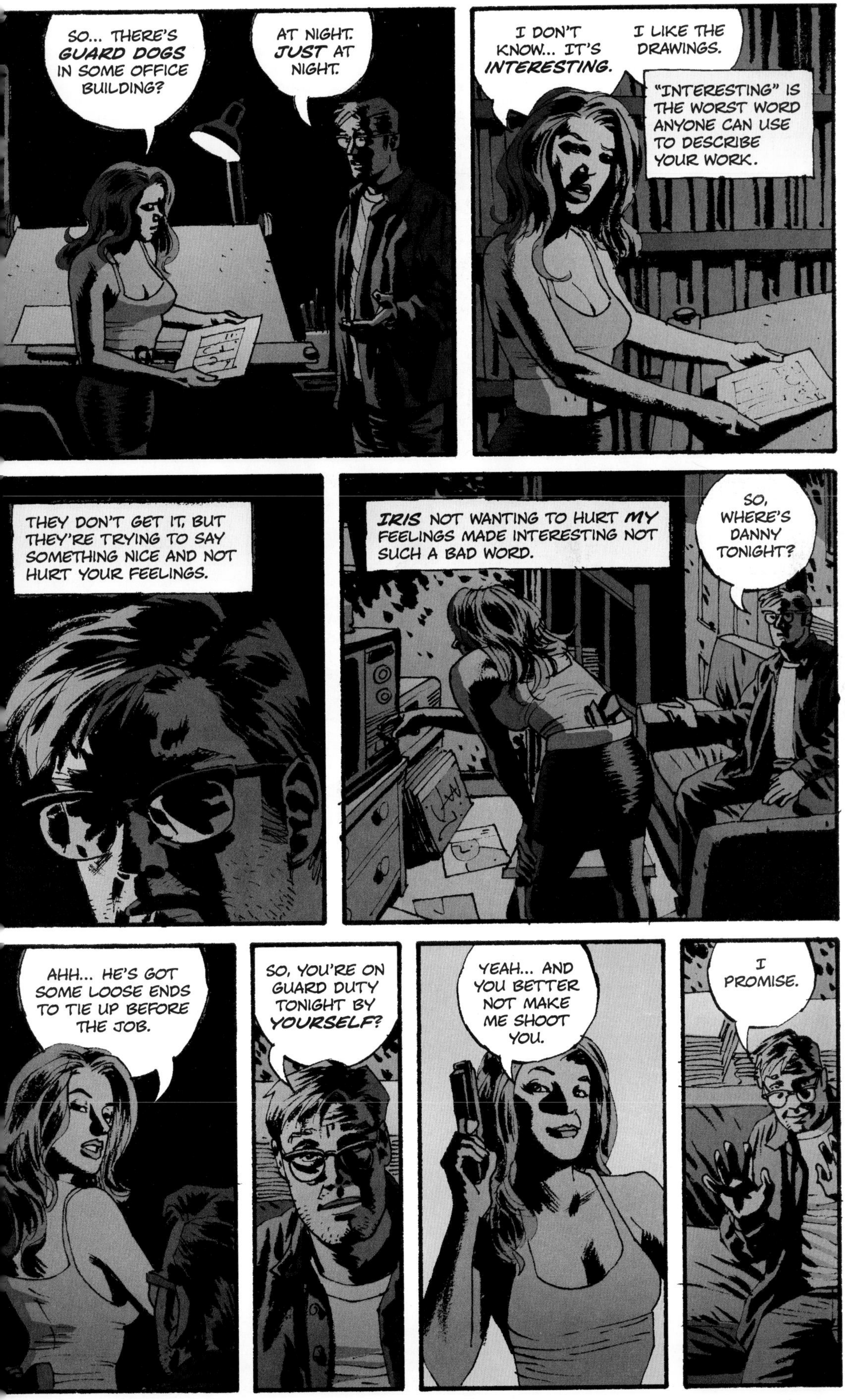

SO... THERE'S GUARD DOGS IN SOME OFFICE BUILDING?
AT NIGHT. JUST AT NIGHT.
I DON'T KNOW... IT'S INTERESTING.
I LIKE THE DRAWINGS.
"INTERESTING" IS THE WORST WORD ANYONE CAN USE TO DESCRIBE YOUR WORK.
THEY DON'T GET IT, BUT THEY'RE TRYING TO SAY SOMETHING NICE AND NOT HURT YOUR FEELINGS.
IRIS NOT WANTING TO HURT MY FEELINGS MADE INTERESTING NOT SUCH A BAD WORD.
SO, WHERE'S DANNY TONIGHT?
AHH... HE'S GOT SOME LOOSE ENDS TO TIE UP BEFORE THE JOB.
SO, YOU'RE ON GUARD DUTY TONIGHT BY YOURSELF?
YEAH... AND YOU BETTER NOT MAKE ME SHOOT YOU.
I PROMISE.

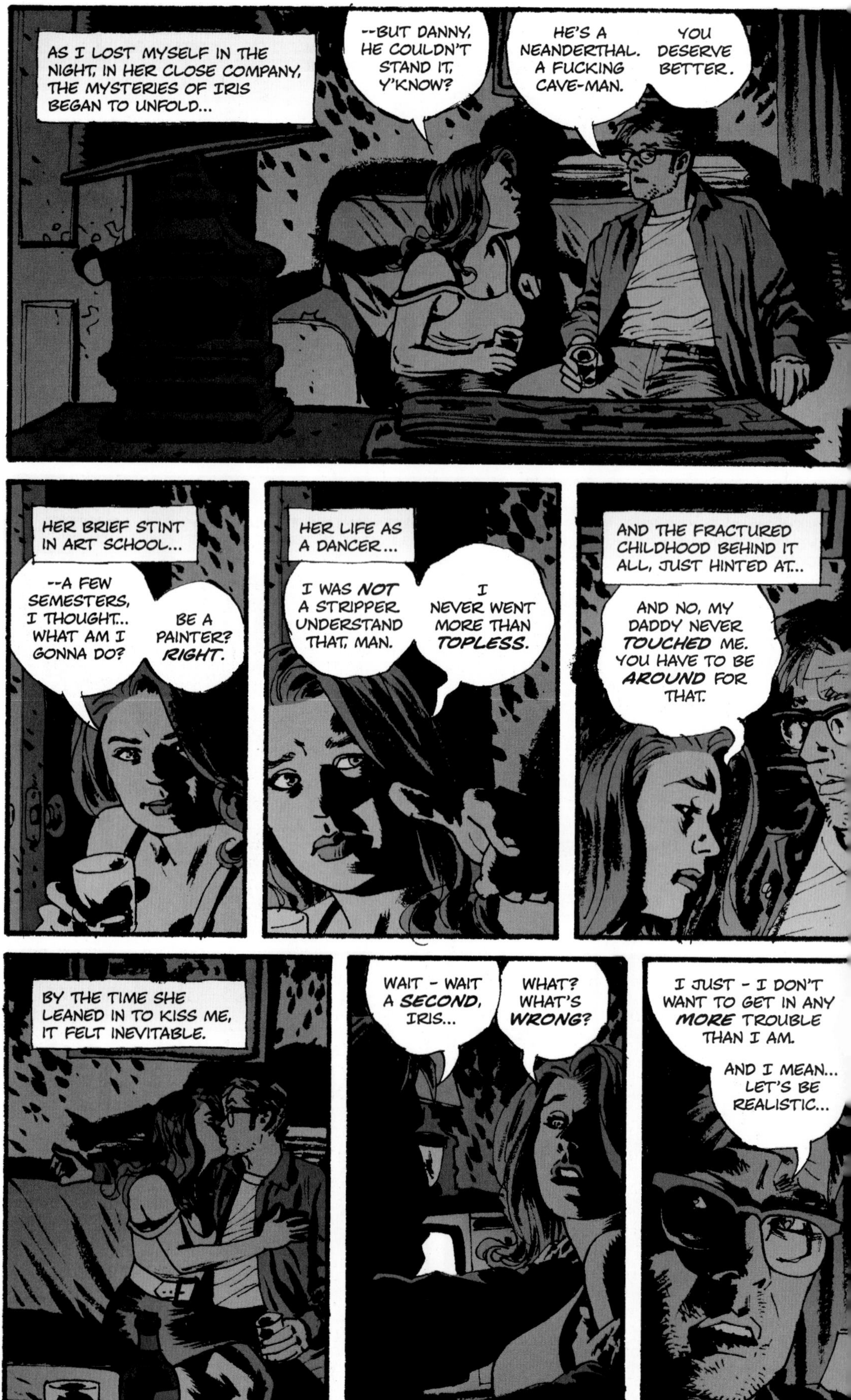
AS I LOST MYSELF IN THE NIGHT, IN HER CLOSE COMPANY, THE MYSTERIES OF IRIS BEGAN TO UNFOLD...
--BUT DANNY, HE COULDN'T STAND IT, Y'KNOW?
HE'S A NEANDERTHAL. A FUCKING CAVE-MAN.
YOU DESERVE BETTER.
HER BRIEF STINT IN ART SCHOOL...
--A FEW SEMESTERS, I THOUGHT... WHAT AM I GONNA DO?
BE A PAINTER? RIGHT.
HER LIFE AS A DANCER...
I WAS NOT A STRIPPER UNDERSTAND THAT, MAN.
I NEVER WENT MORE THAN TOPLESS.
AND THE FRACTURED CHILDHOOD BEHIND IT ALL, JUST HINTED AT...
AND NO, MY DADDY NEVER TOUCHED ME. YOU HAVE TO BE AROUND FOR THAT.
BY THE TIME SHE LEANED IN TO KISS ME, IT FELT INEVITABLE.
WAIT - WAIT A SECOND, IRIS...
WHAT? WHAT'S WRONG?
I JUST - I DON'T WANT TO GET IN ANY MORE TROUBLE THAN I AM.
AND I MEAN... LET'S BE REALISTIC...

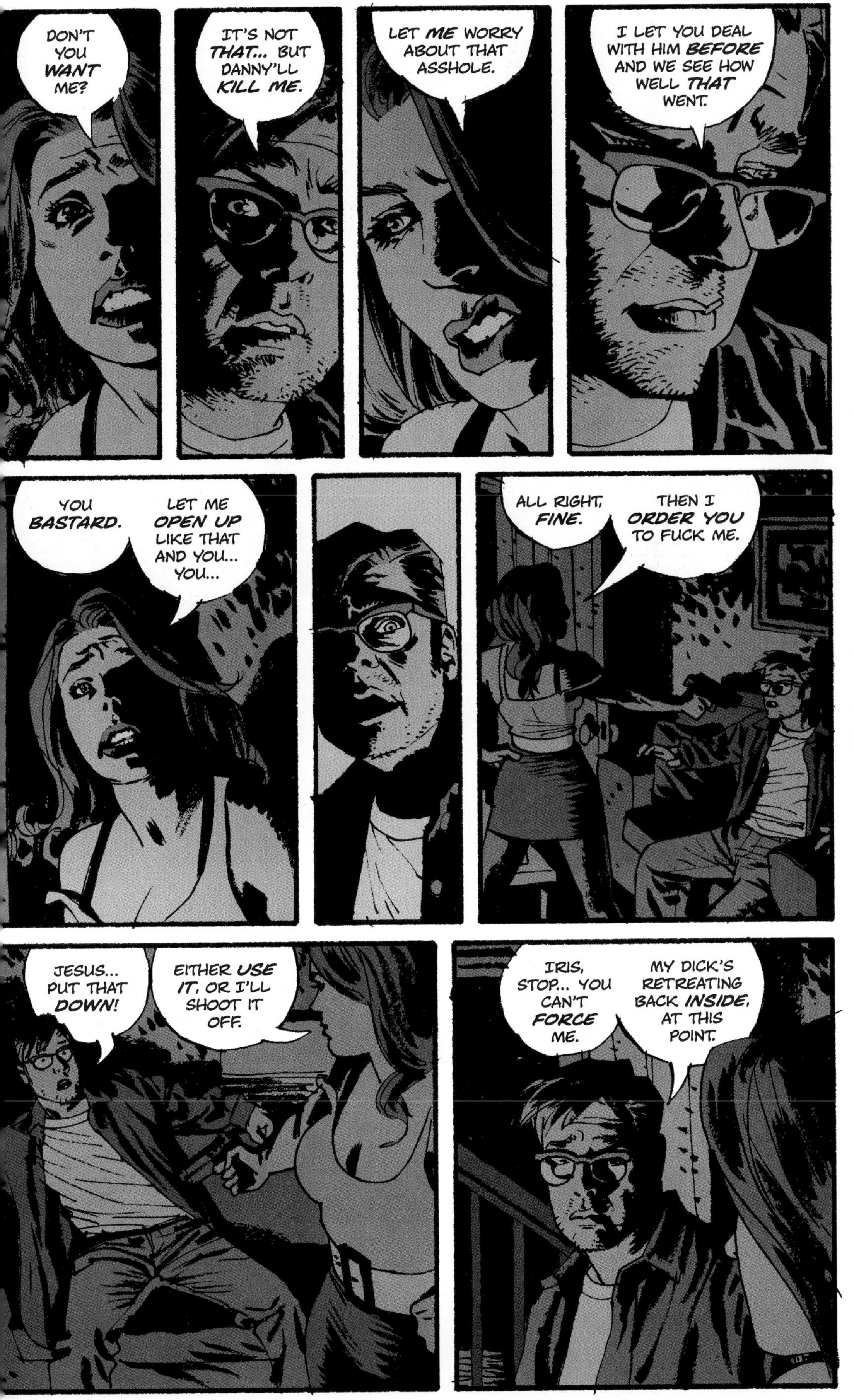
DON'T YOU WANT ME?
IT'S NOT THAT... BUT DANNY'LL KILL ME.
LET ME WORRY ABOUT THAT ASSHOLE.
I LET YOU DEAL WITH HIM BEFORE AND WE SEE HOW WELL THAT WENT.
YOU BASTARD.
LET ME OPEN UP LIKE THAT AND YOU... YOU...
ALL RIGHT, FINE.
THEN I ORDER YOU TO FUCK ME.
JESUS... PUT THAT DOWN!
EITHER USE IT, OR I'LL SHOOT IT OFF.
IRIS, STOP... YOU CAN'T FORCE ME.
MY DICK'S RETREATING BACK INSIDE, AT THIS POINT.

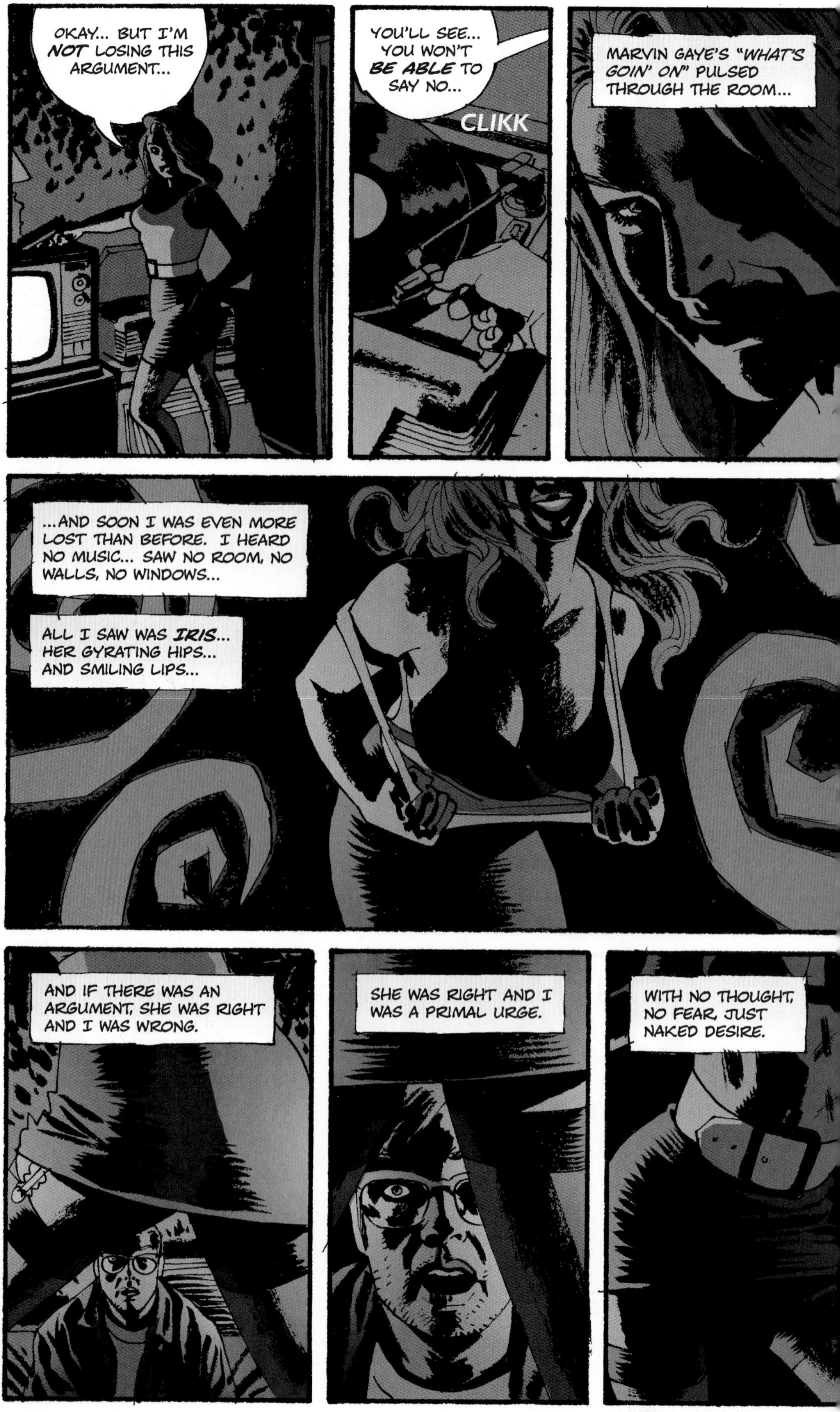

OKAY... BUT I'M *NOT* LOSING THIS ARGUMENT...
YOU'LL SEE... YOU WON'T *BE ABLE* TO SAY NO...
CLIKK
MARVIN GAYE'S "*WHAT'S GOIN' ON*" PULSED THROUGH THE ROOM...
...AND SOON I WAS EVEN MORE LOST THAN BEFORE. I HEARD NO MUSIC... SAW NO ROOM, NO WALLS, NO WINDOWS...
ALL I SAW WAS *IRIS*... HER GYRATING HIPS... AND SMILING LIPS...
AND IF THERE WAS AN ARGUMENT, SHE WAS RIGHT AND I WAS WRONG.
SHE WAS RIGHT AND I WAS A PRIMAL URGE.
WITH NO THOUGHT, NO FEAR, JUST NAKED DESIRE.

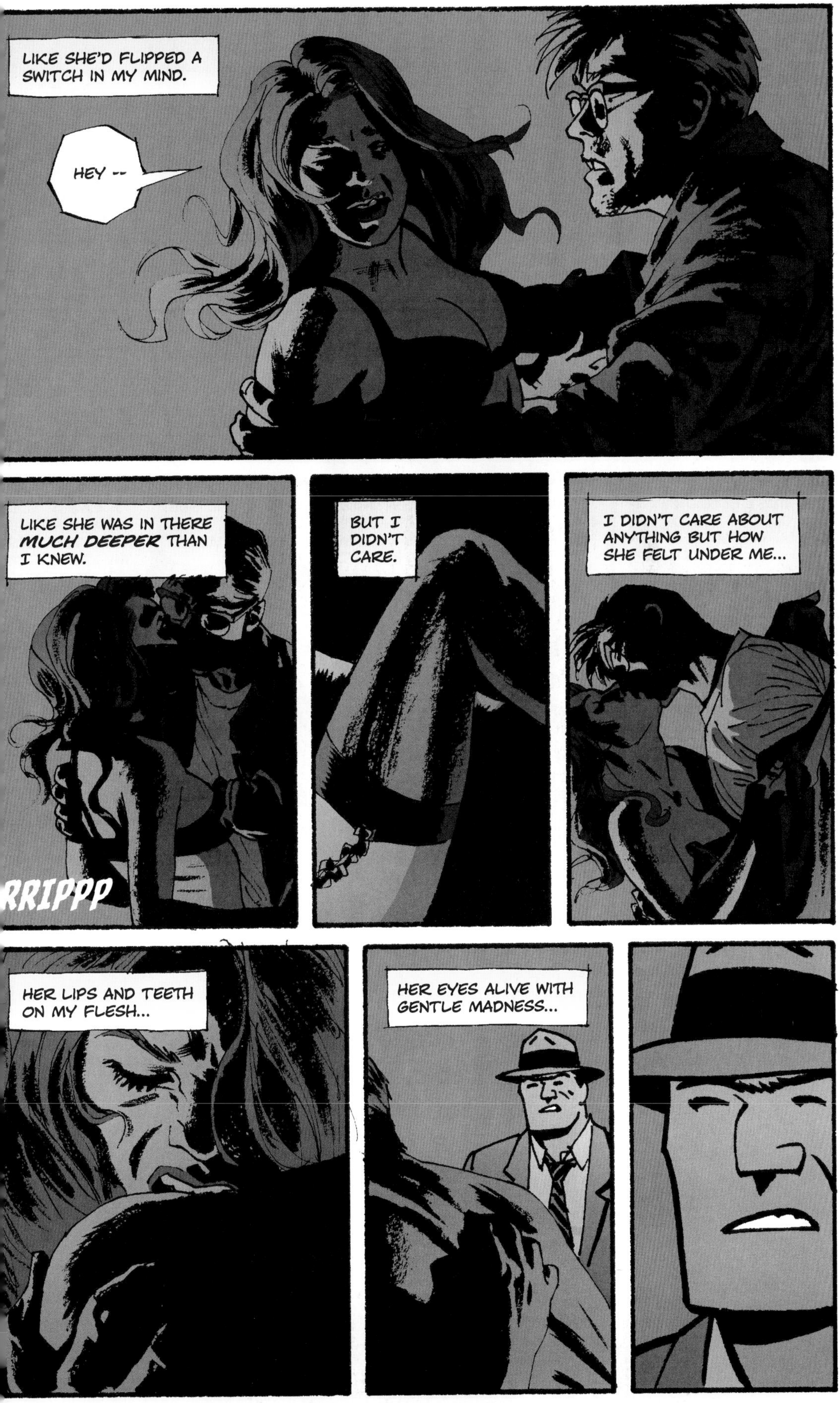
LIKE SHE'D FLIPPED A SWITCH IN MY MIND.
HEY --
LIKE SHE WAS IN THERE *MUCH DEEPER* THAN I KNEW.
RRIPPP
BUT I DIDN'T CARE.
I DIDN'T CARE ABOUT ANYTHING BUT HOW SHE FELT UNDER ME...
HER LIPS AND TEETH ON MY FLESH...
HER EYES ALIVE WITH GENTLE MADNESS...

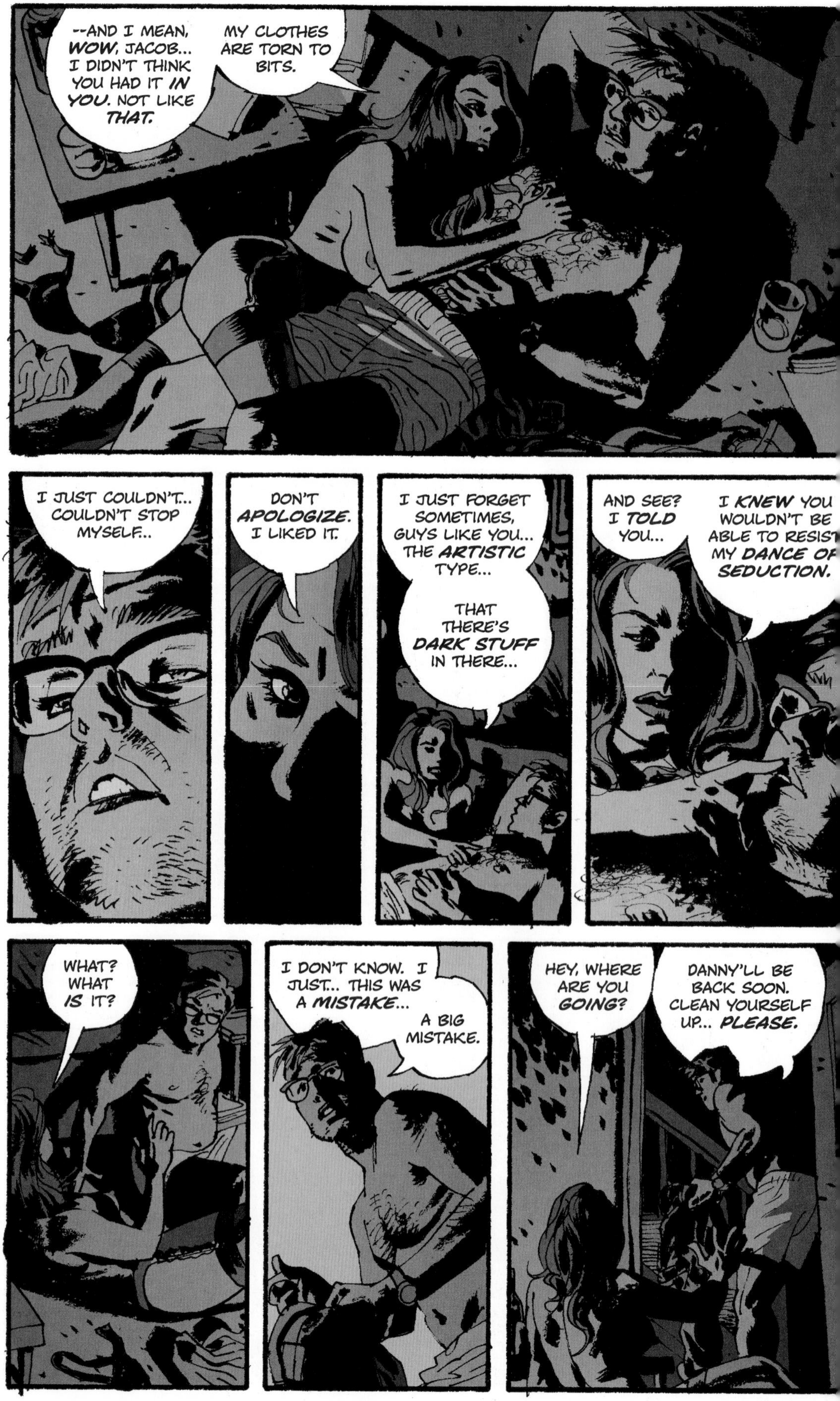
--AND I MEAN, WOW, JACOB... I DIDN'T THINK YOU HAD IT IN YOU. NOT LIKE THAT.
MY CLOTHES ARE TORN TO BITS.
I JUST COULDN'T... COULDN'T STOP MYSELF...
DON'T APOLOGIZE. I LIKED IT.
I JUST FORGET SOMETIMES, GUYS LIKE YOU... THE ARTISTIC TYPE...
THAT THERE'S DARK STUFF IN THERE...
AND SEE? I TOLD YOU...
I KNEW YOU WOULDN'T BE ABLE TO RESIST MY DANCE OF SEDUCTION.
WHAT? WHAT IS IT?
I DON'T KNOW. I JUST... THIS WAS A MISTAKE...
A BIG MISTAKE.
HEY, WHERE ARE YOU GOING?
DANNY'LL BE BACK SOON. CLEAN YOURSELF UP... PLEASE.

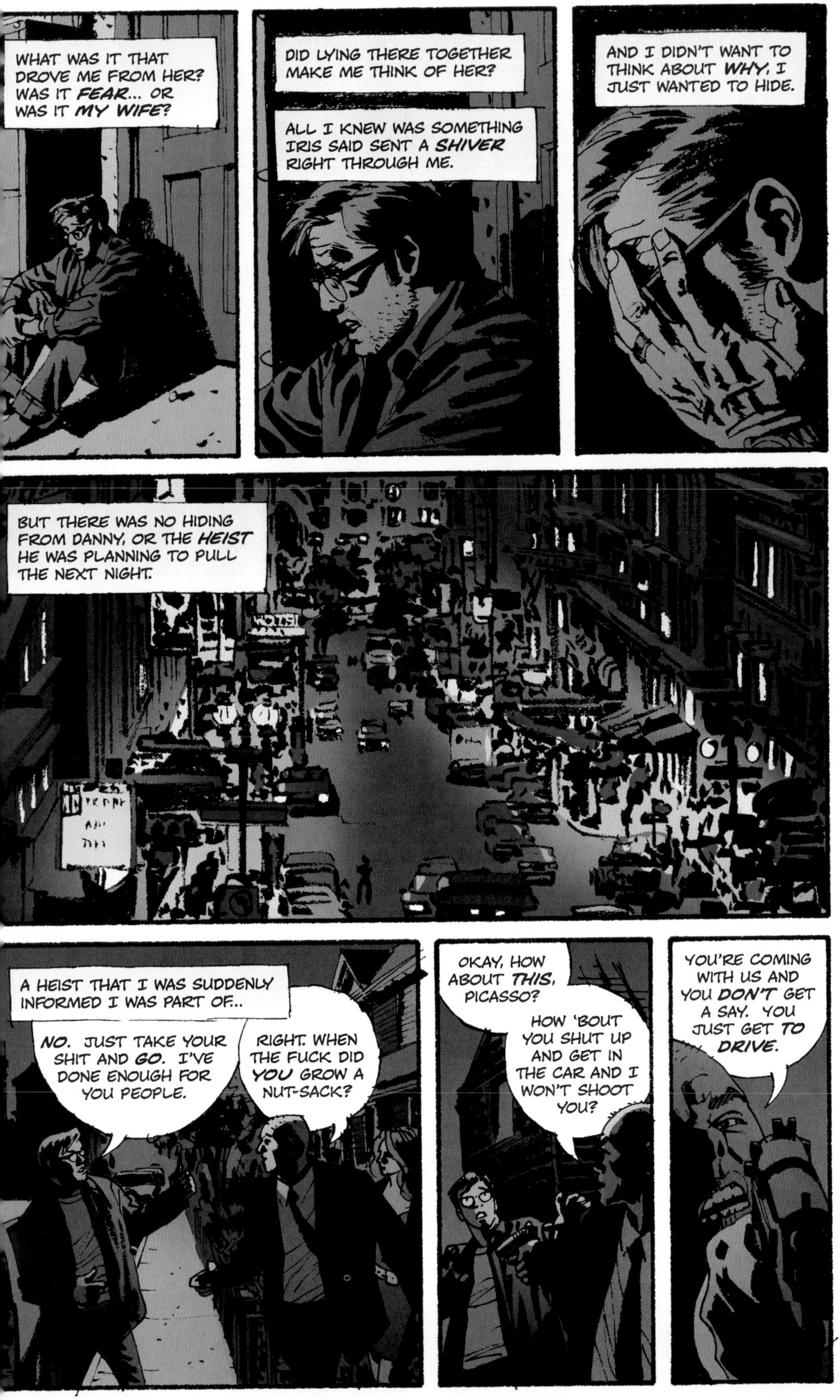
WHAT WAS IT THAT DROVE ME FROM HER? WAS IT FEAR... OR WAS IT MY WIFE?
DID LYING THERE TOGETHER MAKE ME THINK OF HER?
ALL I KNEW WAS SOMETHING IRIS SAID SENT A SHIVER RIGHT THROUGH ME.
AND I DIDN'T WANT TO THINK ABOUT WHY, I JUST WANTED TO HIDE.
BUT THERE WAS NO HIDING FROM DANNY, OR THE HEIST HE WAS PLANNING TO PULL THE NEXT NIGHT.
A HEIST THAT I WAS SUDDENLY INFORMED I WAS PART OF...
NO. JUST TAKE YOUR SHIT AND GO. I'VE DONE ENOUGH FOR YOU PEOPLE.
RIGHT. WHEN THE FUCK DID YOU GROW A NUT-SACK?
OKAY, HOW ABOUT THIS, PICASSO?
HOW 'BOUT YOU SHUT UP AND GET IN THE CAR AND I WON'T SHOOT YOU?
YOU'RE COMING WITH US AND YOU DON'T GET A SAY. YOU JUST GET TO DRIVE.

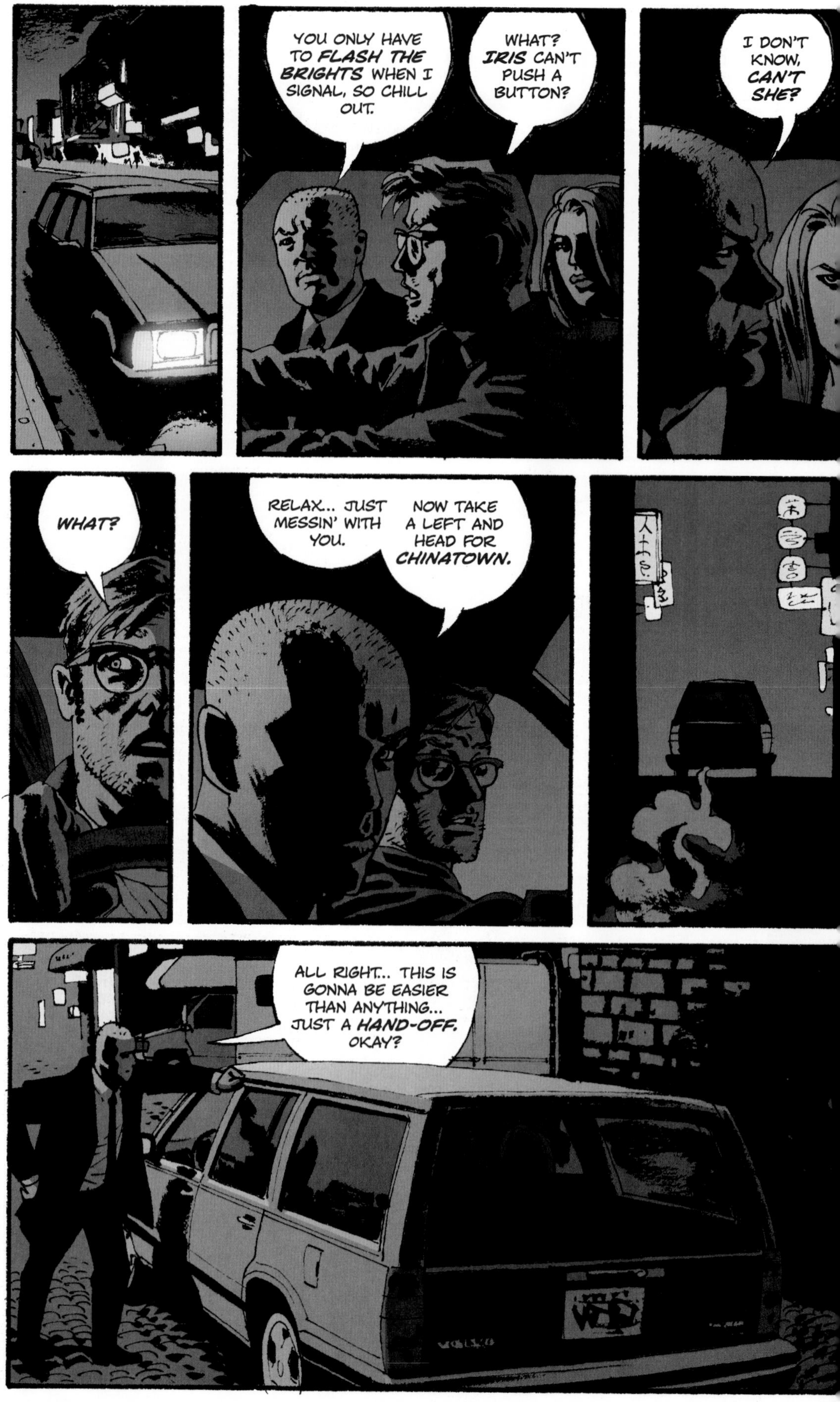
YOU ONLY HAVE TO FLASH THE BRIGHTS WHEN I SIGNAL, SO CHILL OUT.
WHAT? IRIS CAN'T PUSH A BUTTON?
I DON'T KNOW, CAN'T SHE?
WHAT?
RELAX... JUST MESSIN' WITH YOU.
NOW TAKE A LEFT AND HEAD FOR CHINATOWN.
ALL RIGHT... THIS IS GONNA BE EASIER THAN ANYTHING... JUST A HAND-OFF. OKAY?

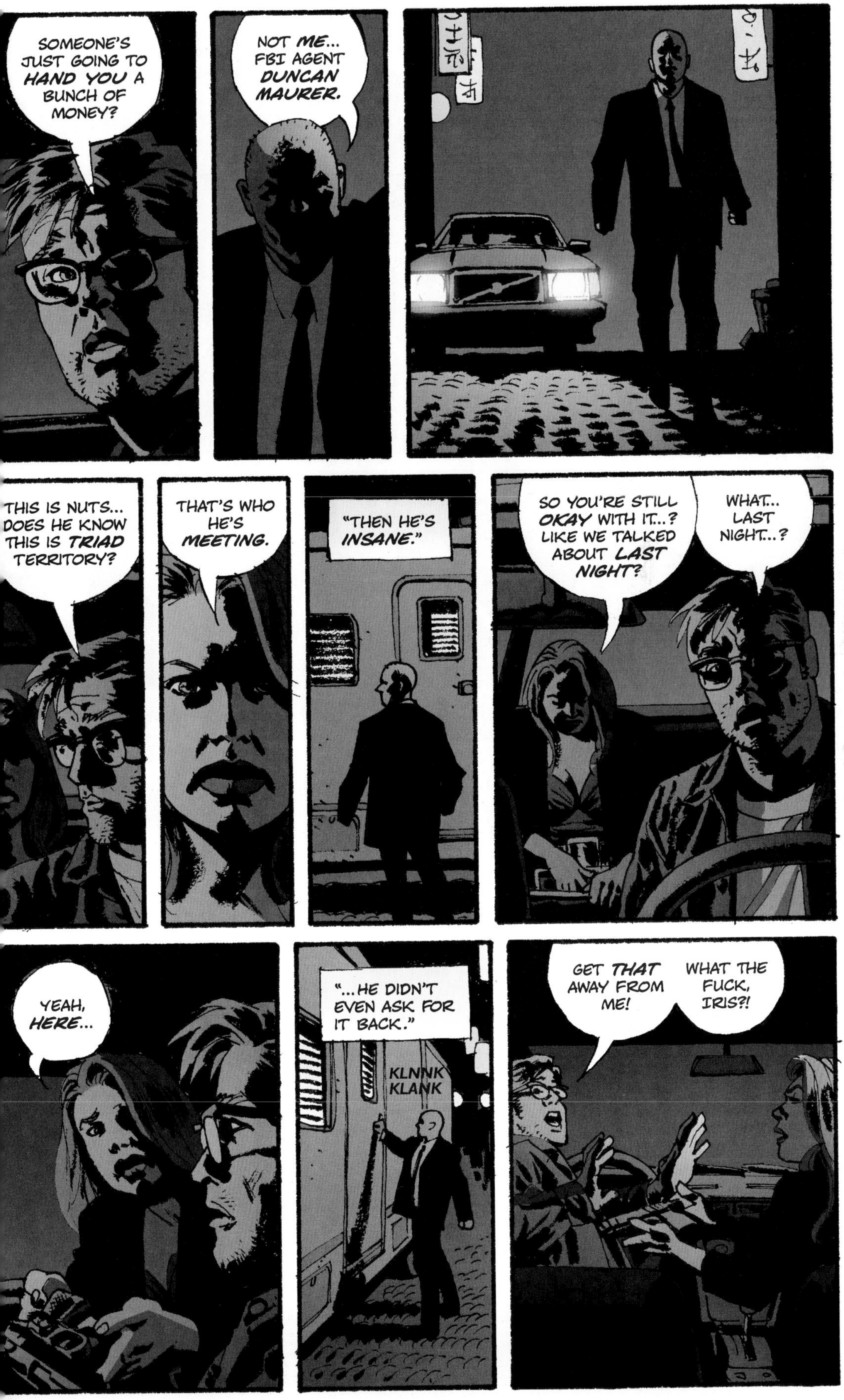
SOMEONE'S JUST GOING TO HAND YOU A BUNCH OF MONEY?
NOT ME... FBI AGENT DUNCAN MAURER.
THIS IS NUTS... DOES HE KNOW THIS IS TRIAD TERRITORY?
THAT'S WHO HE'S MEETING.
"THEN HE'S INSANE."
SO YOU'RE STILL OKAY WITH IT...? LIKE WE TALKED ABOUT LAST NIGHT?
WHAT... LAST NIGHT...?
YEAH, HERE...
"...HE DIDN'T EVEN ASK FOR IT BACK."
KLNNK KLANK
GET THAT AWAY FROM ME!
WHAT THE FUCK, IRIS?!

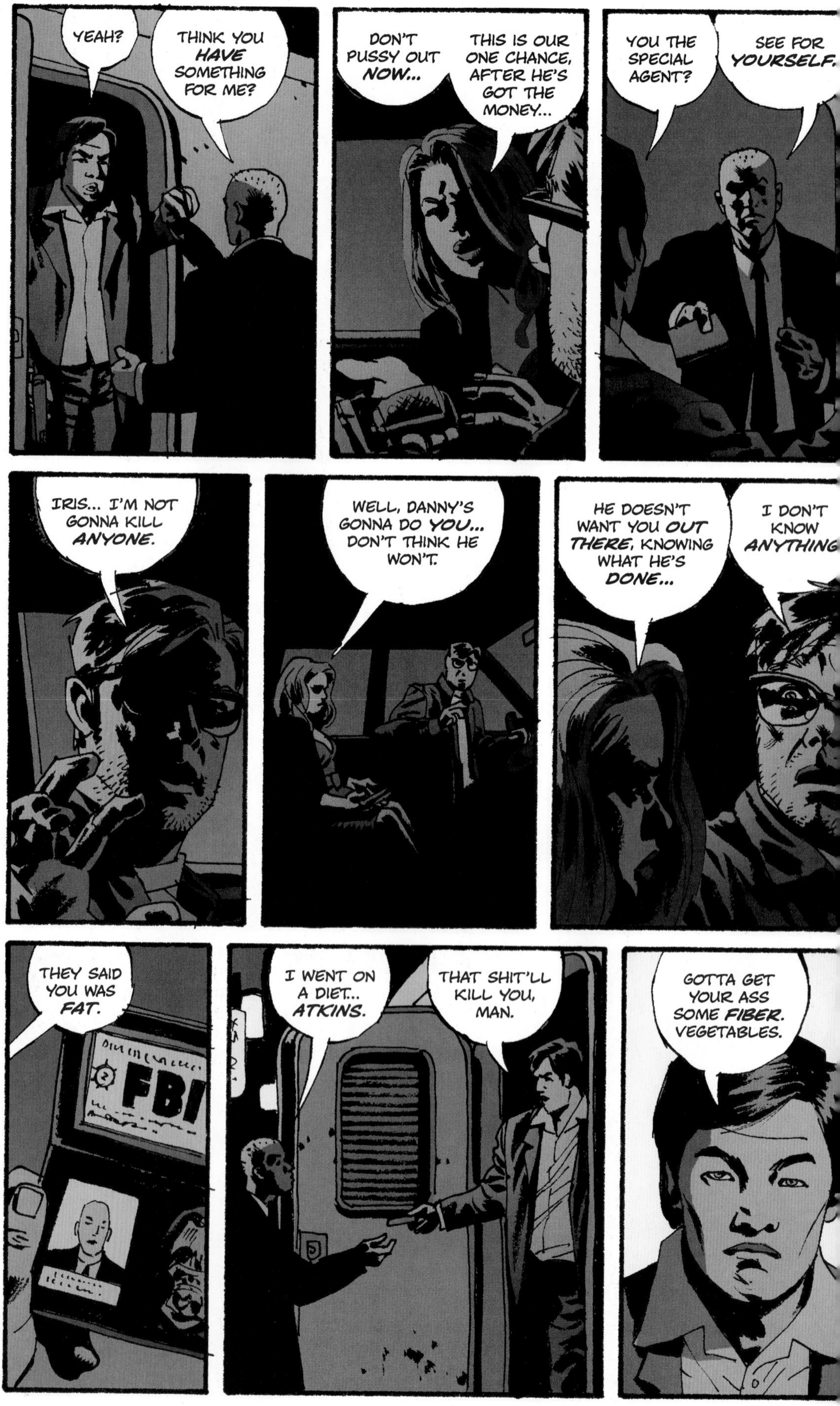
YEAH?
THINK YOU HAVE SOMETHING FOR ME?
DON'T PUSSY OUT NOW...
THIS IS OUR ONE CHANCE, AFTER HE'S GOT THE MONEY...
YOU THE SPECIAL AGENT?
SEE FOR YOURSELF.
IRIS... I'M NOT GONNA KILL ANYONE.
WELL, DANNY'S GONNA DO YOU... DON'T THINK HE WON'T.
HE DOESN'T WANT YOU OUT THERE, KNOWING WHAT HE'S DONE...
I DON'T KNOW ANYTHING
THEY SAID YOU WAS FAT.
FBI
I WENT ON A DIET... ATKINS.
THAT SHIT'LL KILL YOU, MAN.
GOTTA GET YOUR ASS SOME FIBER. VEGETABLES.

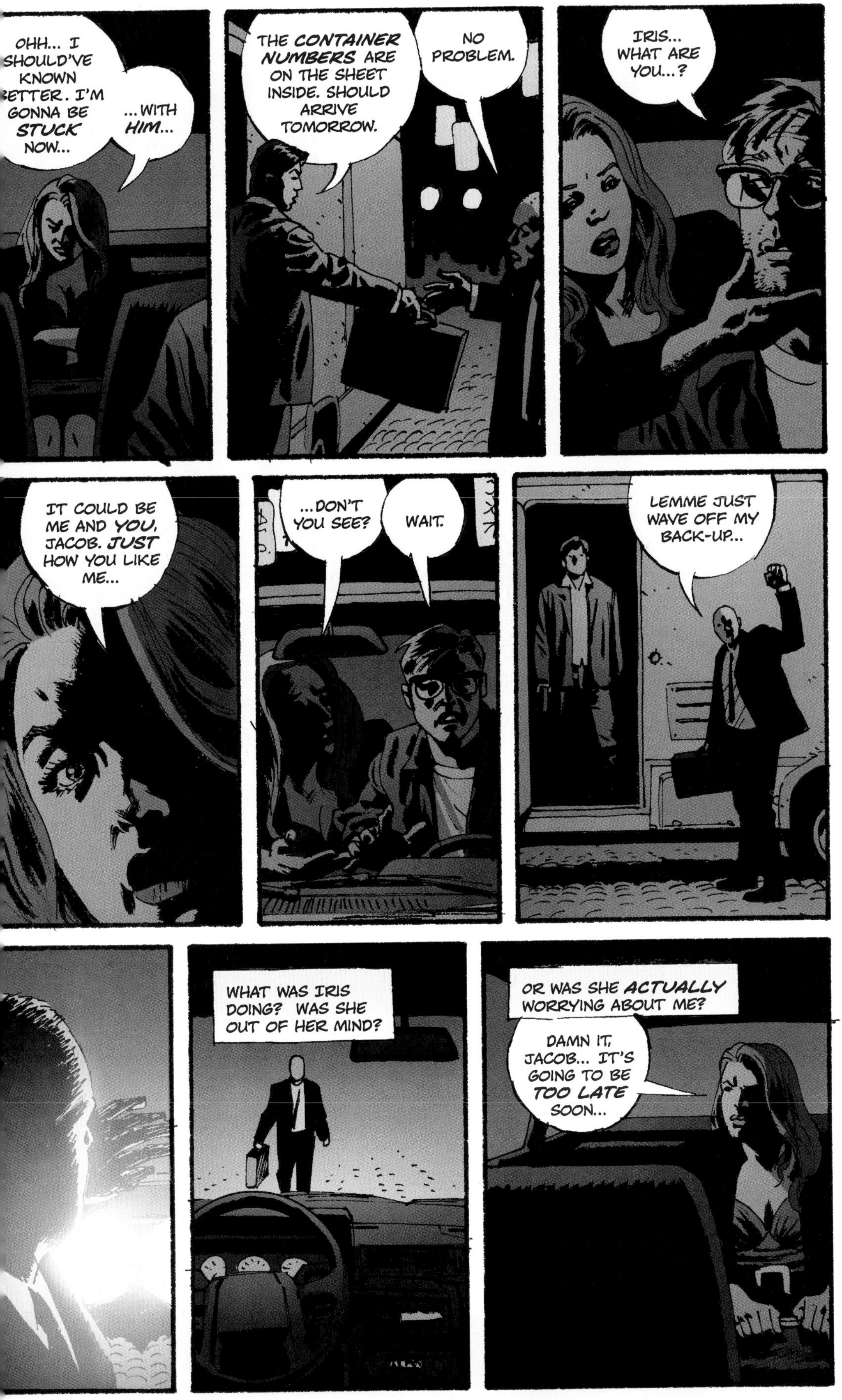
OHH... I SHOULD'VE KNOWN BETTER. I'M GONNA BE STUCK NOW...
...WITH HIM...
THE CONTAINER NUMBERS ARE ON THE SHEET INSIDE. SHOULD ARRIVE TOMORROW.
NO PROBLEM.
IRIS... WHAT ARE YOU...?
IT COULD BE ME AND YOU, JACOB. JUST HOW YOU LIKE ME...
...DON'T YOU SEE?
WAIT.
LEMME JUST WAVE OFF MY BACK-UP...
WHAT WAS IRIS DOING? WAS SHE OUT OF HER MIND?
OR WAS SHE ACTUALLY WORRYING ABOUT ME?
DAMN IT, JACOB... IT'S GOING TO BE TOO LATE SOON...

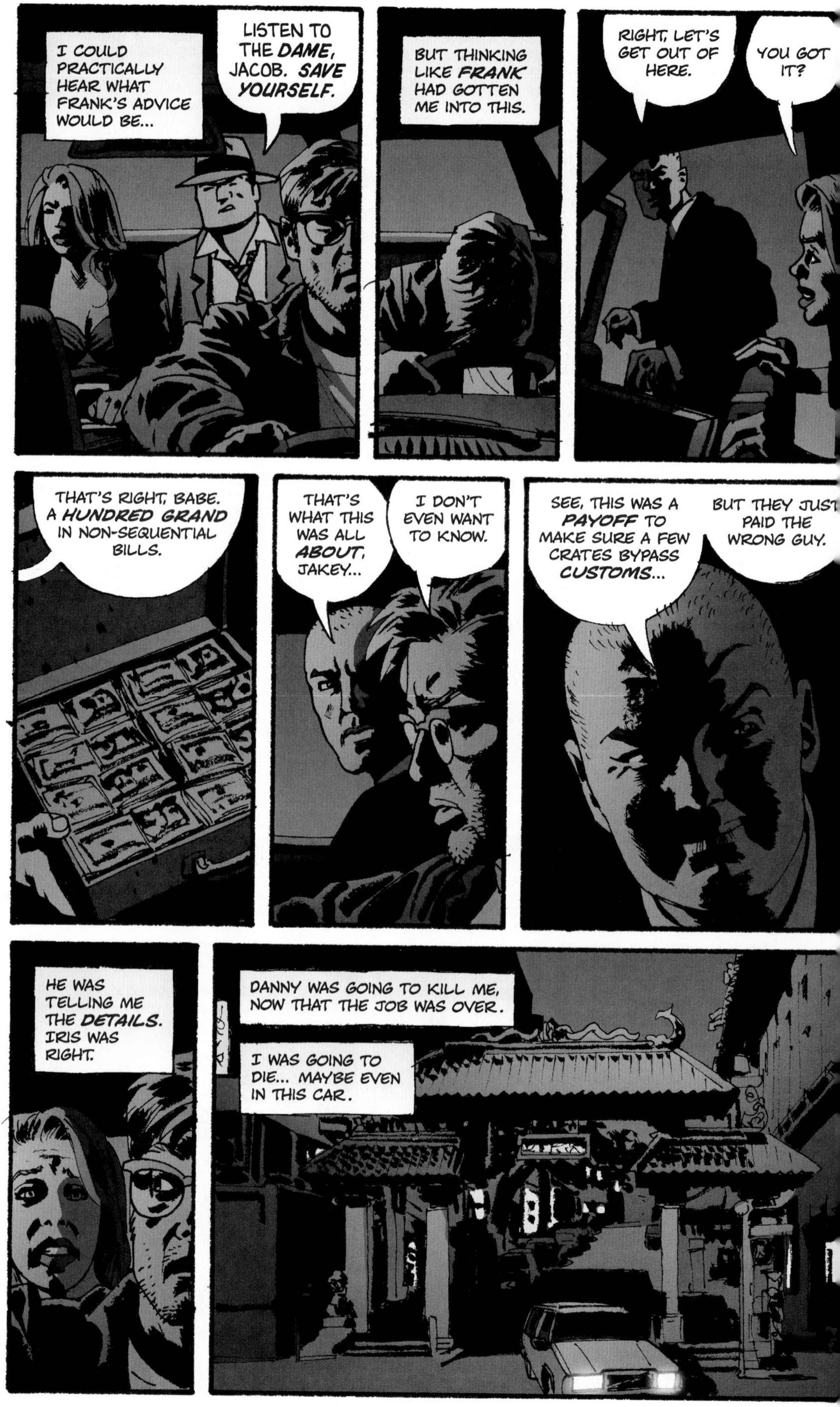
I COULD PRACTICALLY HEAR WHAT FRANK'S ADVICE WOULD BE...
LISTEN TO THE DAME, JACOB. SAVE YOURSELF.
BUT THINKING LIKE FRANK HAD GOTTEN ME INTO THIS.
RIGHT, LET'S GET OUT OF HERE.
YOU GOT IT?
THAT'S RIGHT, BABE. A HUNDRED GRAND IN NON-SEQUENTIAL BILLS.
THAT'S WHAT THIS WAS ALL ABOUT, JAKEY...
I DON'T EVEN WANT TO KNOW.
SEE, THIS WAS A PAYOFF TO MAKE SURE A FEW CRATES BYPASS CUSTOMS...
BUT THEY JUST PAID THE WRONG GUY.
HE WAS TELLING ME THE DETAILS. IRIS WAS RIGHT.
DANNY WAS GOING TO KILL ME, NOW THAT THE JOB WAS OVER.
I WAS GOING TO DIE... MAYBE EVEN IN THIS CAR.

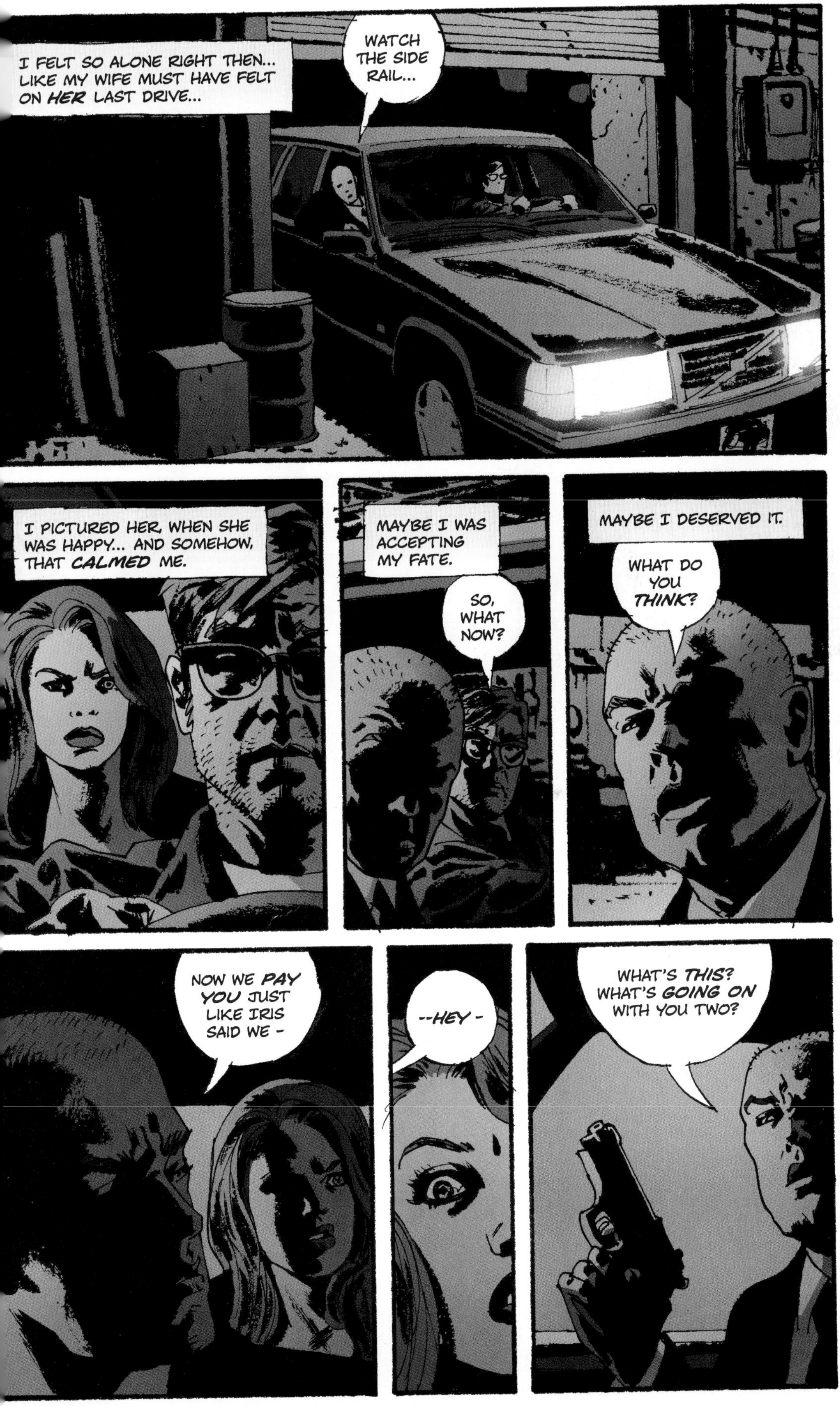
I FELT SO ALONE RIGHT THEN... LIKE MY WIFE MUST HAVE FELT ON *HER* LAST DRIVE...
WATCH THE SIDE RAIL...
I PICTURED HER, WHEN SHE WAS HAPPY... AND SOMEHOW, THAT *CALMED* ME.
MAYBE I WAS ACCEPTING MY FATE.
SO, WHAT NOW?
MAYBE I DESERVED IT.
WHAT DO YOU *THINK?*
NOW WE *PAY YOU* JUST LIKE IRIS SAID WE -
--*HEY* -
WHAT'S *THIS?* WHAT'S *GOING ON* WITH YOU TWO?

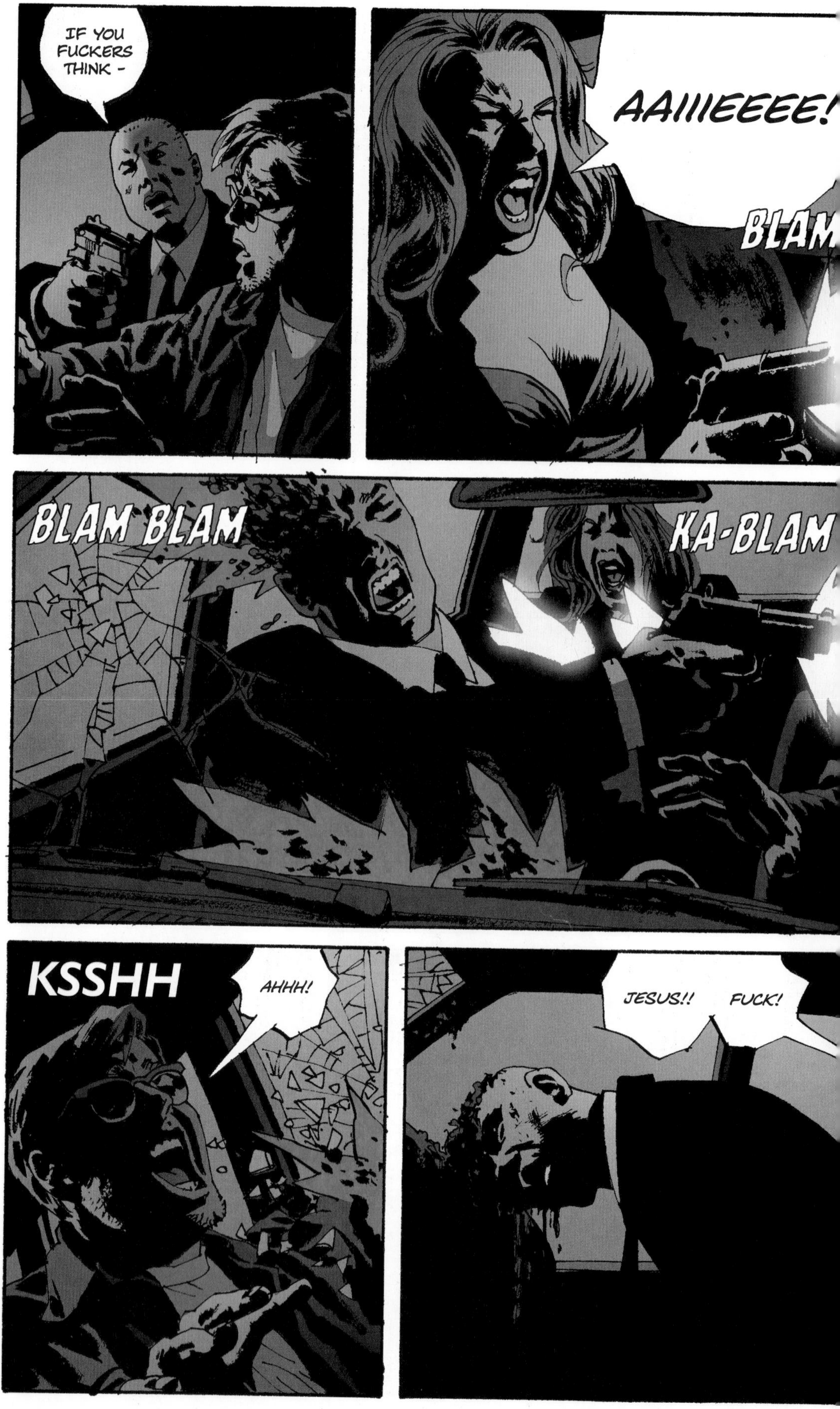
IF YOU FUCKERS THINK -
AAIIIEEEE!
BLAM
BLAM BLAM
KA-BLAM
KSSHH
AHHH!
JESUS!!
FUCK!

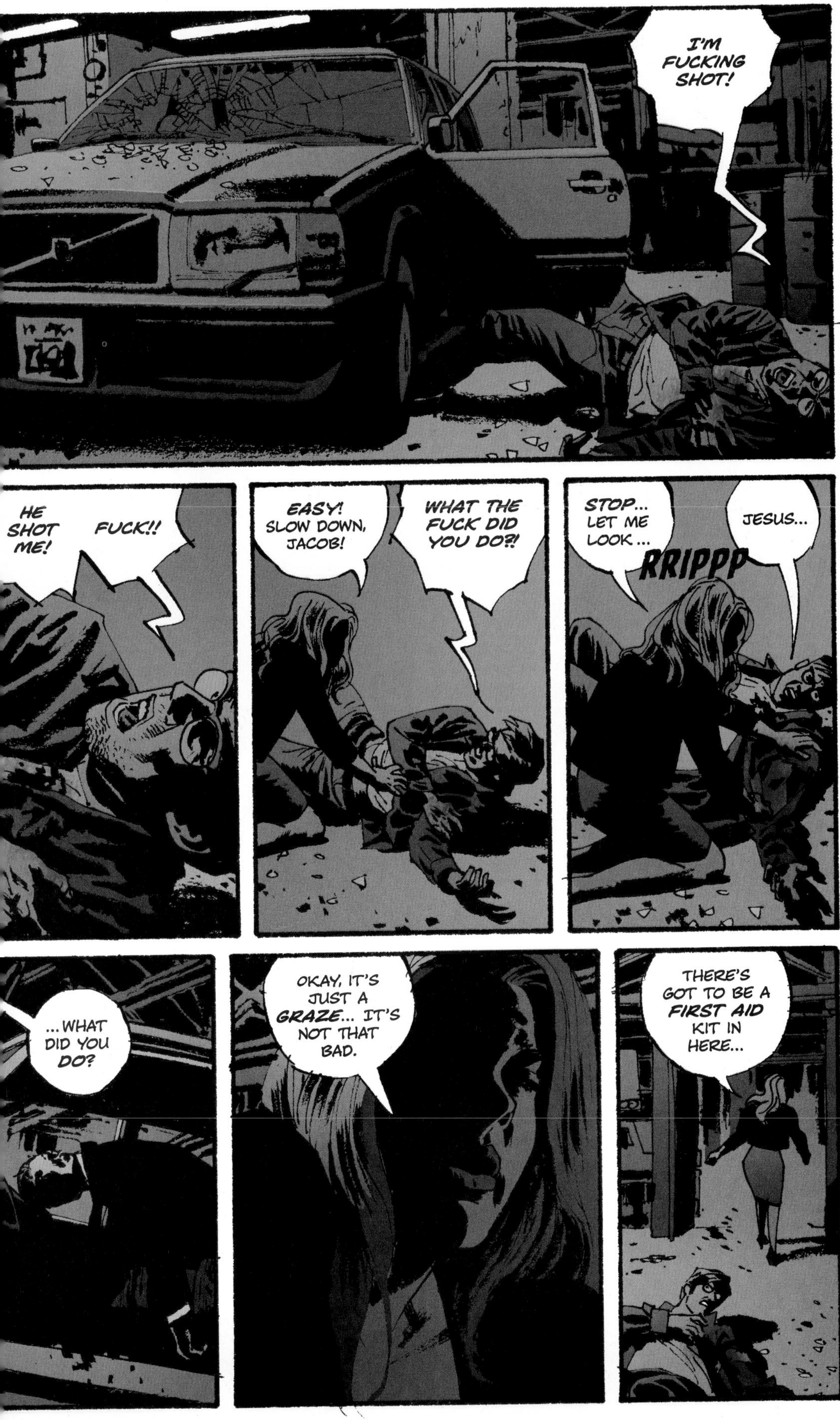
I'M FUCKING SHOT!
HE SHOT ME!
FUCK!!
EASY! SLOW DOWN, JACOB!
WHAT THE FUCK DID YOU DO?!
STOP... LET ME LOOK...
RRIPPP
JESUS...
...WHAT DID YOU DO?
OKAY, IT'S JUST A GRAZE... IT'S NOT THAT BAD.
THERE'S GOT TO BE A FIRST AID KIT IN HERE...

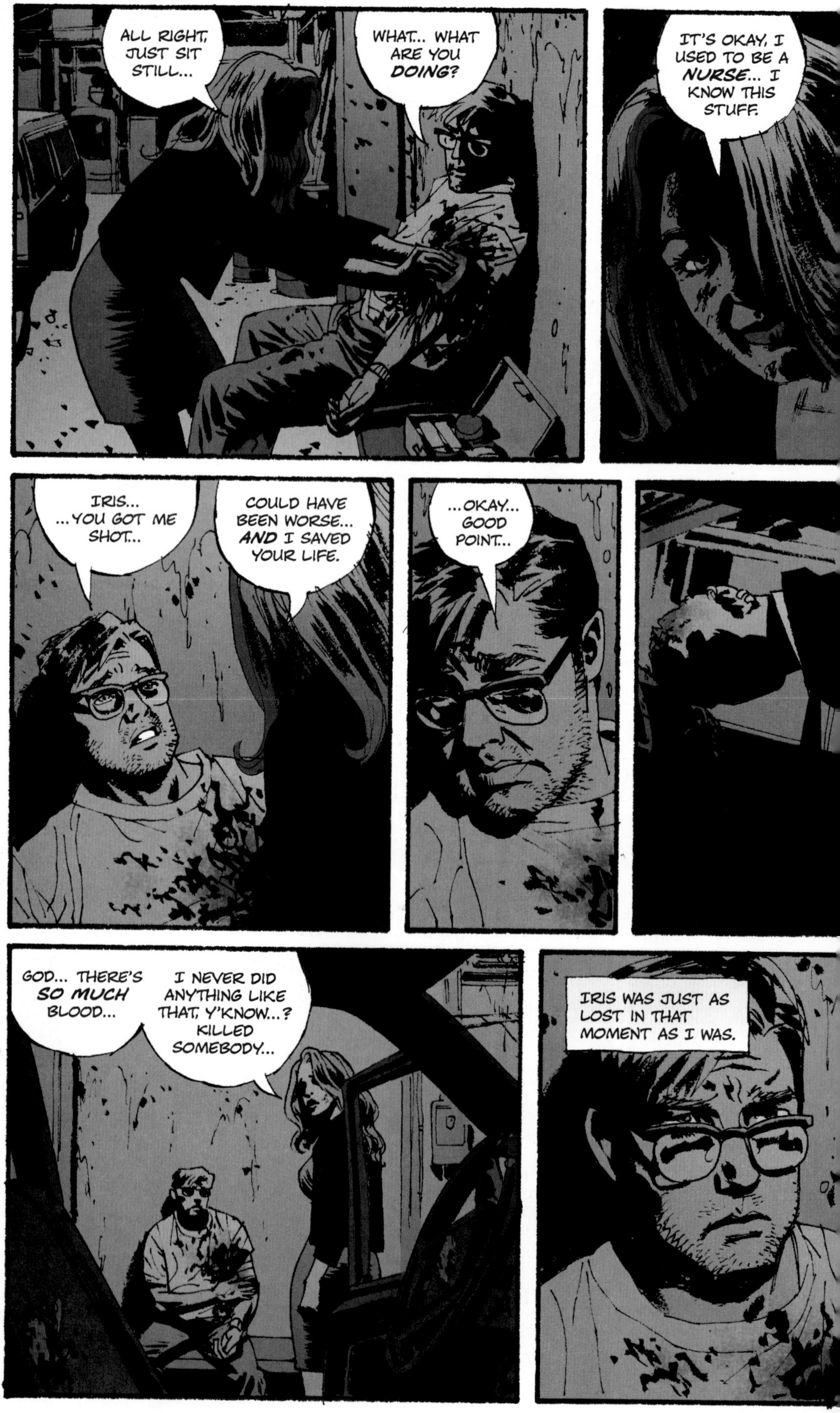
ALL RIGHT, JUST SIT STILL...
WHAT... WHAT ARE YOU *DOING?*
IT'S OKAY, I USED TO BE A *NURSE*... I KNOW THIS STUFF.
IRIS... ...YOU GOT ME SHOT...
COULD HAVE BEEN WORSE... ***AND*** I SAVED YOUR LIFE.
...OKAY... GOOD POINT...
GOD... THERE'S ***SO MUCH*** BLOOD...
I NEVER DID ANYTHING LIKE THAT, Y'KNOW...? KILLED SOMEBODY...
IRIS WAS JUST AS LOST IN THAT MOMENT AS I WAS.

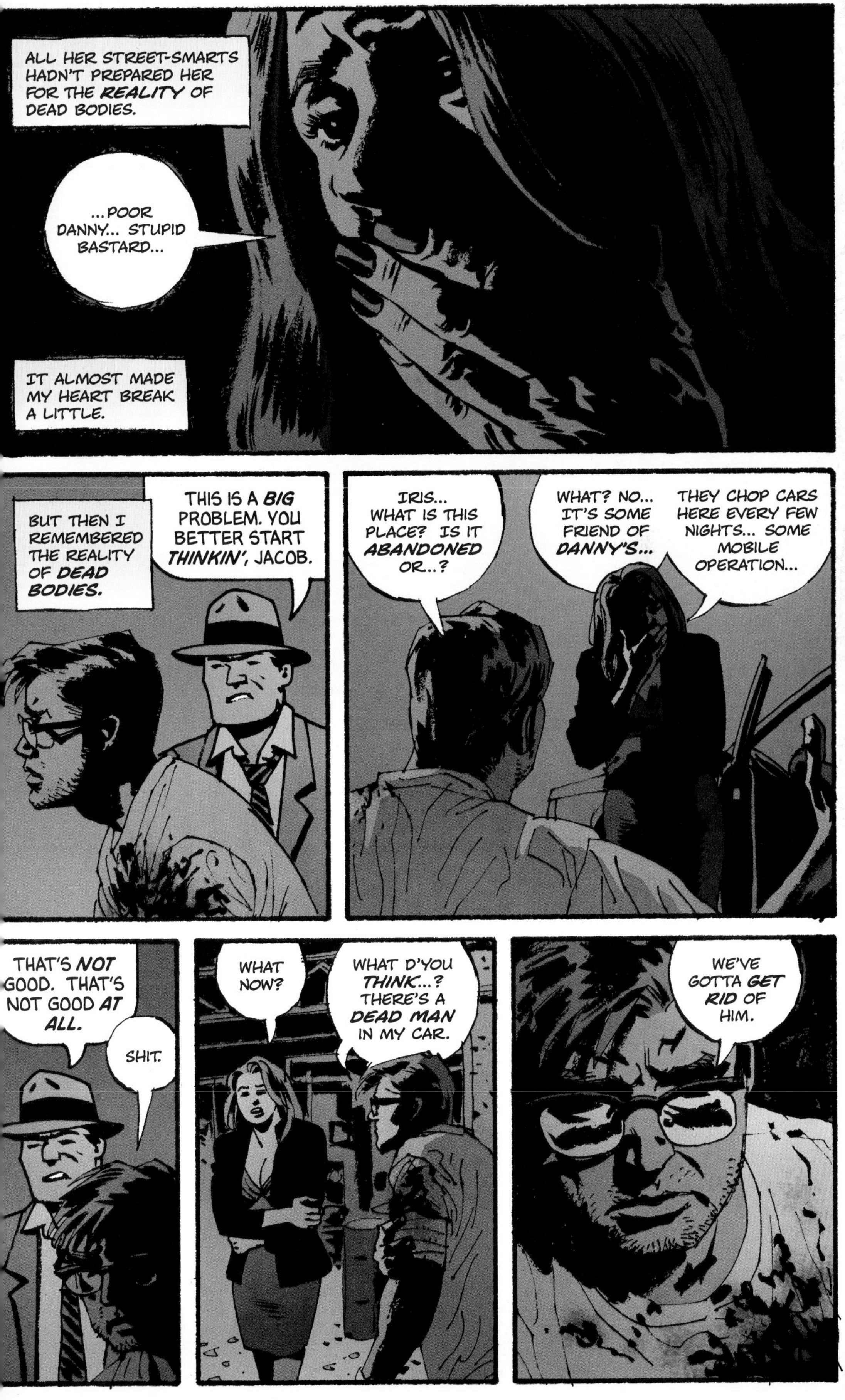
ALL HER STREET-SMARTS HADN'T PREPARED HER FOR THE REALITY OF DEAD BODIES.
...POOR DANNY... STUPID BASTARD...
IT ALMOST MADE MY HEART BREAK A LITTLE.
BUT THEN I REMEMBERED THE REALITY OF DEAD BODIES.
THIS IS A BIG PROBLEM. YOU BETTER START THINKIN', JACOB.
IRIS... WHAT IS THIS PLACE? IS IT ABANDONED OR...?
WHAT? NO... IT'S SOME FRIEND OF DANNY'S...
THEY CHOP CARS HERE EVERY FEW NIGHTS... SOME MOBILE OPERATION...
THAT'S NOT GOOD. THAT'S NOT GOOD AT ALL.
SHIT.
WHAT NOW?
WHAT D'YOU THINK...? THERE'S A DEAD MAN IN MY CAR.
WE'VE GOTTA GET RID OF HIM.

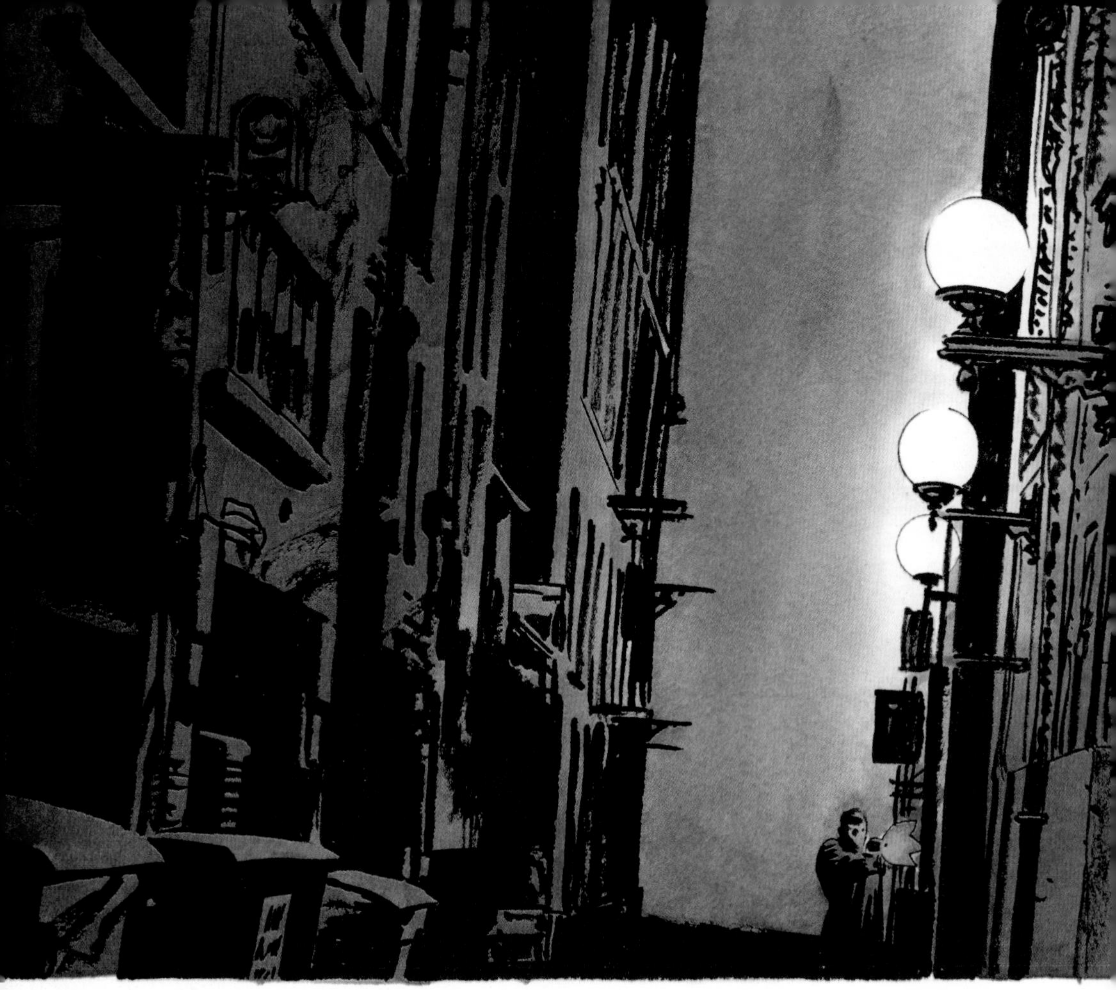

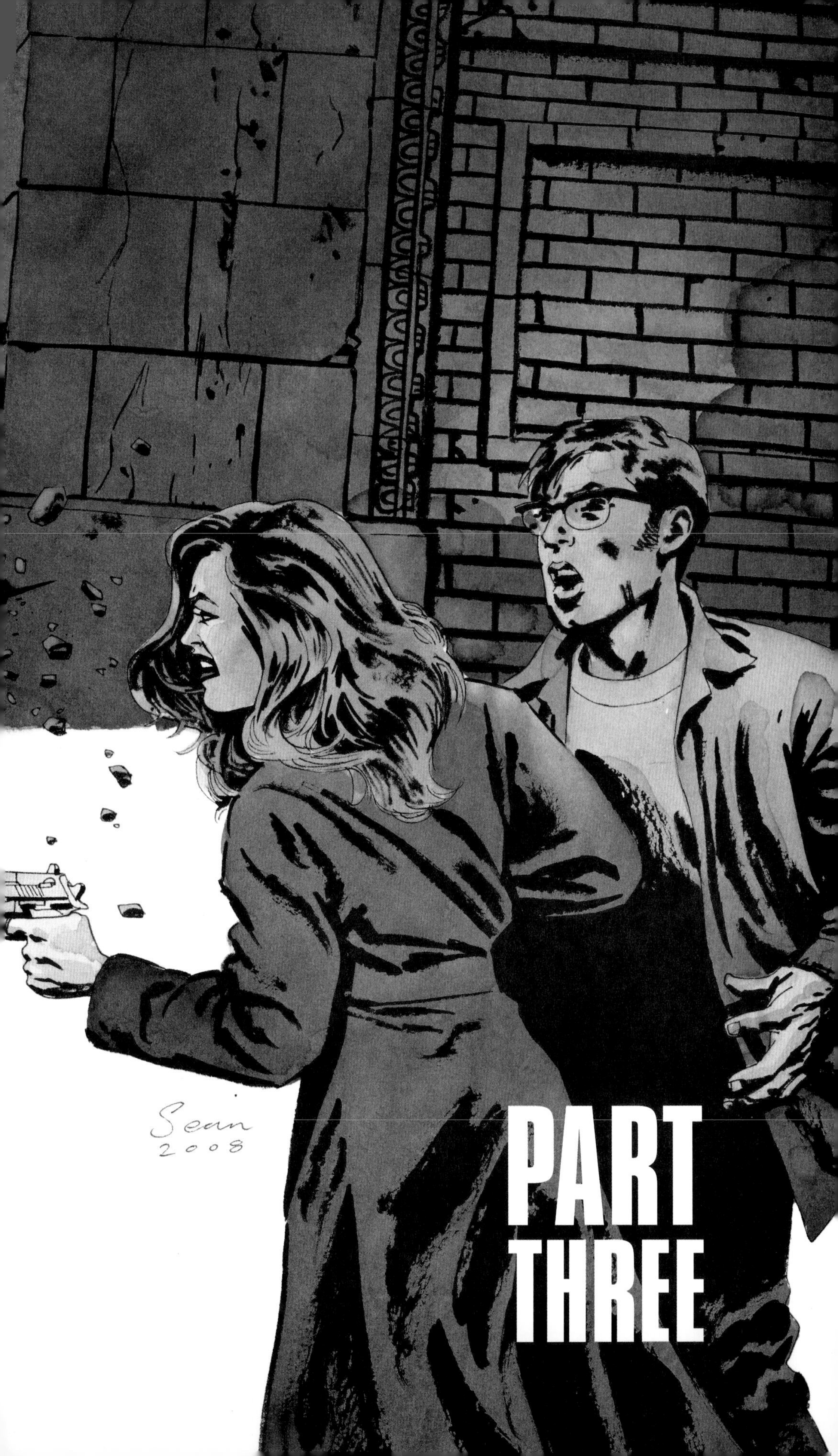
Sean
2008

PART THREE

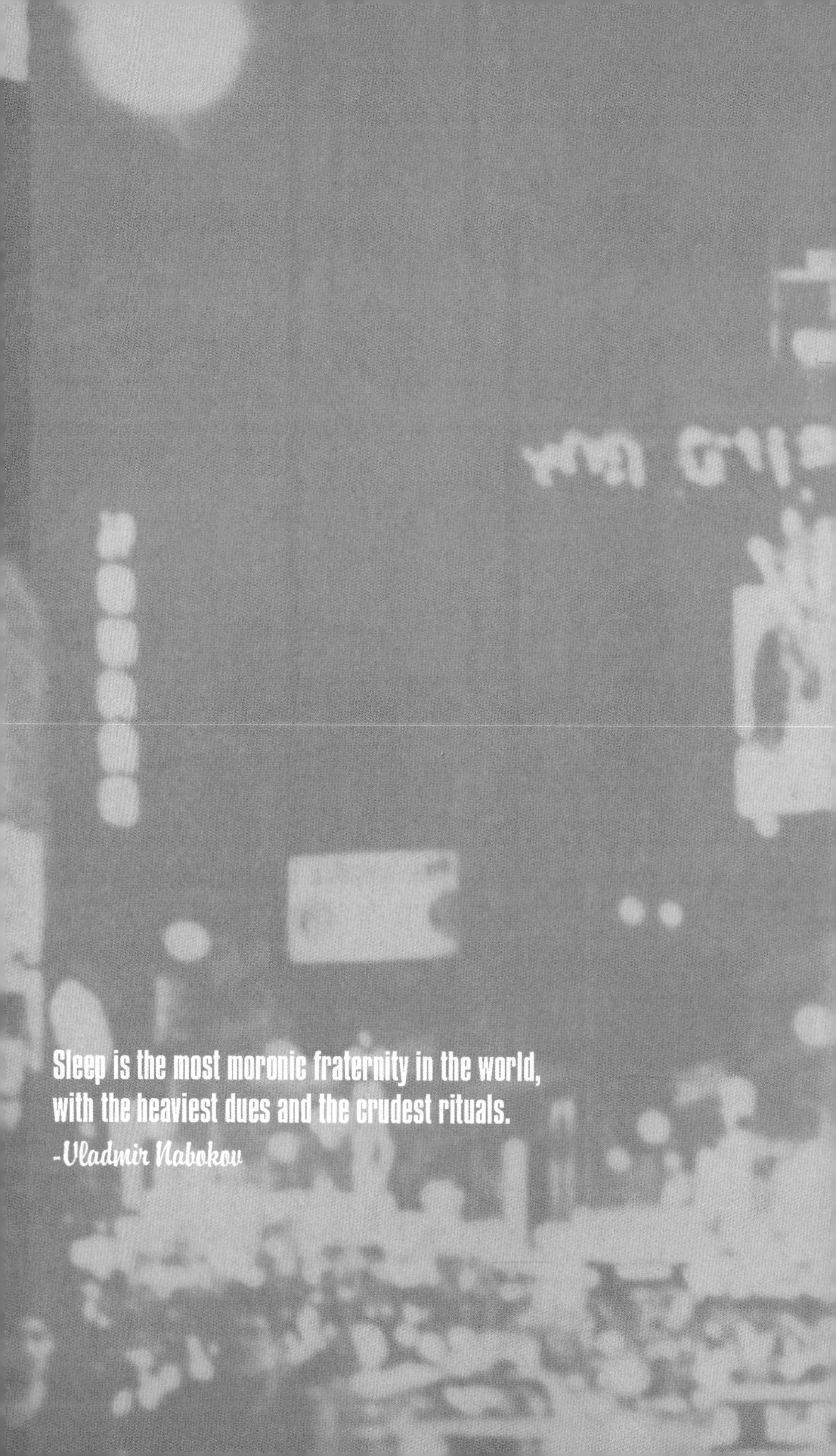

Sleep is the most moronic fraternity in the world,
with the heaviest dues and the crudest rituals.

-Vladmir Nabokov

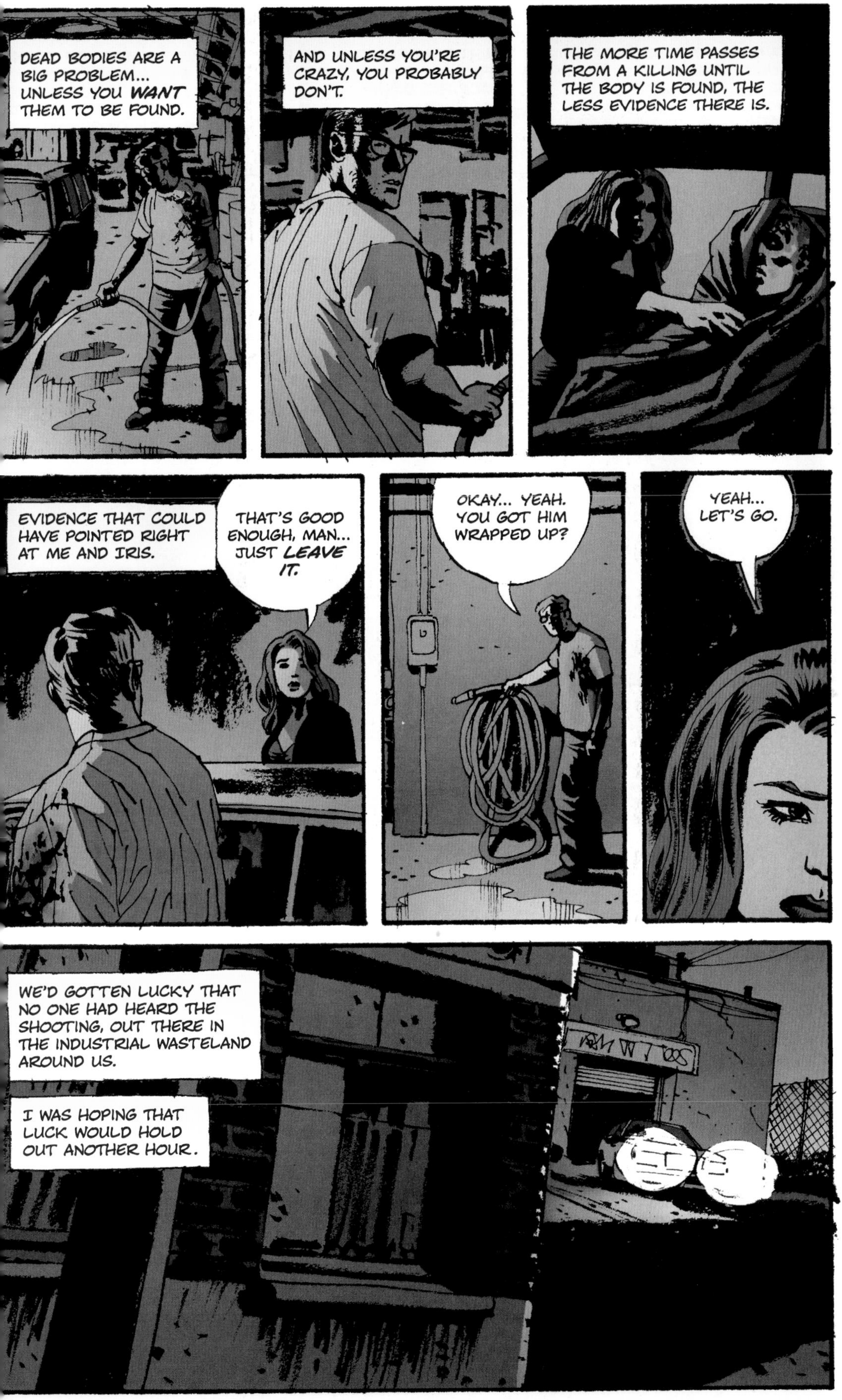
DEAD BODIES ARE A BIG PROBLEM... UNLESS YOU *WANT* THEM TO BE FOUND.
AND UNLESS YOU'RE CRAZY, YOU PROBABLY DON'T.
THE MORE TIME PASSES FROM A KILLING UNTIL THE BODY IS FOUND, THE LESS EVIDENCE THERE IS.
EVIDENCE THAT COULD HAVE POINTED RIGHT AT ME AND IRIS.
THAT'S GOOD ENOUGH, MAN... JUST *LEAVE IT.*
OKAY... YEAH. YOU GOT HIM WRAPPED UP?
YEAH... LET'S GO.
WE'D GOTTEN LUCKY THAT NO ONE HAD HEARD THE SHOOTING, OUT THERE IN THE INDUSTRIAL WASTELAND AROUND US.
I WAS HOPING THAT LUCK WOULD HOLD OUT ANOTHER HOUR.

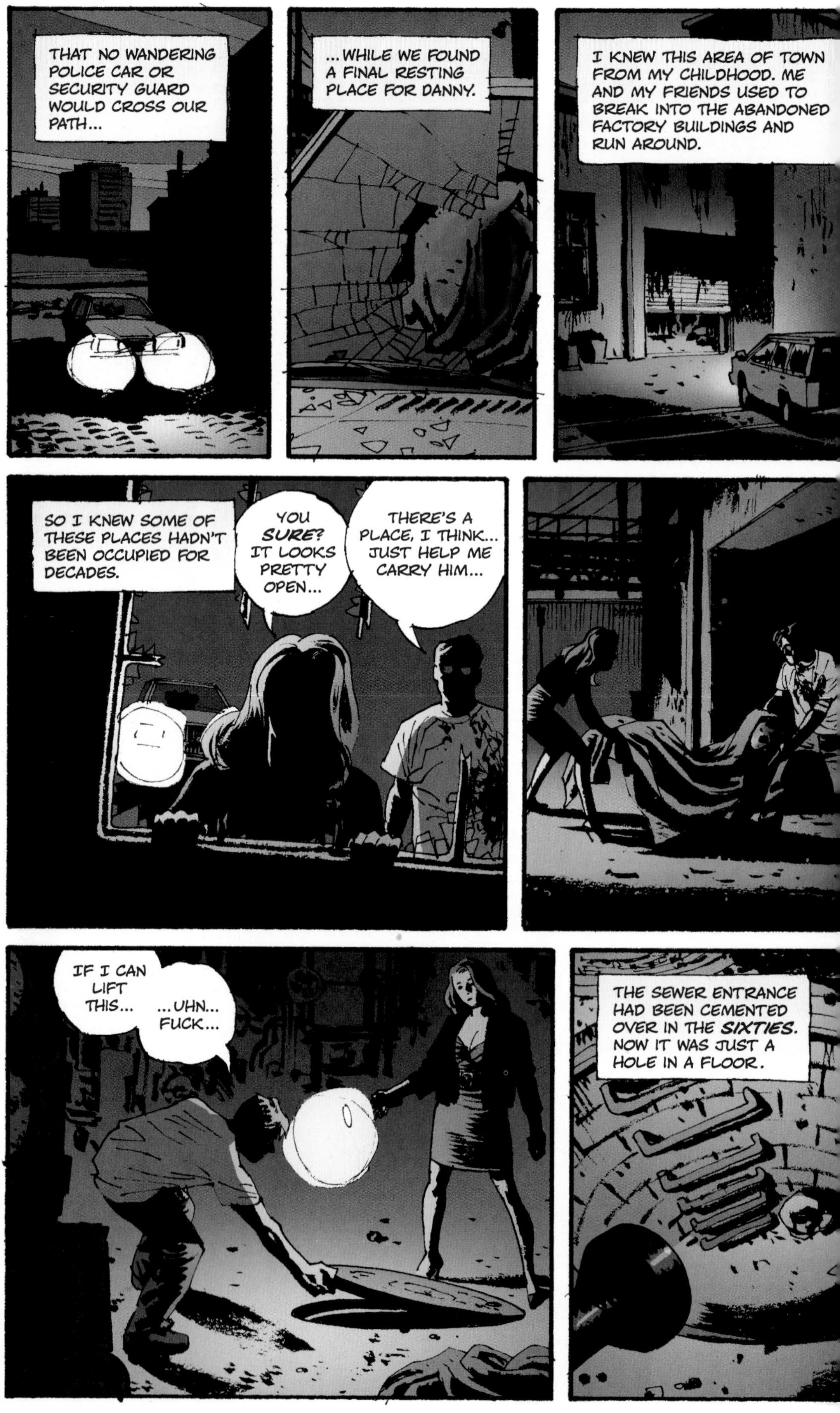
THAT NO WANDERING POLICE CAR OR SECURITY GUARD WOULD CROSS OUR PATH...
...WHILE WE FOUND A FINAL RESTING PLACE FOR DANNY.
I KNEW THIS AREA OF TOWN FROM MY CHILDHOOD. ME AND MY FRIENDS USED TO BREAK INTO THE ABANDONED FACTORY BUILDINGS AND RUN AROUND.
SO I KNEW SOME OF THESE PLACES HADN'T BEEN OCCUPIED FOR DECADES.
YOU *SURE?* IT LOOKS PRETTY OPEN...
THERE'S A PLACE, I THINK... JUST HELP ME CARRY HIM...
IF I CAN LIFT THIS...
...UHN... FUCK...
THE SEWER ENTRANCE HAD BEEN CEMENTED OVER IN THE *SIXTIES.* NOW IT WAS JUST A HOLE IN A FLOOR.

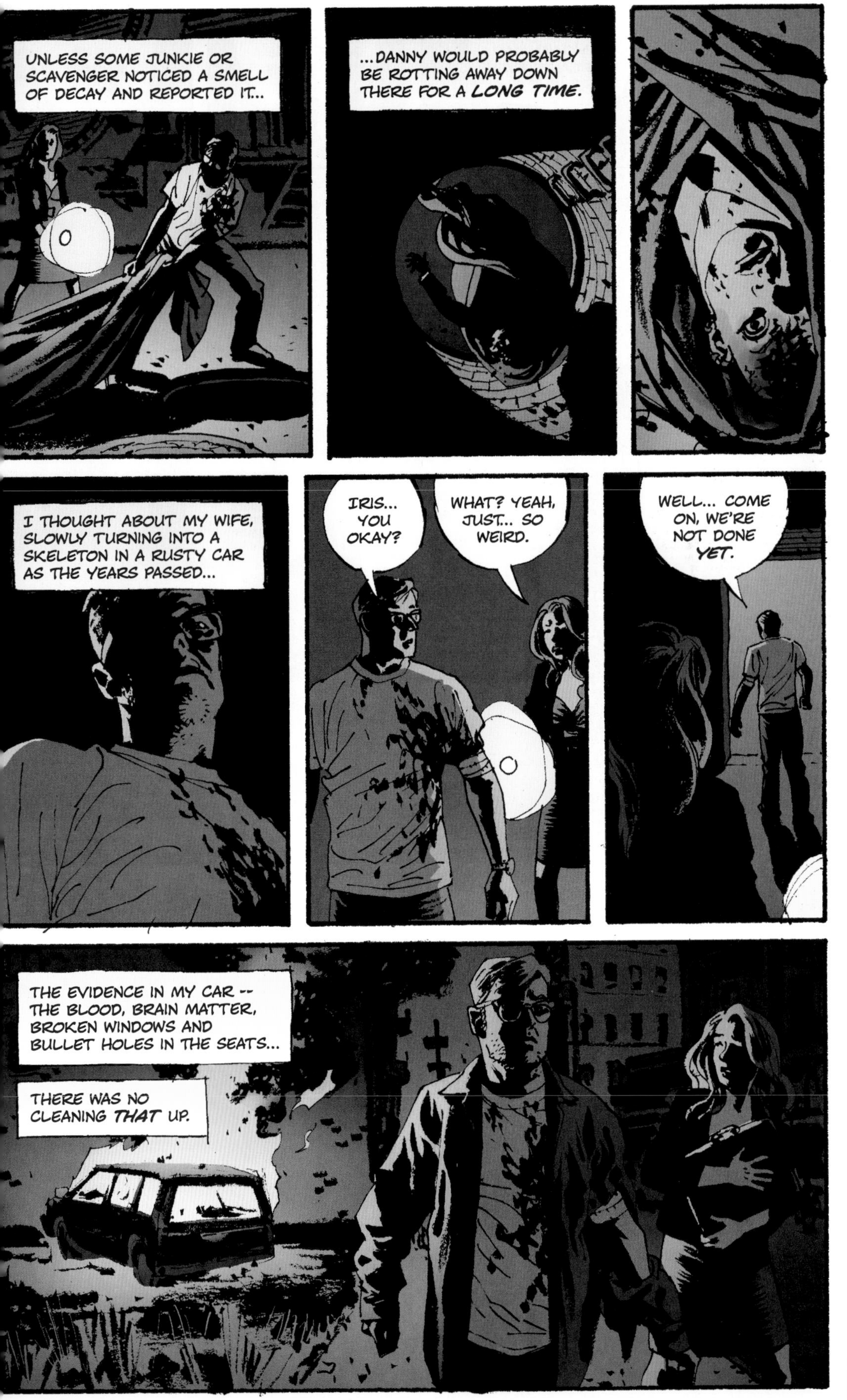
UNLESS SOME JUNKIE OR SCAVENGER NOTICED A SMELL OF DECAY AND REPORTED IT...
...DANNY WOULD PROBABLY BE ROTTING AWAY DOWN THERE FOR A *LONG TIME*.
I THOUGHT ABOUT MY WIFE, SLOWLY TURNING INTO A SKELETON IN A RUSTY CAR AS THE YEARS PASSED...
IRIS... YOU OKAY?
WHAT? YEAH, JUST... SO WEIRD.
WELL... COME ON, WE'RE NOT DONE *YET*.
THE EVIDENCE IN MY CAR -- THE BLOOD, BRAIN MATTER, BROKEN WINDOWS AND BULLET HOLES IN THE SEATS...
THERE WAS NO CLEANING *THAT* UP.

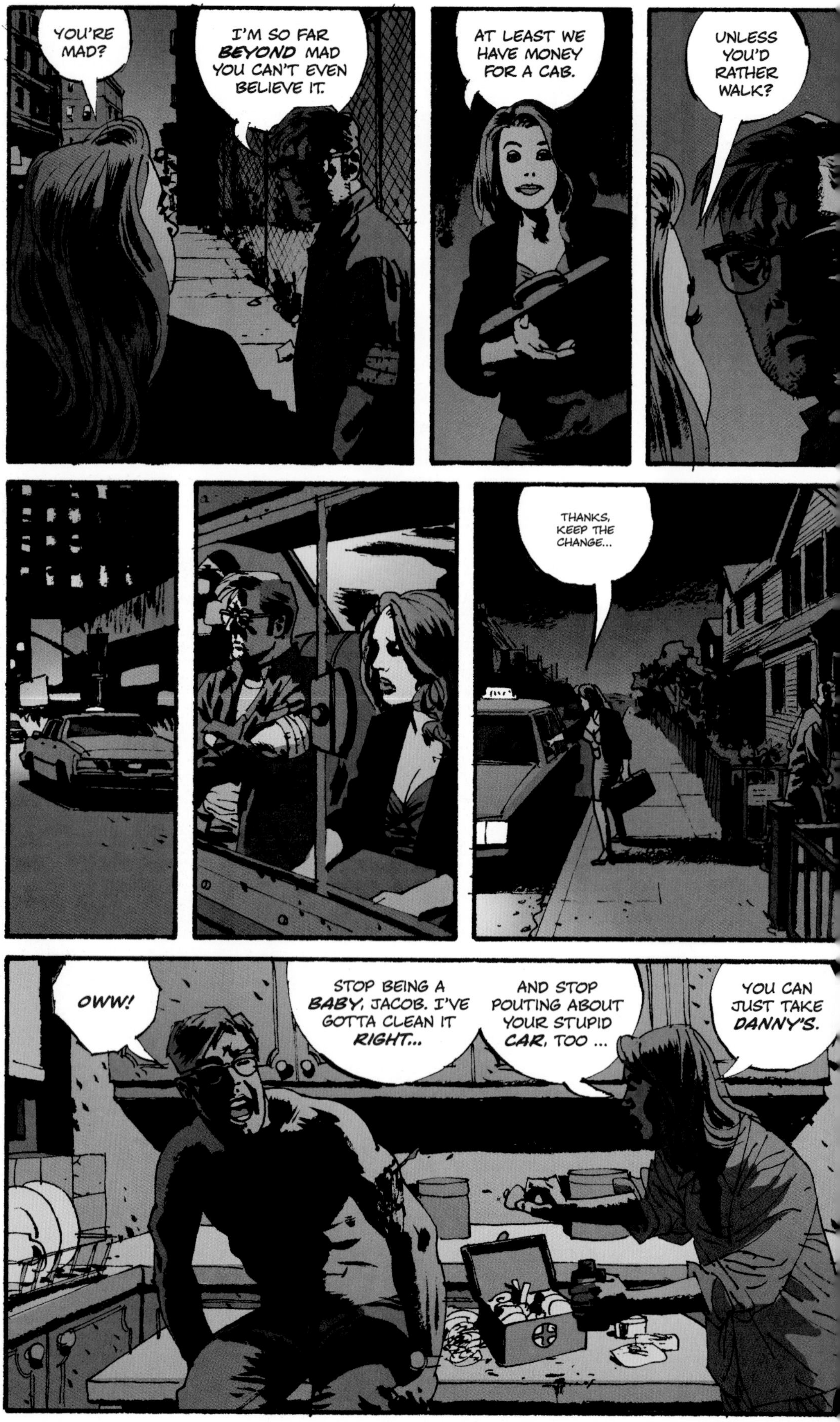

YOU'RE MAD?
I'M SO FAR BEYOND MAD YOU CAN'T EVEN BELIEVE IT.
AT LEAST WE HAVE MONEY FOR A CAB.
UNLESS YOU'D RATHER WALK?
THANKS, KEEP THE CHANGE...
OWW!
STOP BEING A BABY, JACOB. I'VE GOTTA CLEAN IT RIGHT...
AND STOP POUTING ABOUT YOUR STUPID CAR, TOO ...
YOU CAN JUST TAKE DANNY'S.

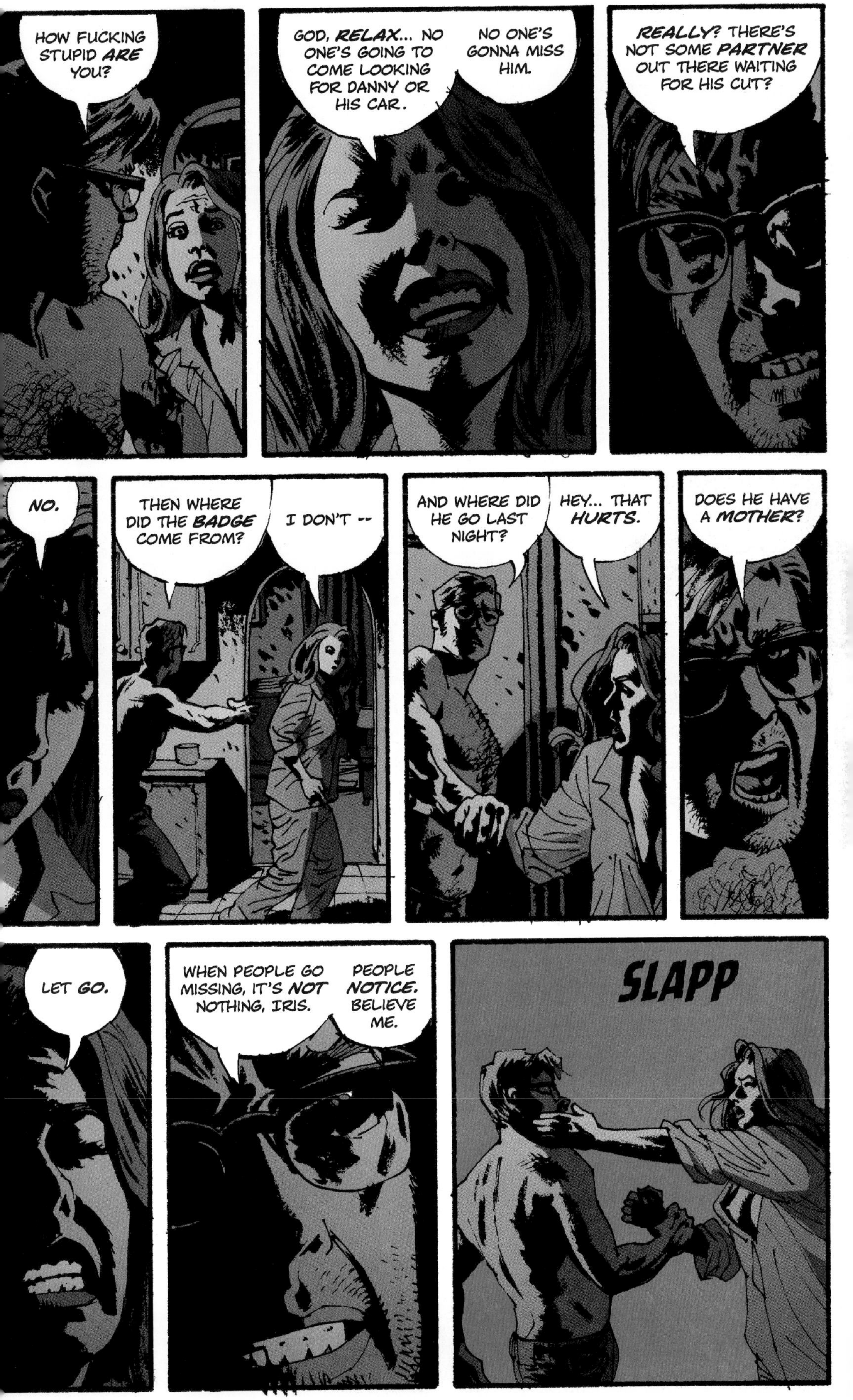

HOW FUCKING STUPID ARE YOU?
GOD, RELAX... NO ONE'S GOING TO COME LOOKING FOR DANNY OR HIS CAR.
NO ONE'S GONNA MISS HIM.
REALLY? THERE'S NOT SOME PARTNER OUT THERE WAITING FOR HIS CUT?
NO.
THEN WHERE DID THE BADGE COME FROM?
I DON'T --
AND WHERE DID HE GO LAST NIGHT?
HEY... THAT HURTS.
DOES HE HAVE A MOTHER?
LET GO.
WHEN PEOPLE GO MISSING, IT'S NOT NOTHING, IRIS.
PEOPLE NOTICE. BELIEVE ME.
SLAPP

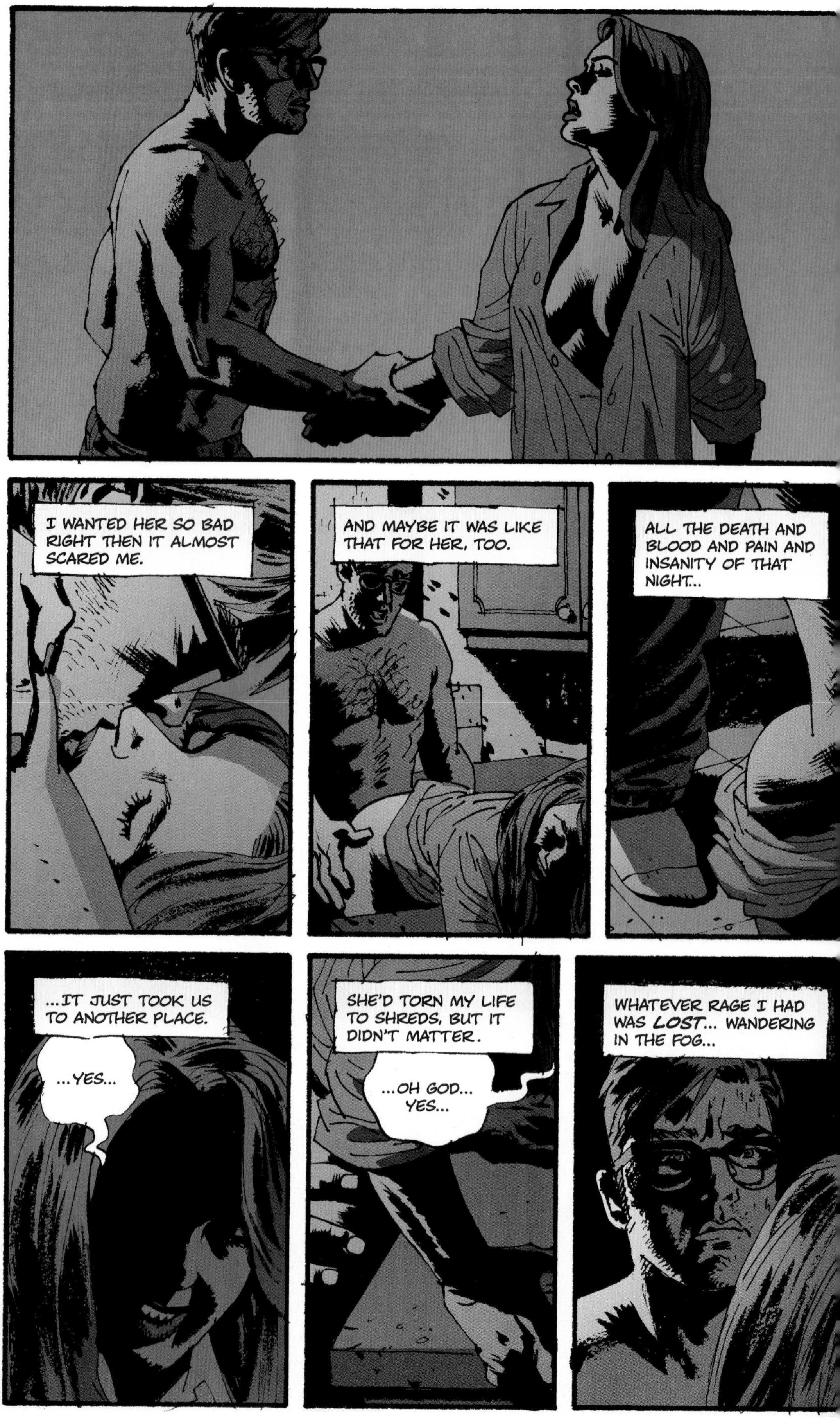
I WANTED HER SO BAD RIGHT THEN IT ALMOST SCARED ME.
AND MAYBE IT WAS LIKE THAT FOR HER, TOO.
ALL THE DEATH AND BLOOD AND PAIN AND INSANITY OF THAT NIGHT...
...IT JUST TOOK US TO ANOTHER PLACE.
...YES...
SHE'D TORN MY LIFE TO SHREDS, BUT IT DIDN'T MATTER.
...OH GOD... YES...
WHATEVER RAGE I HAD WAS LOST... WANDERING IN THE FOG...

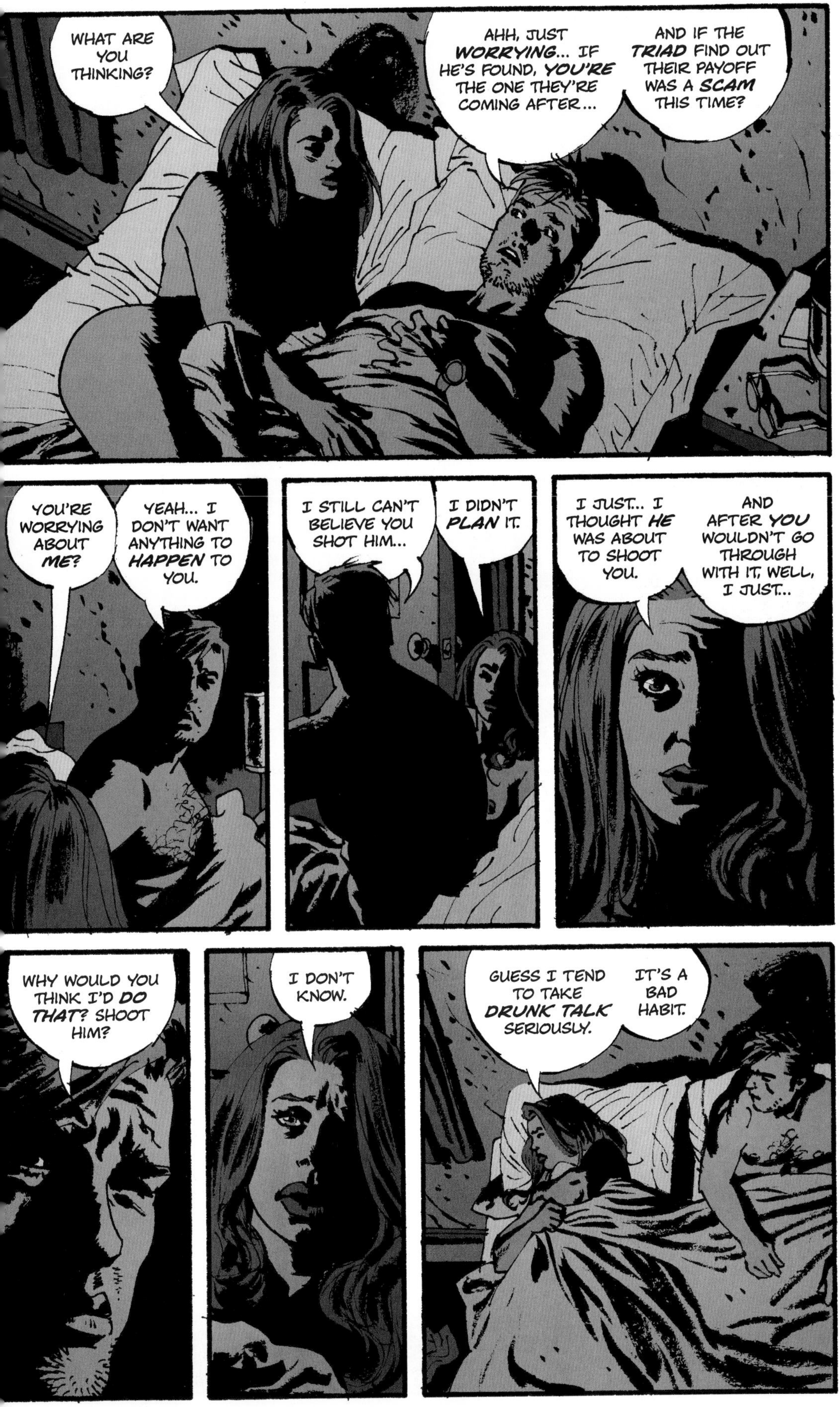
WHAT ARE YOU THINKING?
AHH, JUST *WORRYING*... IF HE'S FOUND, *YOU'RE* THE ONE THEY'RE COMING AFTER...
AND IF THE *TRIAD* FIND OUT THEIR PAYOFF WAS A *SCAM* THIS TIME?
YOU'RE WORRYING ABOUT *ME?*
YEAH... I DON'T WANT ANYTHING TO *HAPPEN* TO YOU.
I STILL CAN'T BELIEVE YOU SHOT HIM...
I DIDN'T *PLAN* IT.
I JUST... I THOUGHT *HE* WAS ABOUT TO SHOOT YOU.
AND AFTER *YOU* WOULDN'T GO THROUGH WITH IT, WELL, I JUST...
WHY WOULD YOU THINK I'D *DO THAT?* SHOOT HIM?
I DON'T KNOW.
GUESS I TEND TO TAKE *DRUNK TALK* SERIOUSLY.
IT'S A BAD HABIT.

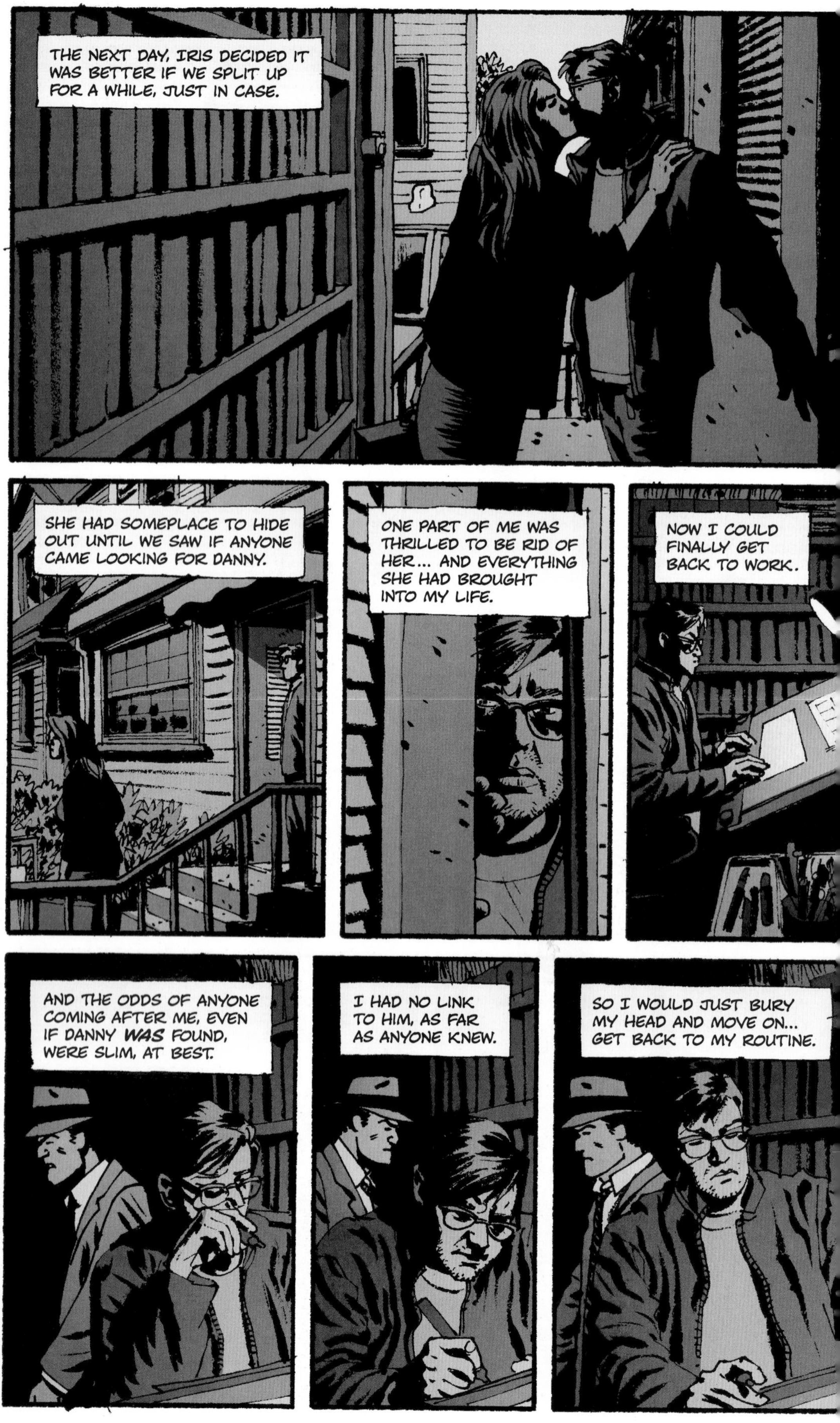
THE NEXT DAY, IRIS DECIDED IT WAS BETTER IF WE SPLIT UP FOR A WHILE, JUST IN CASE.
SHE HAD SOMEPLACE TO HIDE OUT UNTIL WE SAW IF ANYONE CAME LOOKING FOR DANNY.
ONE PART OF ME WAS THRILLED TO BE RID OF HER... AND EVERYTHING SHE HAD BROUGHT INTO MY LIFE.
NOW I COULD FINALLY GET BACK TO WORK.
AND THE ODDS OF ANYONE COMING AFTER ME, EVEN IF DANNY *WAS* FOUND, WERE SLIM, AT BEST.
I HAD NO LINK TO HIM, AS FAR AS ANYONE KNEW.
SO I WOULD JUST BURY MY HEAD AND MOVE ON... GET BACK TO MY ROUTINE.

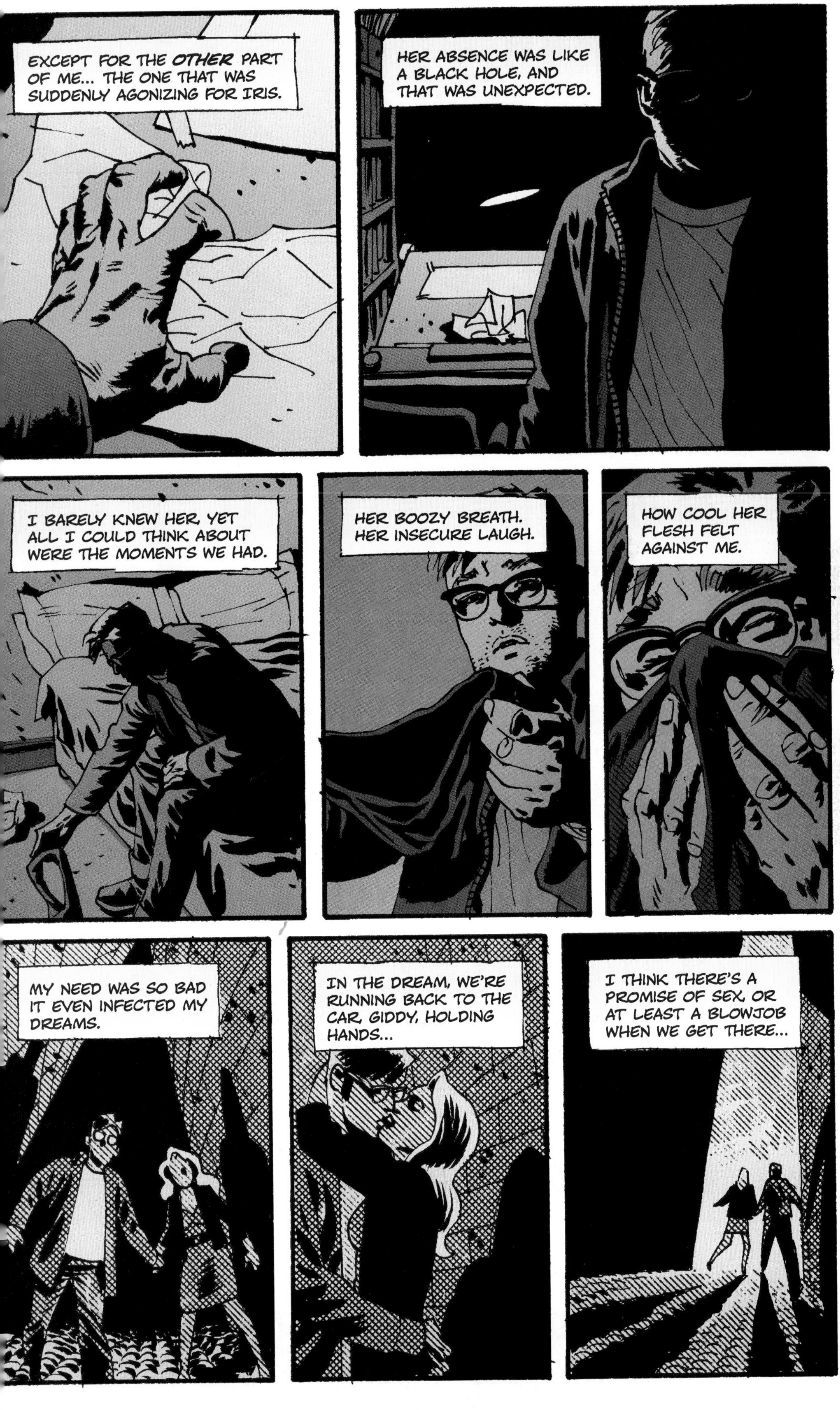
EXCEPT FOR THE *OTHER* PART OF ME... THE ONE THAT WAS SUDDENLY AGONIZING FOR IRIS.
HER ABSENCE WAS LIKE A BLACK HOLE, AND THAT WAS UNEXPECTED.
I BARELY KNEW HER, YET ALL I COULD THINK ABOUT WERE THE MOMENTS WE HAD.
HER BOOZY BREATH. HER INSECURE LAUGH.
HOW COOL HER FLESH FELT AGAINST ME.
MY NEED WAS SO BAD IT EVEN INFECTED MY DREAMS.
IN THE DREAM, WE'RE RUNNING BACK TO THE CAR, GIDDY, HOLDING HANDS...
I THINK THERE'S A PROMISE OF SEX, OR AT LEAST A BLOWJOB WHEN WE GET THERE...

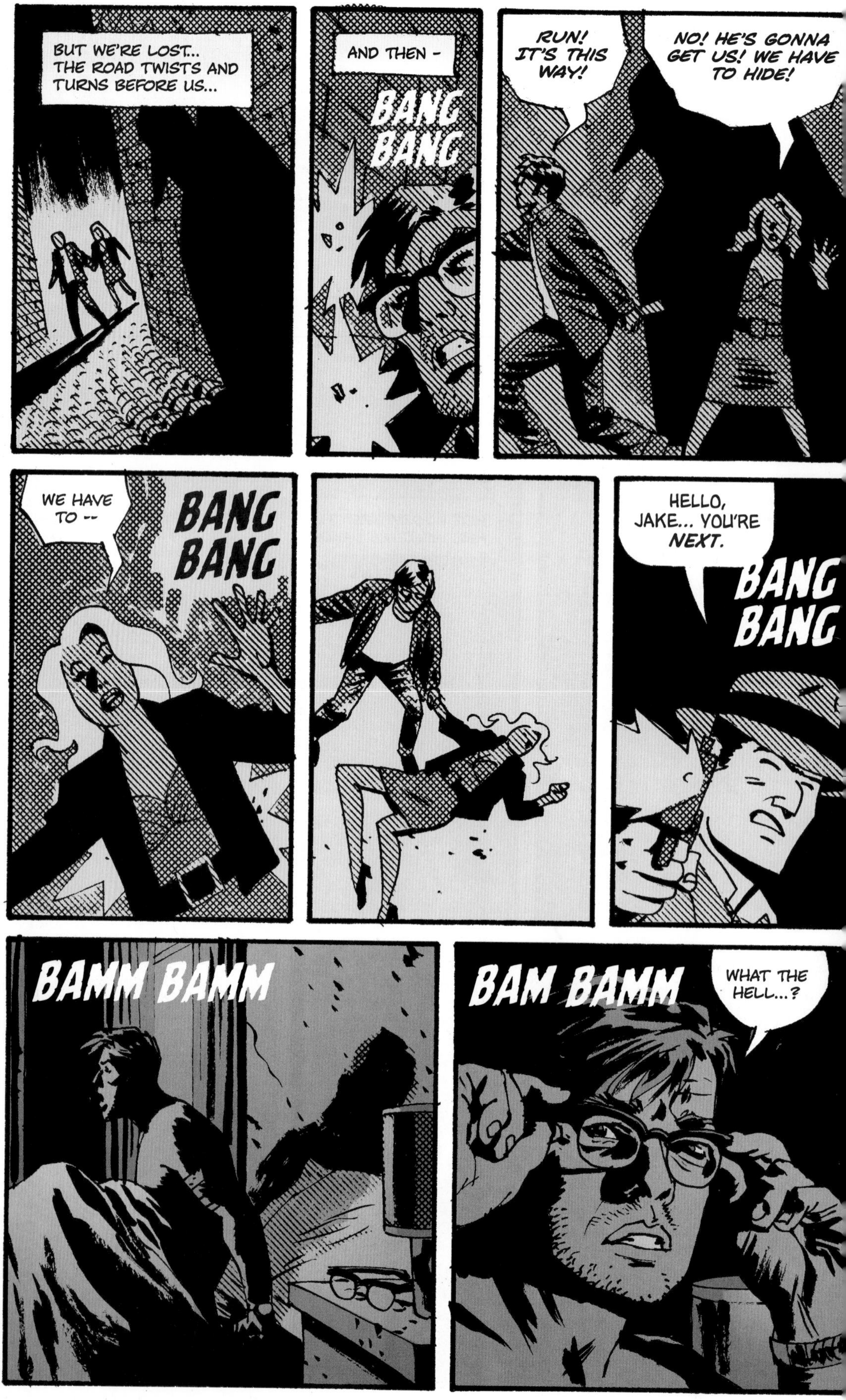

BUT WE'RE LOST... THE ROAD TWISTS AND TURNS BEFORE US...
AND THEN -
BANG BANG
RUN! IT'S THIS WAY!
NO! HE'S GONNA GET US! WE HAVE TO HIDE!
WE HAVE TO --
BANG BANG
HELLO, JAKE... YOU'RE NEXT.
BANG BANG
BAMM BAMM
BAM BAMM
WHAT THE HELL...?

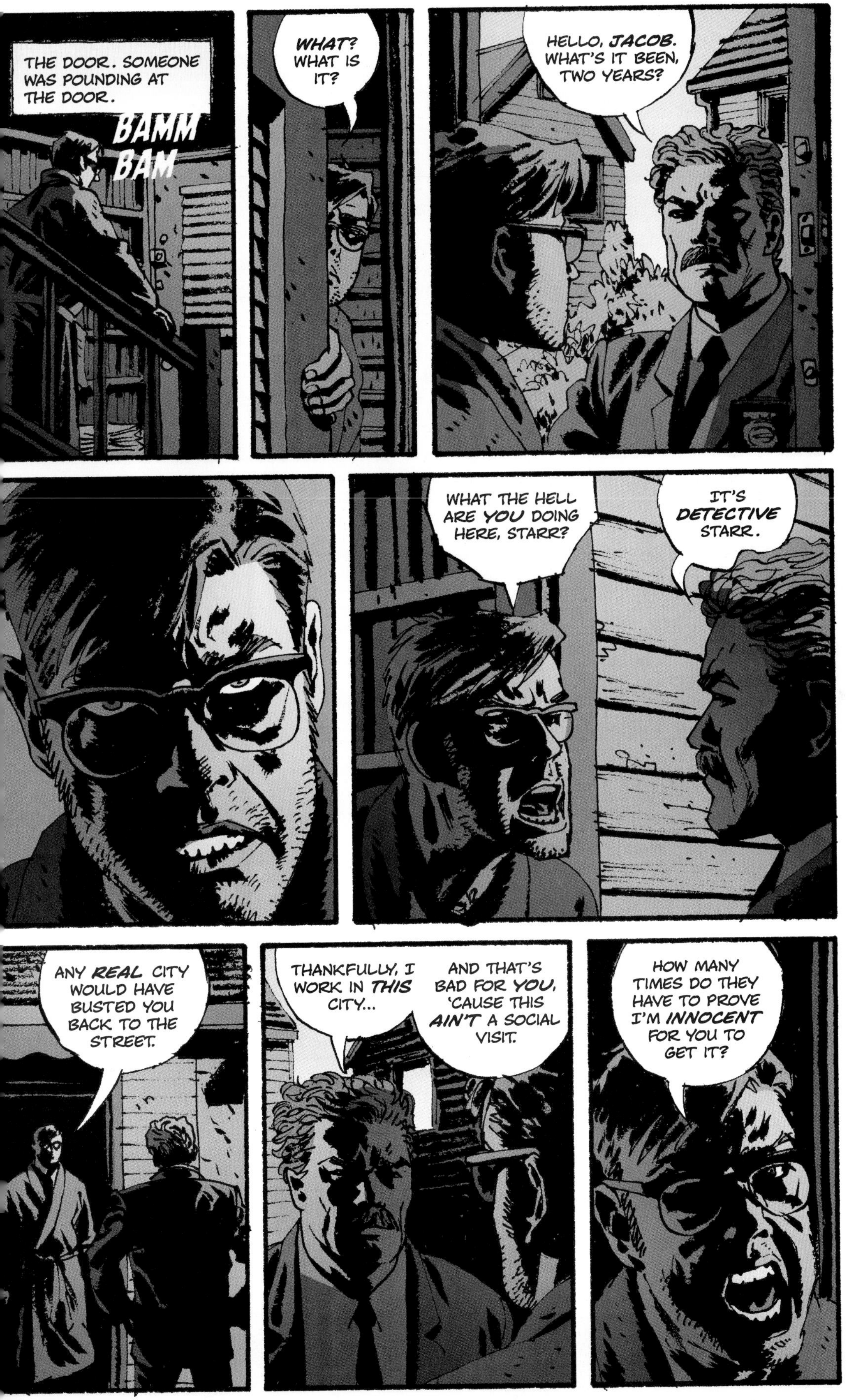
THE DOOR. SOMEONE WAS POUNDING AT THE DOOR.
BAMM BAM
WHAT? WHAT IS IT?
HELLO, *JACOB*. WHAT'S IT BEEN, TWO YEARS?
WHAT THE HELL ARE *YOU* DOING HERE, STARR?
IT'S *DETECTIVE* STARR.
ANY *REAL* CITY WOULD HAVE BUSTED YOU BACK TO THE STREET.
THANKFULLY, I WORK IN *THIS* CITY...
AND THAT'S BAD FOR *YOU*, 'CAUSE THIS *AIN'T* A SOCIAL VISIT.
HOW MANY TIMES DO THEY HAVE TO PROVE I'M *INNOCENT* FOR YOU TO GET IT?

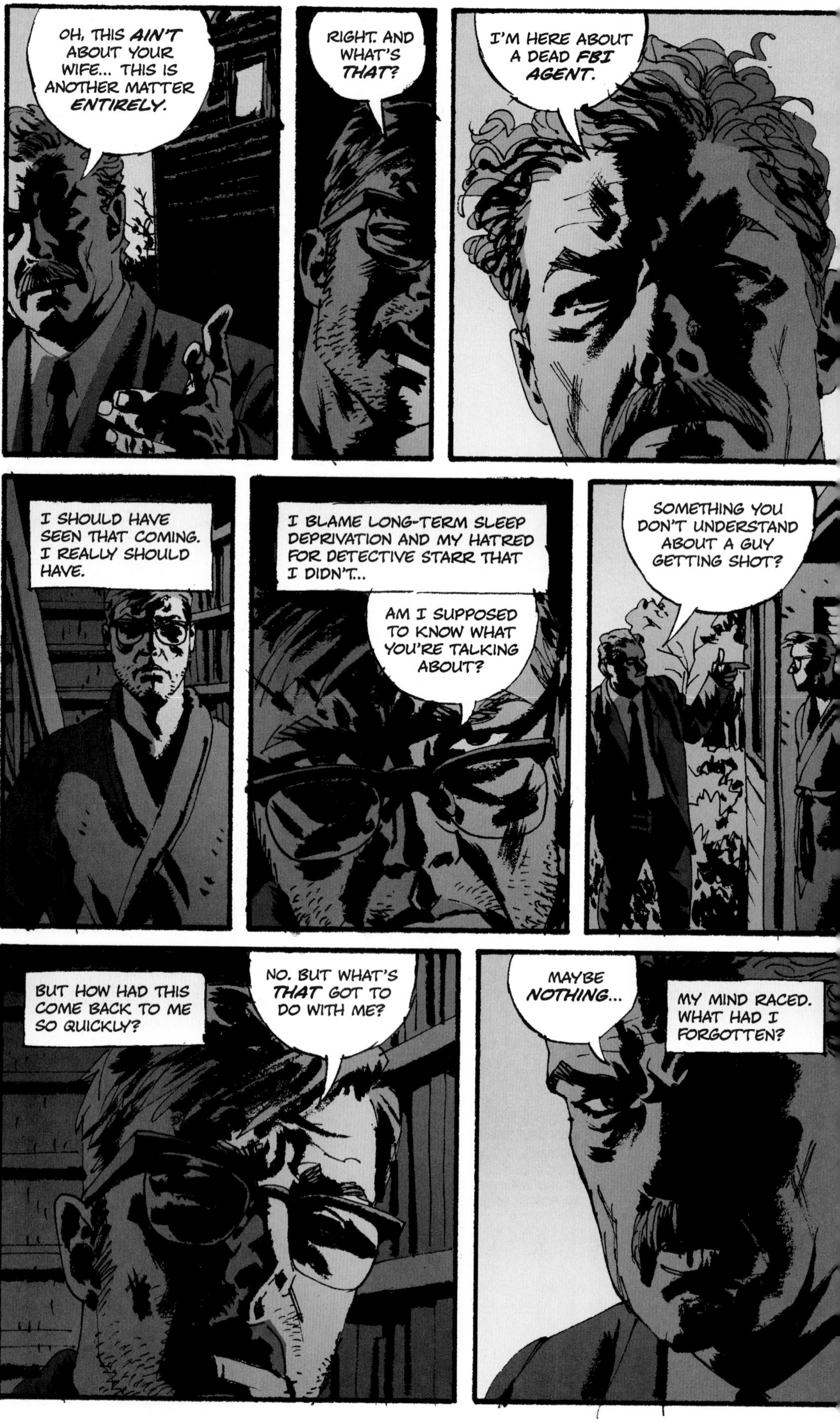

OH, THIS AIN'T ABOUT YOUR WIFE... THIS IS ANOTHER MATTER ENTIRELY.
RIGHT. AND WHAT'S THAT?
I'M HERE ABOUT A DEAD FBI AGENT.
I SHOULD HAVE SEEN THAT COMING. I REALLY SHOULD HAVE.
I BLAME LONG-TERM SLEEP DEPRIVATION AND MY HATRED FOR DETECTIVE STARR THAT I DIDN'T...
AM I SUPPOSED TO KNOW WHAT YOU'RE TALKING ABOUT?
SOMETHING YOU DON'T UNDERSTAND ABOUT A GUY GETTING SHOT?
BUT HOW HAD THIS COME BACK TO ME SO QUICKLY?
NO. BUT WHAT'S THAT GOT TO DO WITH ME?
MAYBE NOTHING...
MY MIND RACED. WHAT HAD I FORGOTTEN?

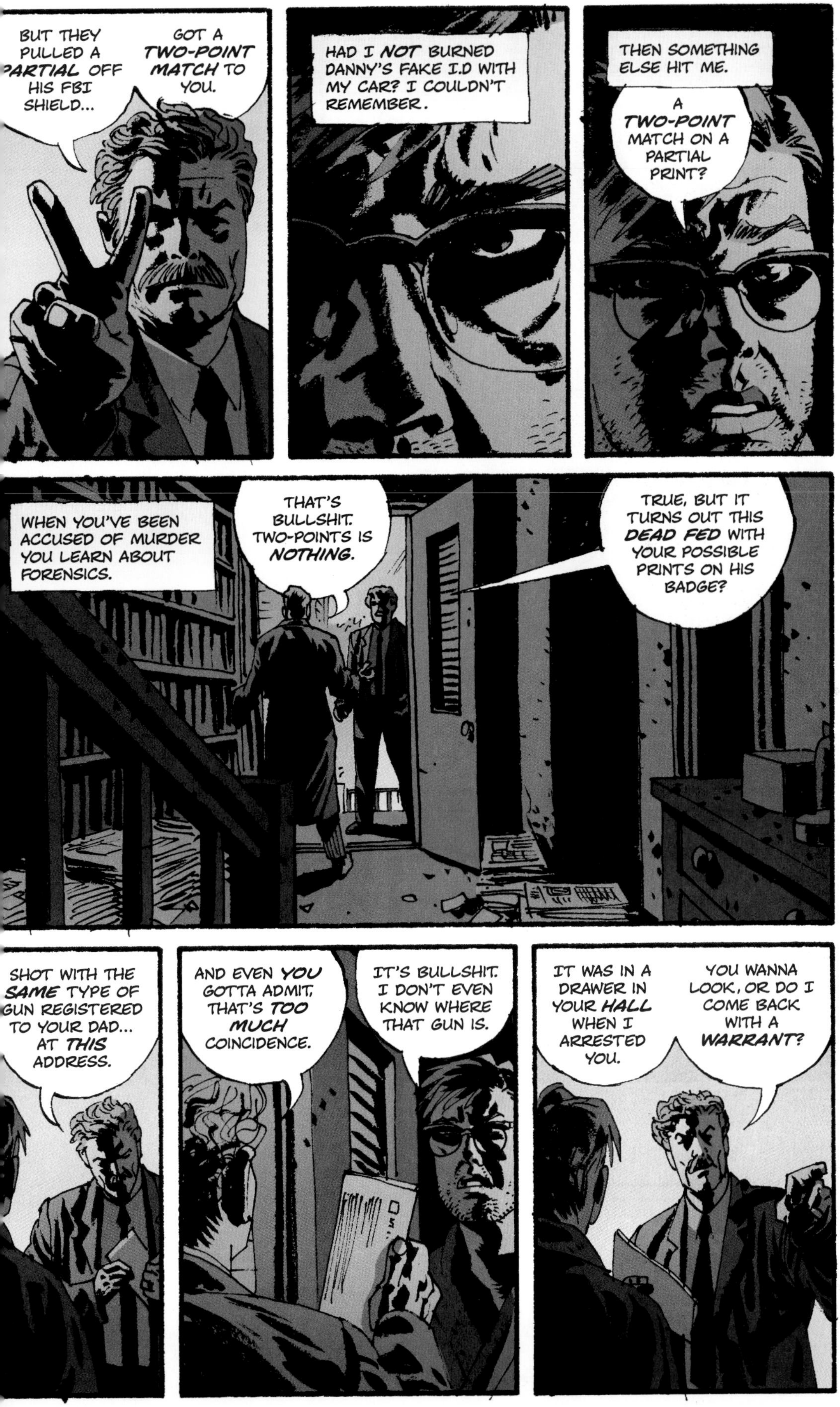
BUT THEY PULLED A PARTIAL OFF HIS FBI SHIELD...
GOT A TWO-POINT MATCH TO YOU.
HAD I NOT BURNED DANNY'S FAKE I.D WITH MY CAR? I COULDN'T REMEMBER.
THEN SOMETHING ELSE HIT ME.
A TWO-POINT MATCH ON A PARTIAL PRINT?
WHEN YOU'VE BEEN ACCUSED OF MURDER YOU LEARN ABOUT FORENSICS.
THAT'S BULLSHIT. TWO-POINTS IS NOTHING.
TRUE, BUT IT TURNS OUT THIS DEAD FED WITH YOUR POSSIBLE PRINTS ON HIS BADGE?
SHOT WITH THE SAME TYPE OF GUN REGISTERED TO YOUR DAD... AT THIS ADDRESS.
AND EVEN YOU GOTTA ADMIT, THAT'S TOO MUCH COINCIDENCE.
IT'S BULLSHIT. I DON'T EVEN KNOW WHERE THAT GUN IS.
IT WAS IN A DRAWER IN YOUR HALL WHEN I ARRESTED YOU.
YOU WANNA LOOK, OR DO I COME BACK WITH A WARRANT?

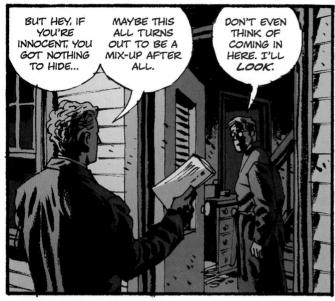

BUT HEY, IF YOU'RE INNOCENT, YOU GOT NOTHING TO HIDE...

MAYBE THIS ALL TURNS OUT TO BE A MIX-UP AFTER ALL.

DON'T EVEN THINK OF COMING IN HERE. I'LL *LOOK*.

THIS WAS BAD. STARR FOLLOWING DANNY'S BODY BACK TO ME, THREATENING WARRANTS...

STILL THINKING HE WAS AN ACTUAL FBI AGENT, NOT SOME SCUMBAG.

YEAH... *THAT* CABINET, THERE.

I'M TELLING YOU, I HAVEN'T SEEN THAT THING IN –

FOUND IT?

YEAH.

GOOD.

GONNA NEED YOU TO SIGN SOME SHIT SO WE CAN DO THE BALLISTICS TEST...

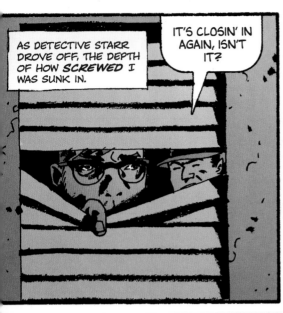

AS DETECTIVE STARR DROVE OFF, THE DEPTH OF HOW *SCREWED* I WAS SUNK IN.

IT'S CLOSIN' IN AGAIN, ISN'T IT?

THAT GUN HAD *NOT* BEEN IN THAT DRAWER A WEEK AGO.

IT'S ALL CLOSIN' IN... DAMN IT.

AND IT *WASN'T* THE GUN IRIS SHOT DANNY WITH. I WAS SURE OF THAT.

SO, WHAT DID THAT MEAN, THEN?

IT WAS THOSE BUMS. THEY *SET YOU UP.*

DANNY WASN'T GONNA *KILL YOU*, HE WAS GONNA HANG YOU OUT TO DRY.

HE JUST DIDN'T TELL *THE TWIST* HIS PLAN.

I *KNEW* WHEN THERE WAS NO CRIME SCENE TAPE. NOTHING DISTURBED.

AND WHEN I SMELLED THE STENCH. BUT I HAD TO BE SURE.

FUCK...

THEY HADN'T FOUND DANNY. THEY'D FOUND A *REAL* FUCKING FBI AGENT.

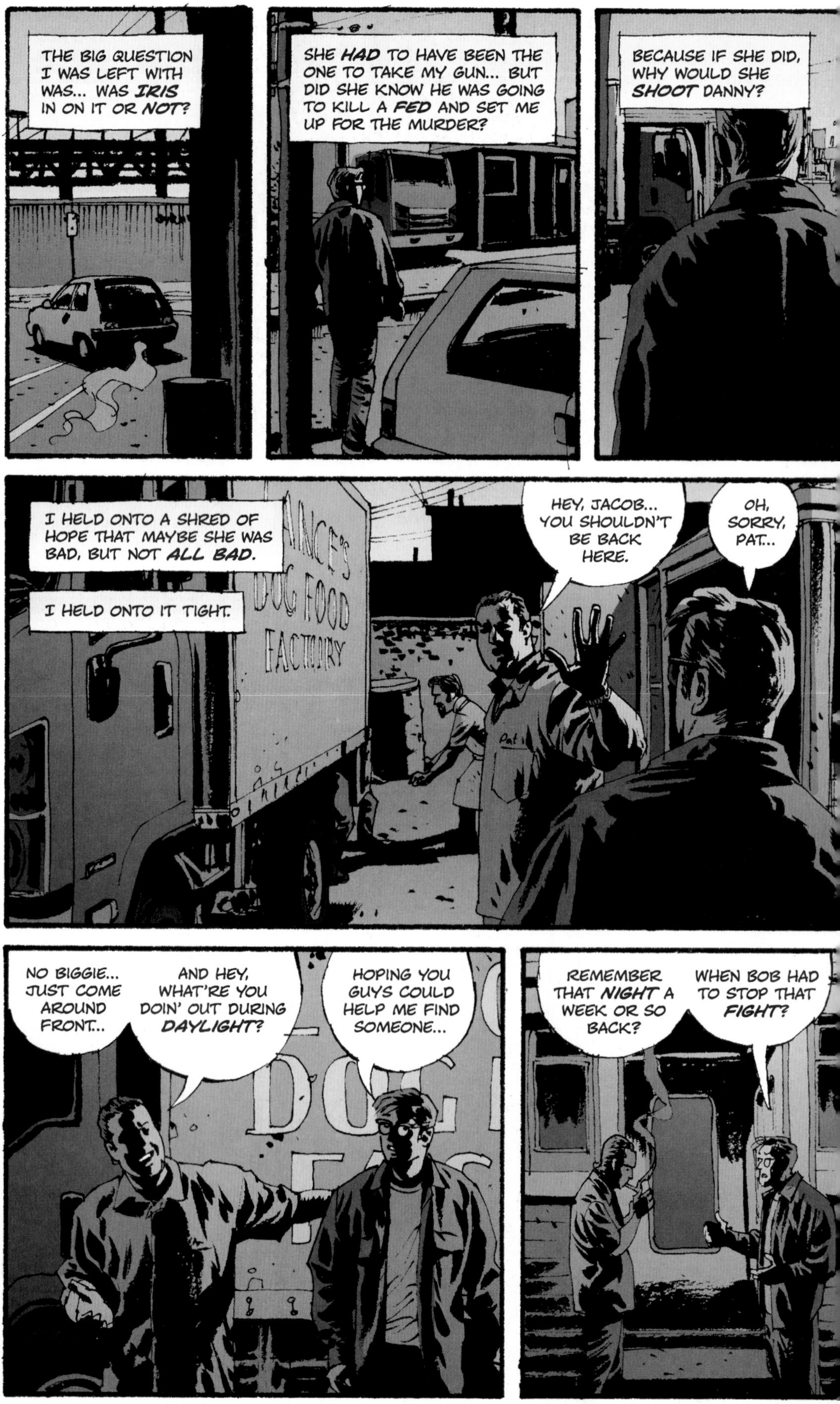
THE BIG QUESTION I WAS LEFT WITH WAS... WAS IRIS IN ON IT OR NOT?
SHE HAD TO HAVE BEEN THE ONE TO TAKE MY GUN... BUT DID SHE KNOW HE WAS GOING TO KILL A FED AND SET ME UP FOR THE MURDER?
BECAUSE IF SHE DID, WHY WOULD SHE SHOOT DANNY?
I HELD ONTO A SHRED OF HOPE THAT MAYBE SHE WAS BAD, BUT NOT ALL BAD.
I HELD ONTO IT TIGHT.
HEY, JACOB... YOU SHOULDN'T BE BACK HERE.
OH, SORRY, PAT...
DOG FOOD FACTORY
NO BIGGIE... JUST COME AROUND FRONT...
AND HEY, WHAT'RE YOU DOIN' OUT DURING DAYLIGHT?
HOPING YOU GUYS COULD HELP ME FIND SOMEONE...
REMEMBER THAT NIGHT A WEEK OR SO BACK?
WHEN BOB HAD TO STOP THAT FIGHT?

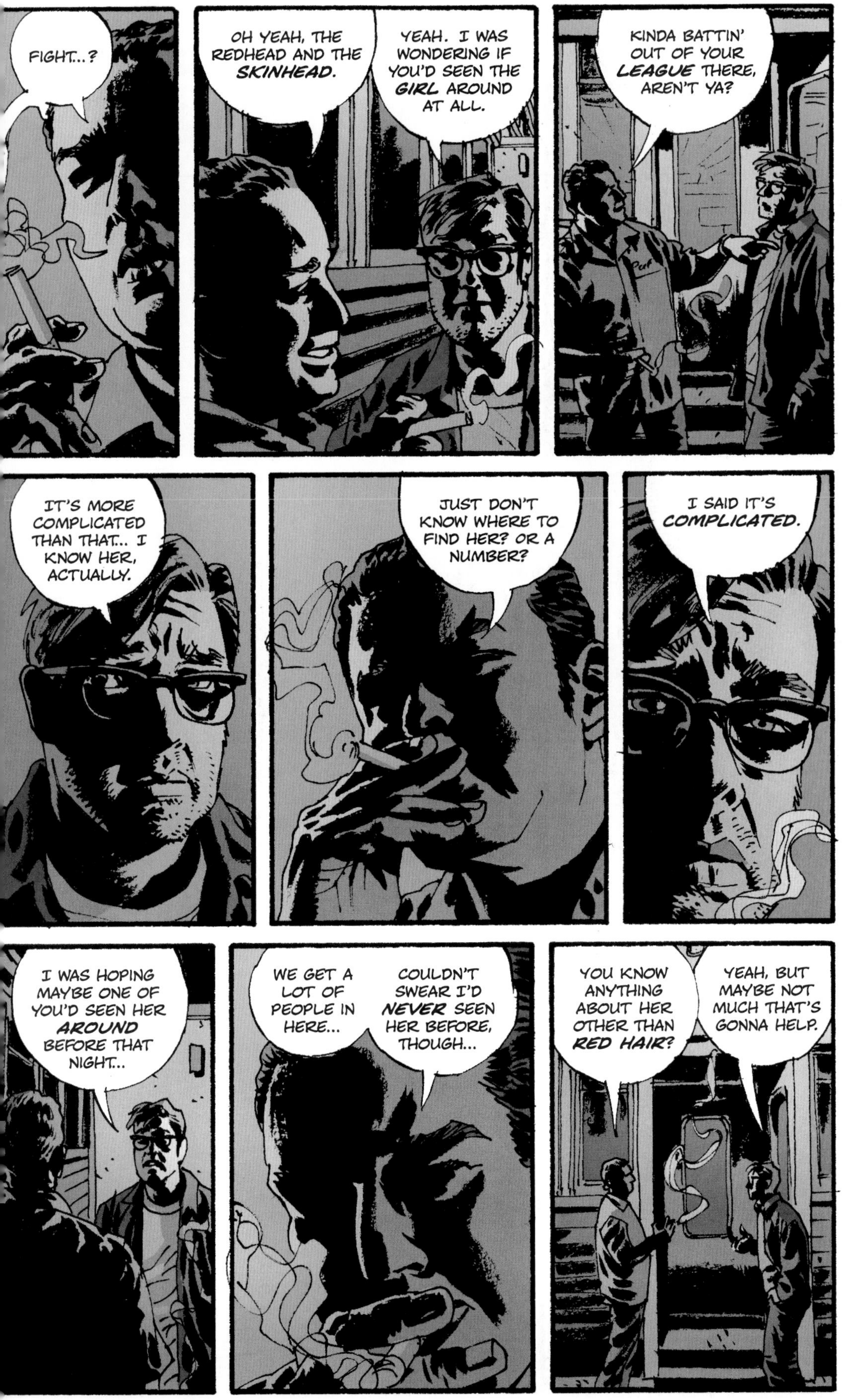
FIGHT...?
OH YEAH, THE REDHEAD AND THE SKINHEAD.
YEAH. I WAS WONDERING IF YOU'D SEEN THE GIRL AROUND AT ALL.
KINDA BATTIN' OUT OF YOUR LEAGUE THERE, AREN'T YA?
IT'S MORE COMPLICATED THAN THAT... I KNOW HER, ACTUALLY.
JUST DON'T KNOW WHERE TO FIND HER? OR A NUMBER?
I SAID IT'S COMPLICATED.
I WAS HOPING MAYBE ONE OF YOU'D SEEN HER AROUND BEFORE THAT NIGHT...
WE GET A LOT OF PEOPLE IN HERE...
COULDN'T SWEAR I'D NEVER SEEN HER BEFORE, THOUGH...
YOU KNOW ANYTHING ABOUT HER OTHER THAN RED HAIR?
YEAH, BUT MAYBE NOT MUCH THAT'S GONNA HELP.

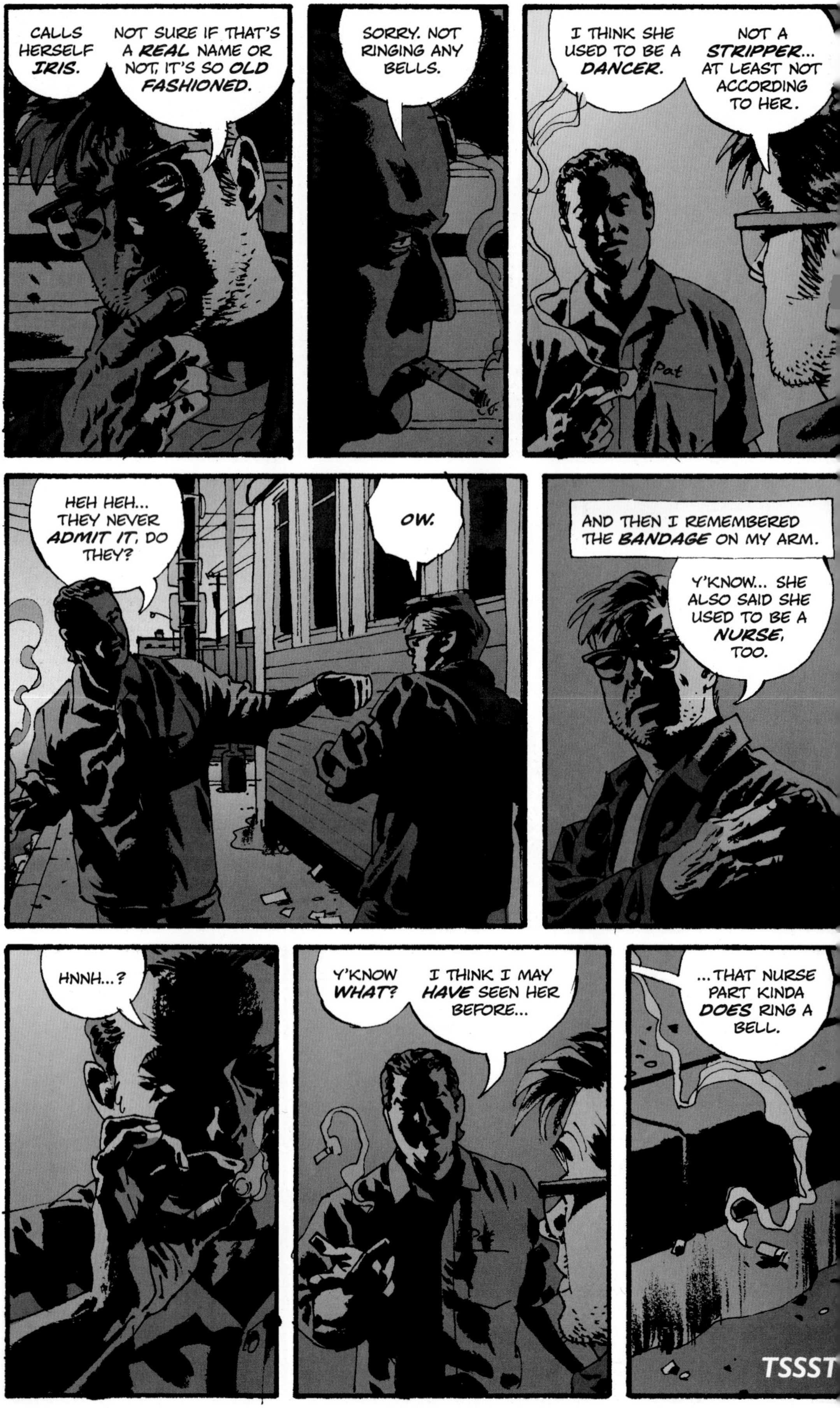
CALLS HERSELF IRIS.
NOT SURE IF THAT'S A REAL NAME OR NOT, IT'S SO OLD FASHIONED.
SORRY. NOT RINGING ANY BELLS.
I THINK SHE USED TO BE A DANCER.
NOT A STRIPPER... AT LEAST NOT ACCORDING TO HER.
Pat
HEH HEH... THEY NEVER ADMIT IT, DO THEY?
OW.
AND THEN I REMEMBERED THE BANDAGE ON MY ARM.
Y'KNOW... SHE ALSO SAID SHE USED TO BE A NURSE, TOO.
HNNH...?
Y'KNOW WHAT?
I THINK I MAY HAVE SEEN HER BEFORE...
...THAT NURSE PART KINDA DOES RING A BELL.
TSSST

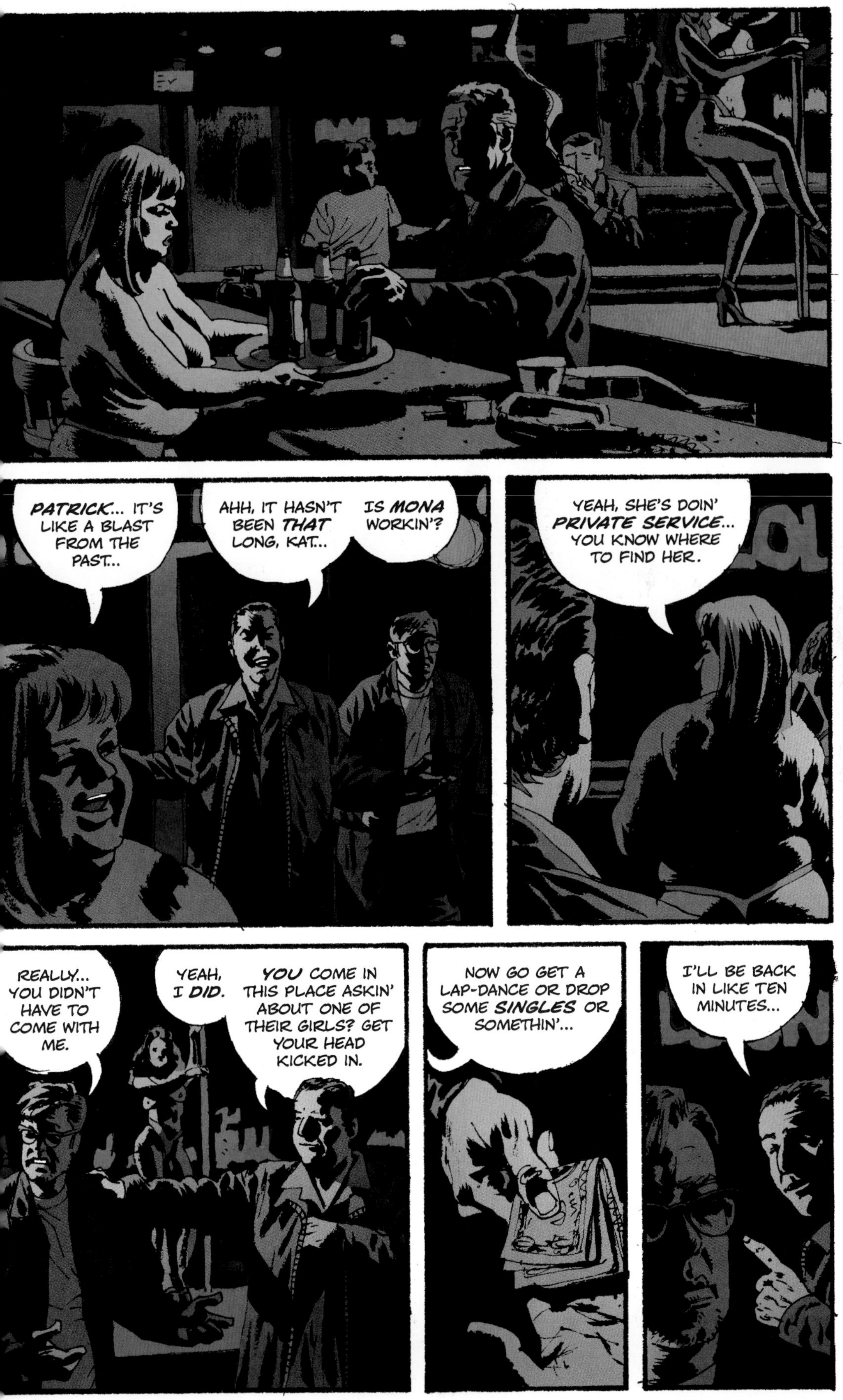
PATRICK... IT'S LIKE A BLAST FROM THE PAST...
AHH, IT HASN'T BEEN THAT LONG, KAT...
IS MONA WORKIN'?
YEAH, SHE'S DOIN' PRIVATE SERVICE... YOU KNOW WHERE TO FIND HER.
REALLY... YOU DIDN'T HAVE TO COME WITH ME.
YEAH, I DID.
YOU COME IN THIS PLACE ASKIN' ABOUT ONE OF THEIR GIRLS? GET YOUR HEAD KICKED IN.
NOW GO GET A LAP-DANCE OR DROP SOME SINGLES OR SOMETHIN'...
I'LL BE BACK IN LIKE TEN MINUTES...

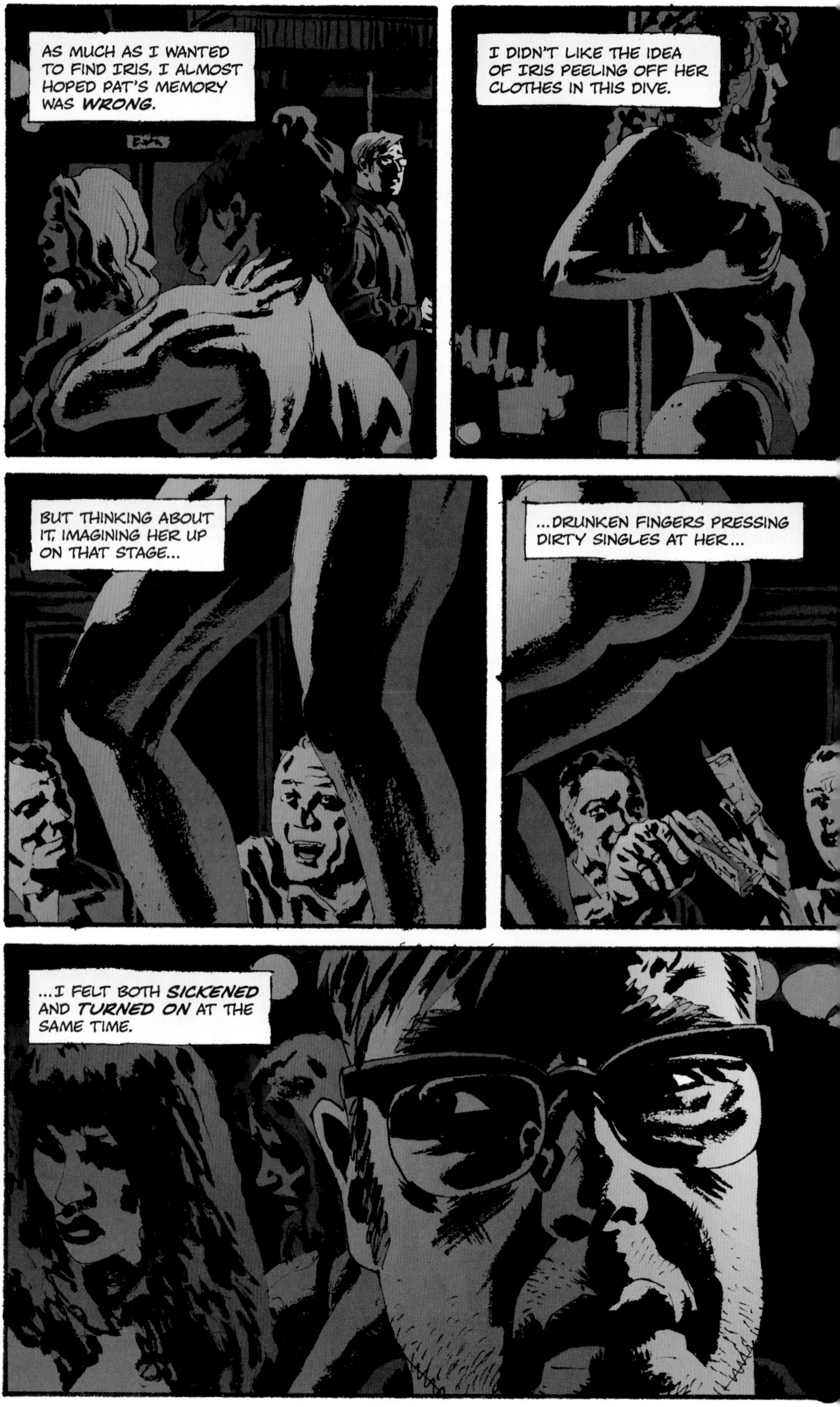
AS MUCH AS I WANTED TO FIND IRIS, I ALMOST HOPED PAT'S MEMORY WAS *WRONG*.
I DIDN'T LIKE THE IDEA OF IRIS PEELING OFF HER CLOTHES IN THIS DIVE.
BUT THINKING ABOUT IT, IMAGINING HER UP ON THAT STAGE...
...DRUNKEN FINGERS PRESSING DIRTY SINGLES AT HER...
...I FELT BOTH *SICKENED* AND *TURNED ON* AT THE SAME TIME.

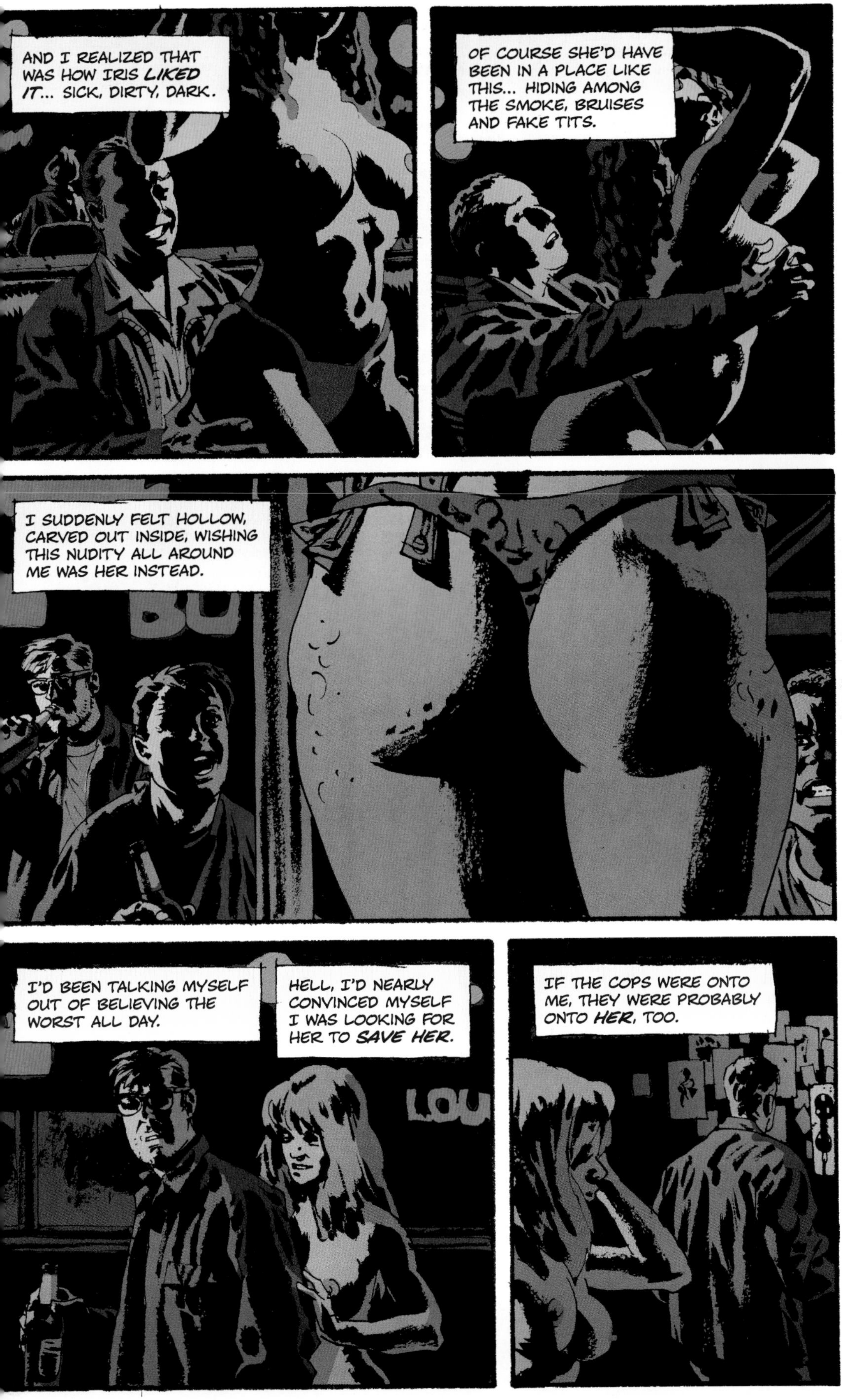
AND I REALIZED THAT WAS HOW IRIS *LIKED IT*... SICK, DIRTY, DARK.
OF COURSE SHE'D HAVE BEEN IN A PLACE LIKE THIS... HIDING AMONG THE SMOKE, BRUISES AND FAKE TITS.
I SUDDENLY FELT HOLLOW, CARVED OUT INSIDE, WISHING THIS NUDITY ALL AROUND ME WAS HER INSTEAD.
I'D BEEN TALKING MYSELF OUT OF BELIEVING THE WORST ALL DAY.
HELL, I'D NEARLY CONVINCED MYSELF I WAS LOOKING FOR HER TO *SAVE HER*.
IF THE COPS WERE ONTO ME, THEY WERE PROBABLY ONTO *HER*, TOO.

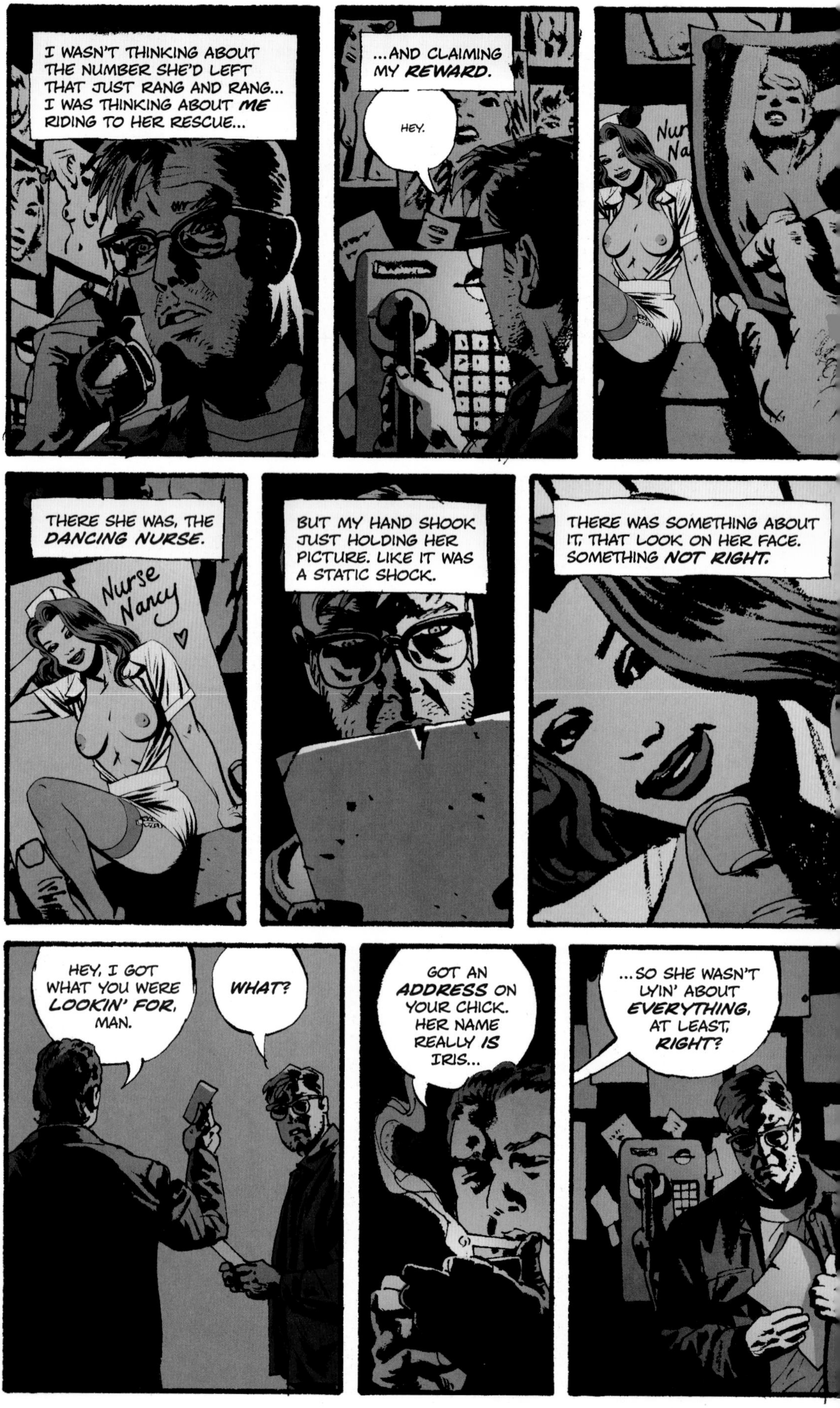
I WASN'T THINKING ABOUT THE NUMBER SHE'D LEFT THAT JUST RANG AND RANG... I WAS THINKING ABOUT *ME* RIDING TO HER RESCUE...
...AND CLAIMING MY *REWARD.*
HEY.
THERE SHE WAS, THE *DANCING NURSE.*
Nurse Nancy
BUT MY HAND SHOOK JUST HOLDING HER PICTURE. LIKE IT WAS A STATIC SHOCK.
THERE WAS SOMETHING ABOUT IT, THAT LOOK ON HER FACE. SOMETHING *NOT RIGHT.*
HEY, I GOT WHAT YOU WERE *LOOKIN' FOR,* MAN.
WHAT?
GOT AN *ADDRESS* ON YOUR CHICK. HER NAME REALLY *IS* IRIS...
...SO SHE WASN'T LYIN' ABOUT *EVERYTHING,* AT LEAST, *RIGHT?*

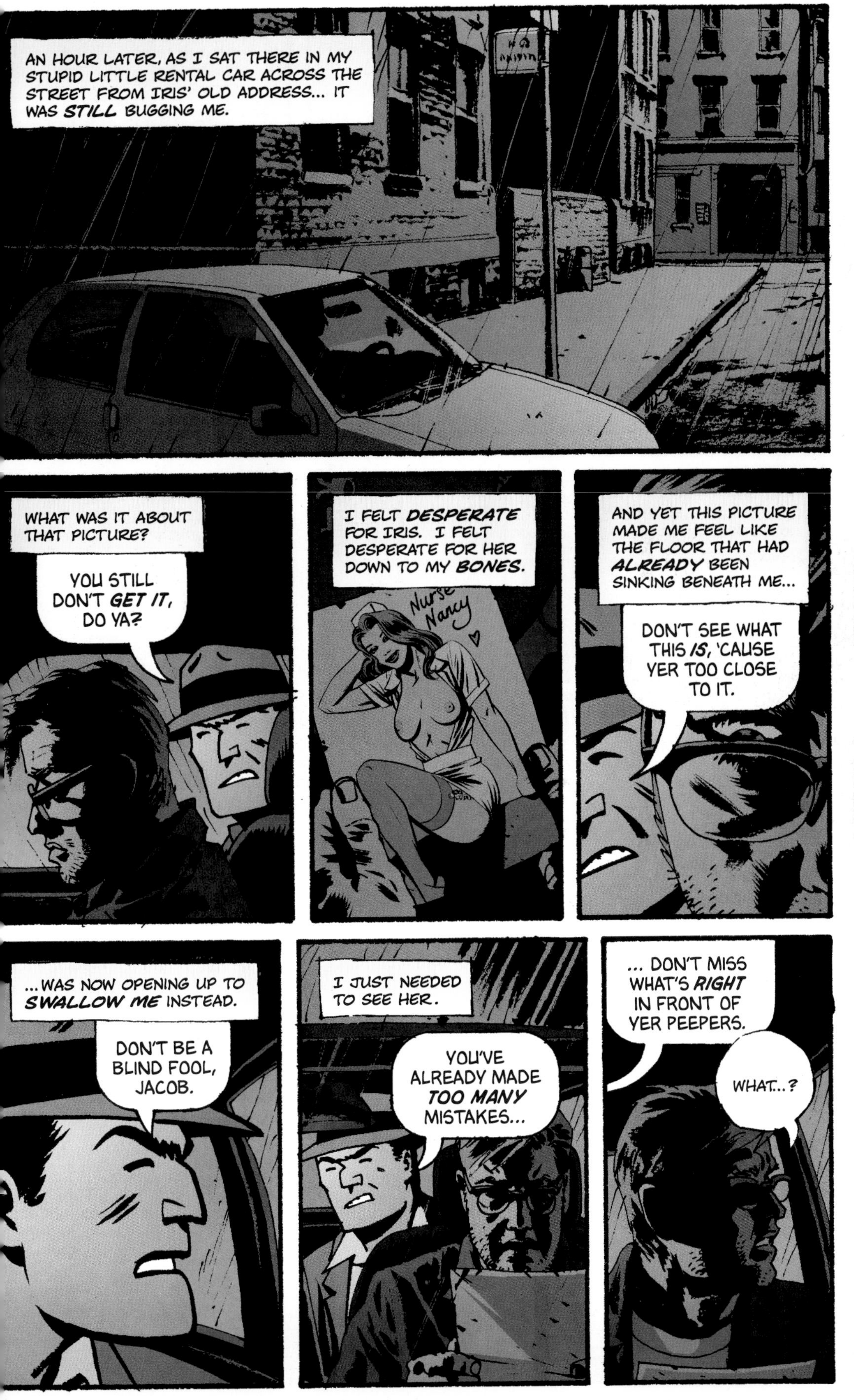
AN HOUR LATER, AS I SAT THERE IN MY STUPID LITTLE RENTAL CAR ACROSS THE STREET FROM IRIS' OLD ADDRESS... IT WAS STILL BUGGING ME.
WHAT WAS IT ABOUT THAT PICTURE?
YOU STILL DON'T GET IT, DO YA?
I FELT DESPERATE FOR IRIS. I FELT DESPERATE FOR HER DOWN TO MY BONES.
Nurse Nancy
AND YET THIS PICTURE MADE ME FEEL LIKE THE FLOOR THAT HAD ALREADY BEEN SINKING BENEATH ME...
DON'T SEE WHAT THIS IS, 'CAUSE YER TOO CLOSE TO IT.
...WAS NOW OPENING UP TO SWALLOW ME INSTEAD.
DON'T BE A BLIND FOOL, JACOB.
I JUST NEEDED TO SEE HER.
YOU'VE ALREADY MADE TOO MANY MISTAKES...
... DON'T MISS WHAT'S RIGHT IN FRONT OF YER PEEPERS.
WHAT...?

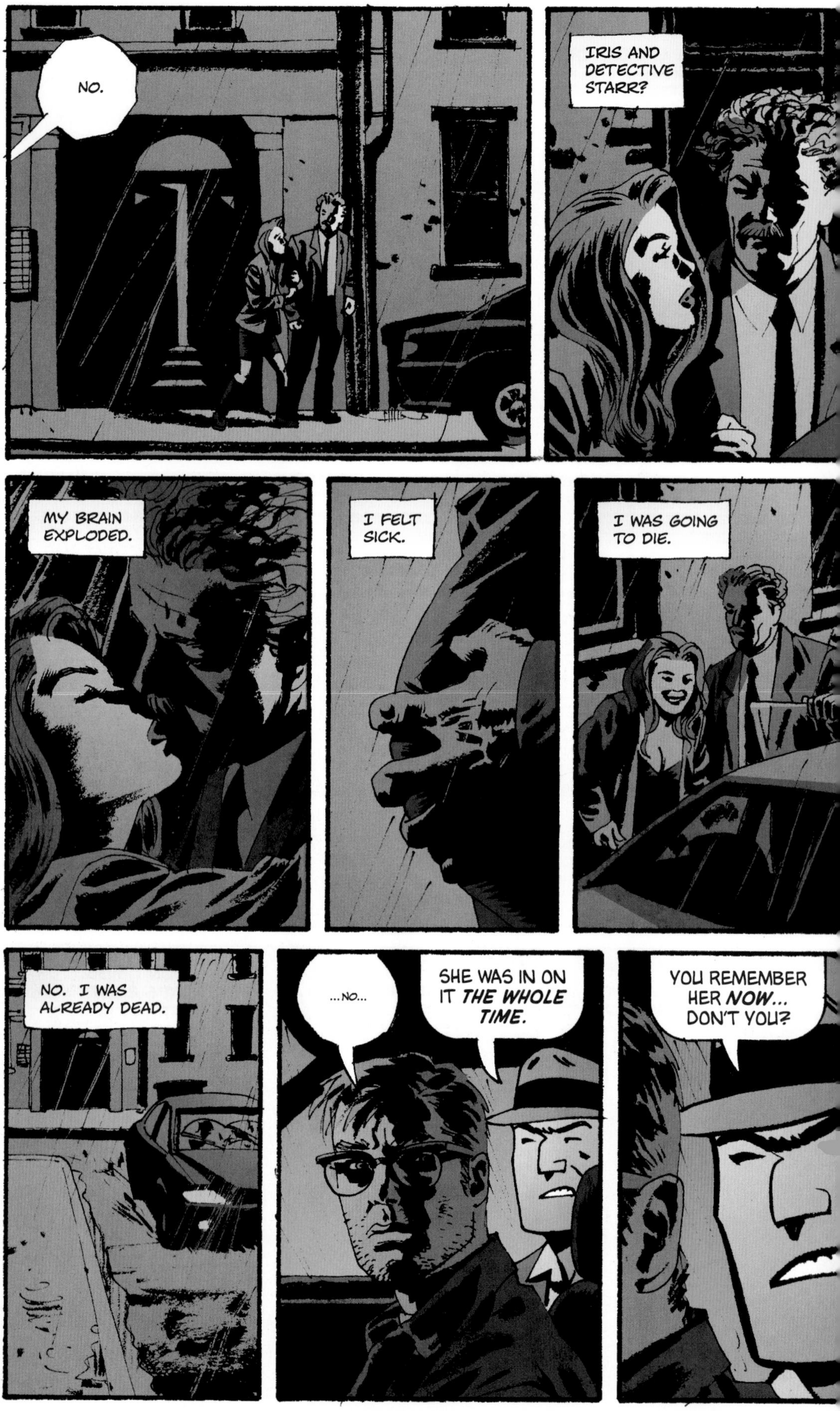
NO.
IRIS AND DETECTIVE STARR?
MY BRAIN EXPLODED.
I FELT SICK.
I WAS GOING TO DIE.
NO. I WAS ALREADY DEAD.
...NO...
SHE WAS IN ON IT THE WHOLE TIME.
YOU REMEMBER HER NOW... DON'T YOU?

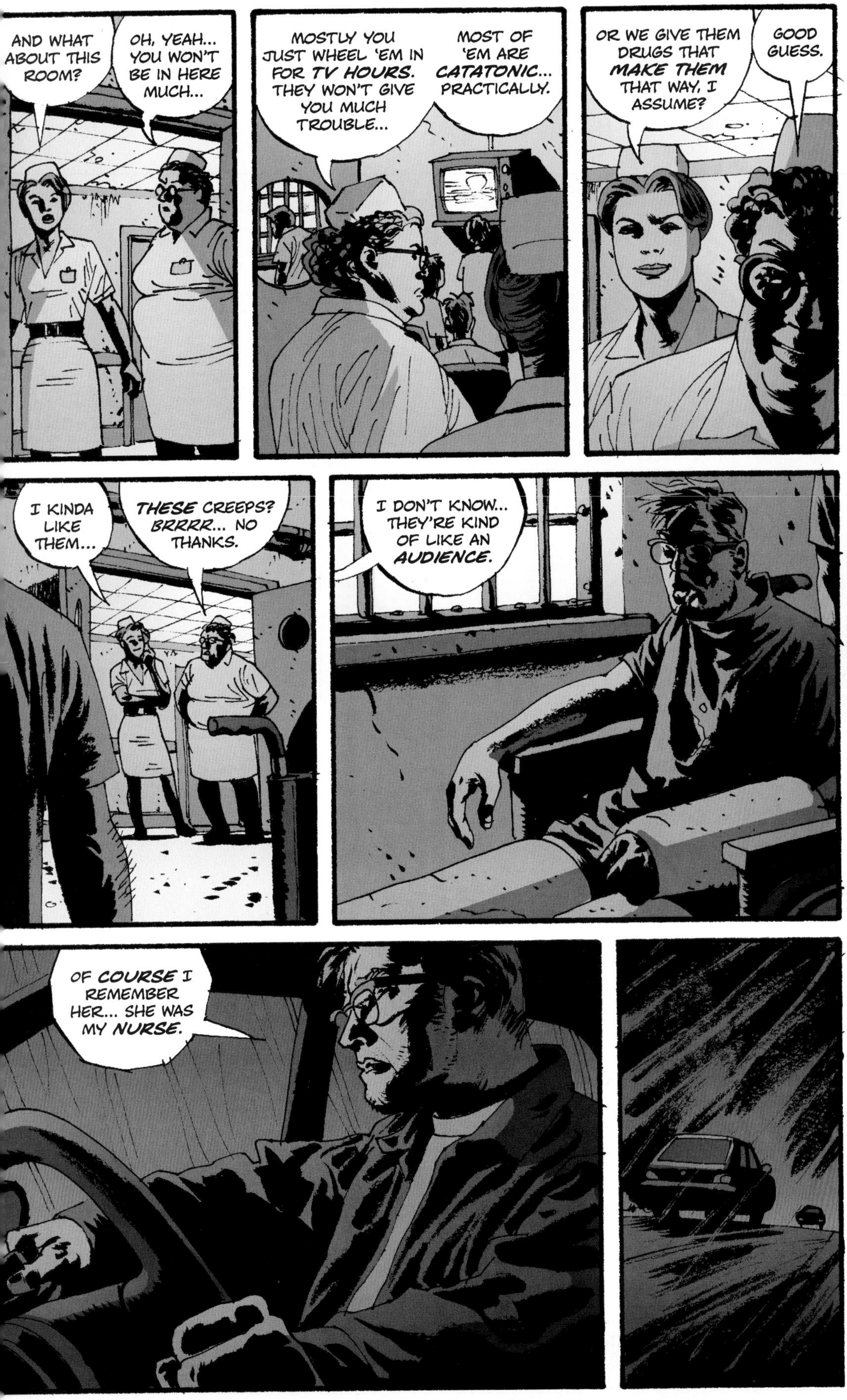
AND WHAT ABOUT THIS ROOM?
OH, YEAH... YOU WON'T BE IN HERE MUCH...
MOSTLY YOU JUST WHEEL 'EM IN FOR TV HOURS. THEY WON'T GIVE YOU MUCH TROUBLE...
MOST OF 'EM ARE CATATONIC... PRACTICALLY.
OR WE GIVE THEM DRUGS THAT MAKE THEM THAT WAY, I ASSUME?
GOOD GUESS.
I KINDA LIKE THEM...
THESE CREEPS? BRRRR... NO THANKS.
I DON'T KNOW... THEY'RE KIND OF LIKE AN AUDIENCE.
OF COURSE I REMEMBER HER... SHE WAS MY NURSE.

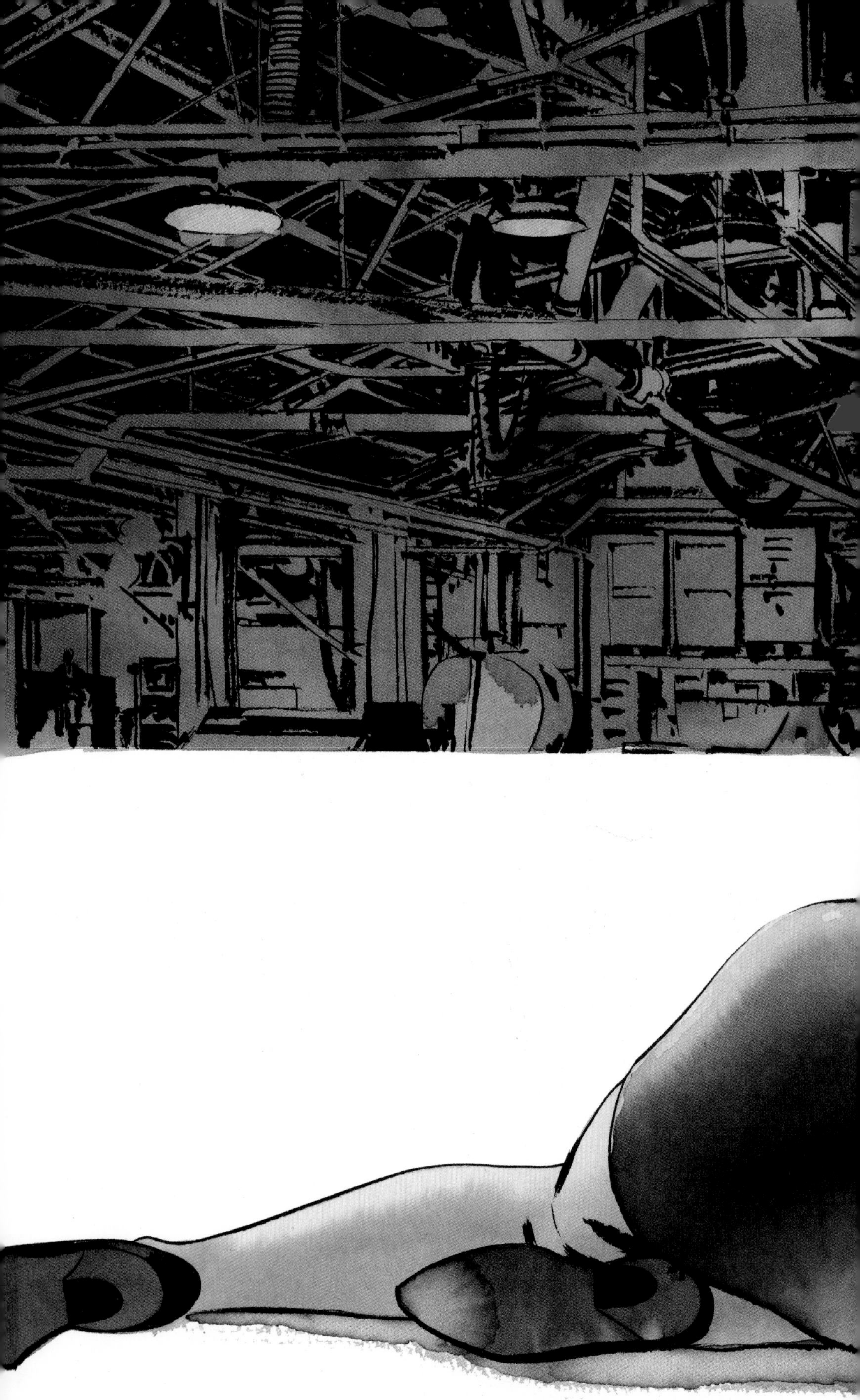

PART FOUR

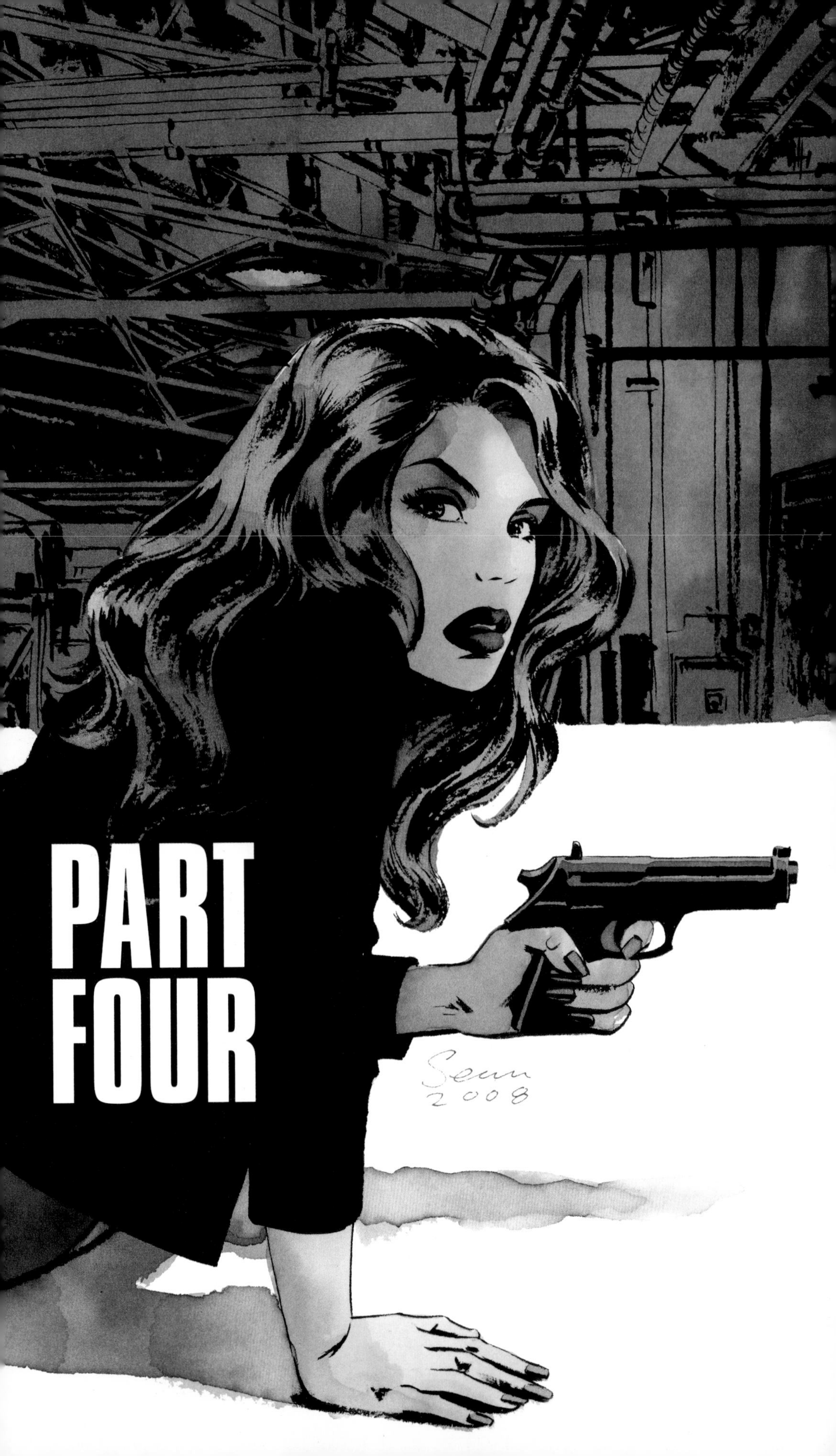
Sean
2008

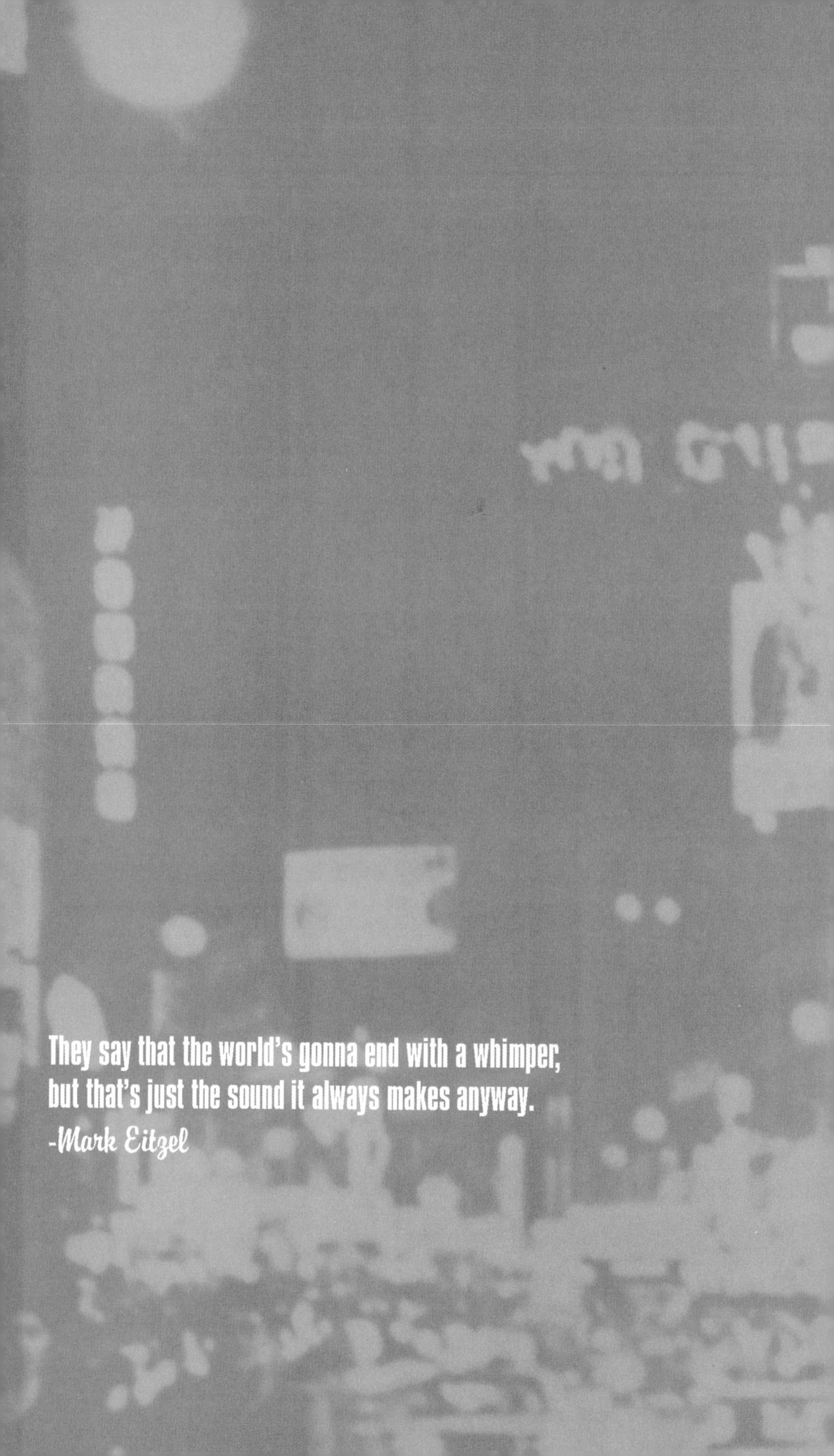

They say that the world's gonna end with a whimper,
but that's just the sound it always makes anyway.
-*Mark Eitzel*

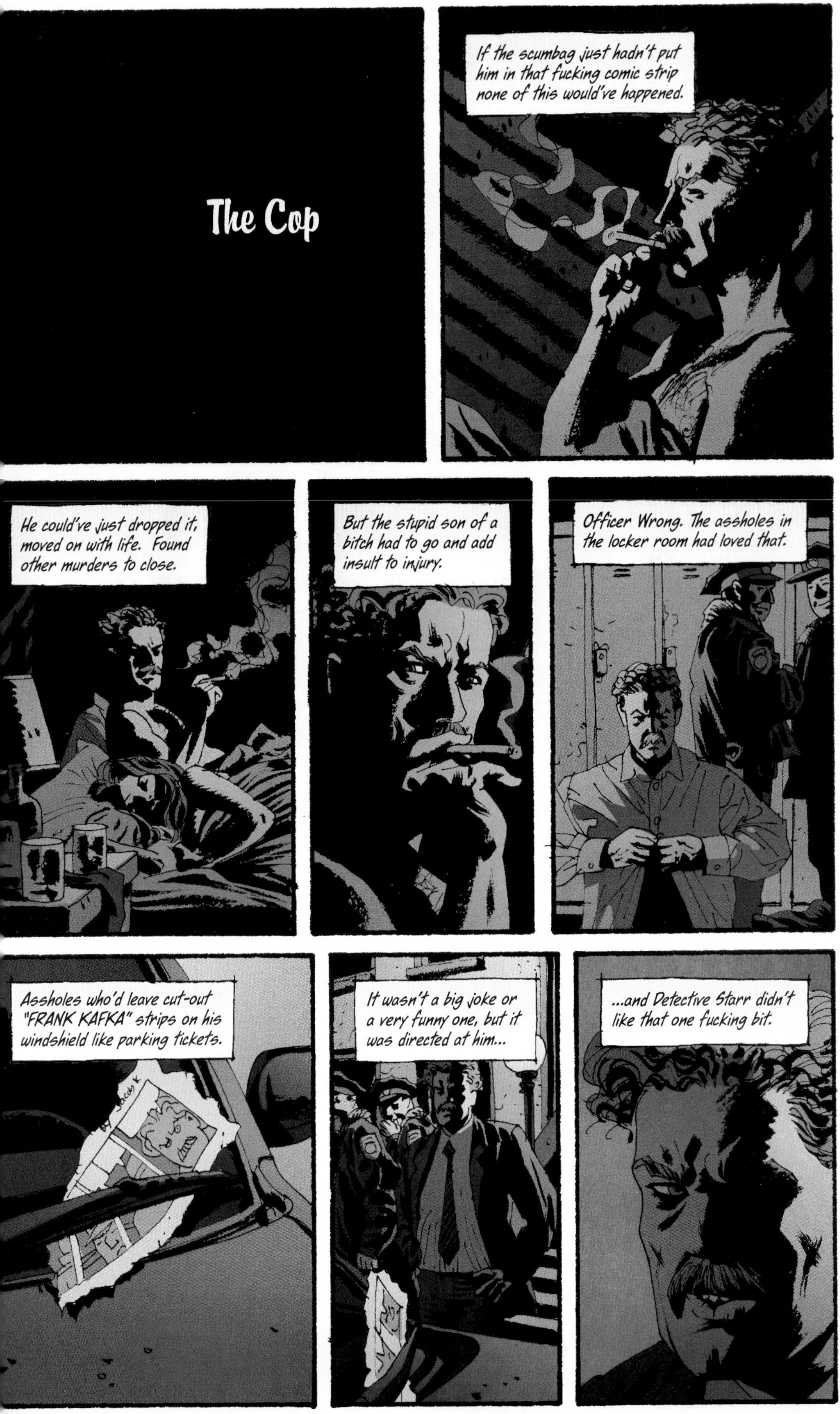
The Cop
If the scumbag just hadn't put him in that fucking comic strip none of this would've happened.
He could've just dropped it, moved on with life. Found other murders to close.
But the stupid son of a bitch had to go and add insult to injury.
Officer Wrong. The assholes in the locker room had loved that.
Assholes who'd leave cut-out "FRANK KAFKA" strips on his windshield like parking tickets.
It wasn't a big joke or a very funny one, but it was directed at him...
...and Detective Starr didn't like that one fucking bit.

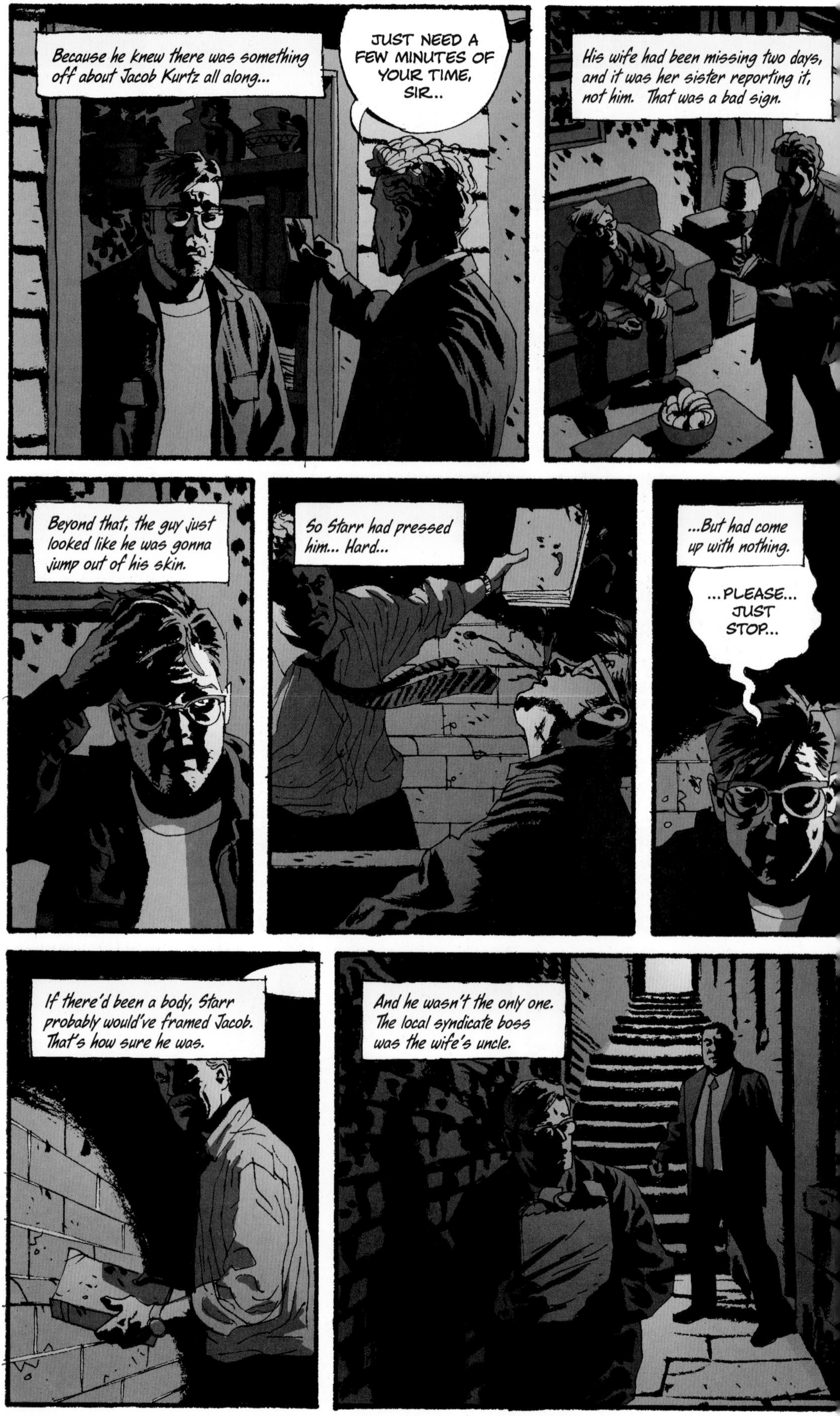
Because he knew there was something off about Jacob Kurtz all along...
JUST NEED A FEW MINUTES OF YOUR TIME, SIR..
His wife had been missing two days, and it was her sister reporting it, not him. That was a bad sign.
Beyond that, the guy just looked like he was gonna jump out of his skin.
So Starr had pressed him... Hard...
...But had come up with nothing.
...PLEASE... JUST STOP...
If there'd been a body, Starr probably would've framed Jacob. That's how sure he was.
And he wasn't the only one. The local syndicate boss was the wife's uncle.

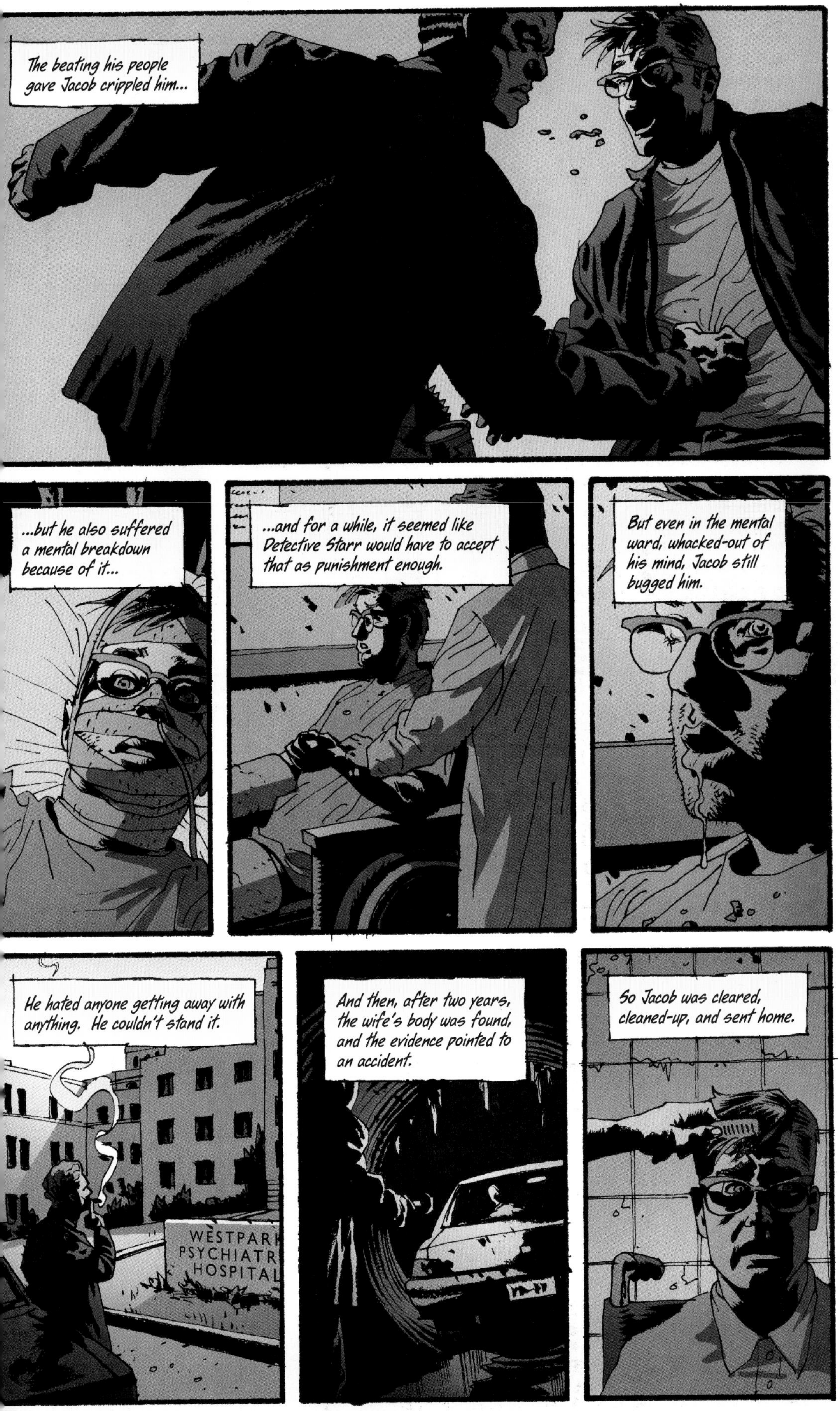
The beating his people gave Jacob crippled him...
...but he also suffered a mental breakdown because of it...
...and for a while, it seemed like Detective Starr would have to accept that as punishment enough.
But even in the mental ward, whacked-out of his mind, Jacob still bugged him.
He hated anyone getting away with anything. He couldn't stand it.
WESTPARK
PSYCHIATR
HOSPITAL
And then, after two years, the wife's body was found, and the evidence pointed to an accident.
So Jacob was cleared, cleaned-up, and sent home.

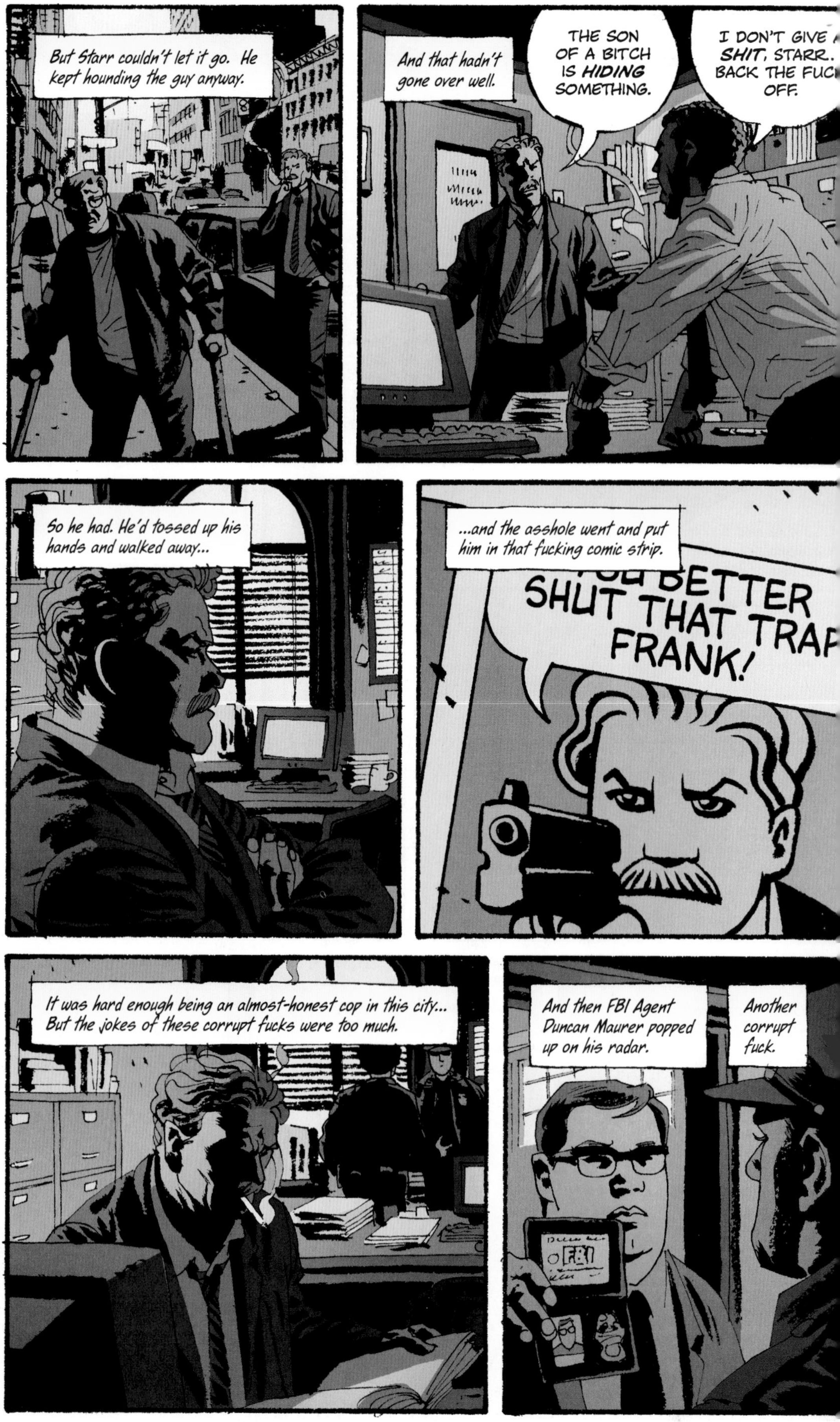
But Starr couldn't let it go. He kept hounding the guy anyway.
And that hadn't gone over well.
THE SON OF A BITCH IS *HIDING* SOMETHING.
I DON'T GIVE A *SHIT*, STARR. BACK THE FUC OFF.
So he had. He'd tossed up his hands and walked away...
...and the asshole went and put him in that fucking comic strip.
BETTER SHUT THAT TRAP FRANK!
It was hard enough being an almost-honest cop in this city... But the jokes of these corrupt fucks were too much.
And then FBI Agent Duncan Maurer popped up on his radar.
Another corrupt fuck.
FBI

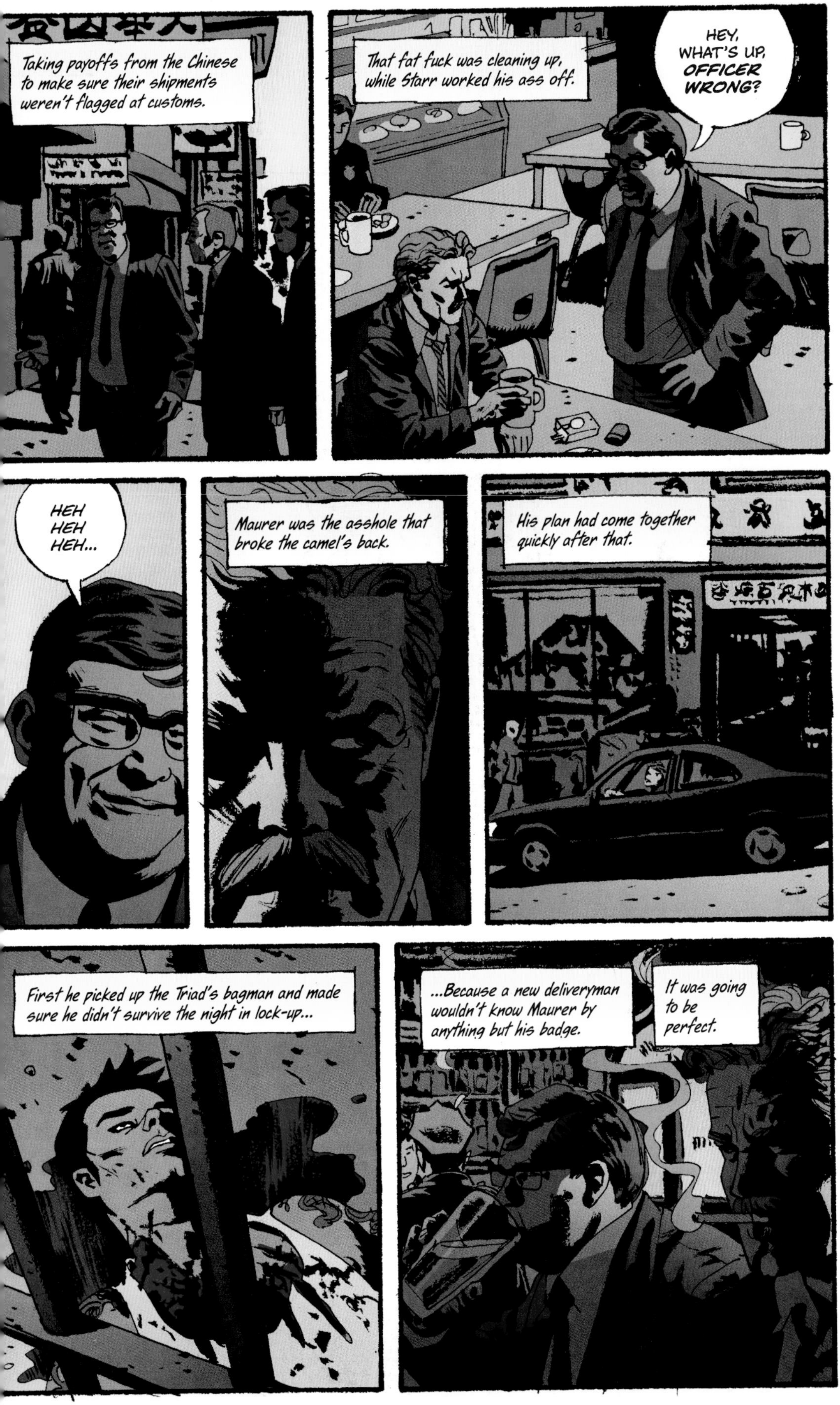
Taking payoffs from the Chinese to make sure their shipments weren't flagged at customs.
That fat fuck was cleaning up, while Starr worked his ass off.
HEY, WHAT'S UP, OFFICER WRONG?
HEH HEH HEH...
Maurer was the asshole that broke the camel's back.
His plan had come together quickly after that.
First he picked up the Triad's bagman and made sure he didn't survive the night in lock-up...
...Because a new deliveryman wouldn't know Maurer by anything but his badge.
It was going to be perfect.

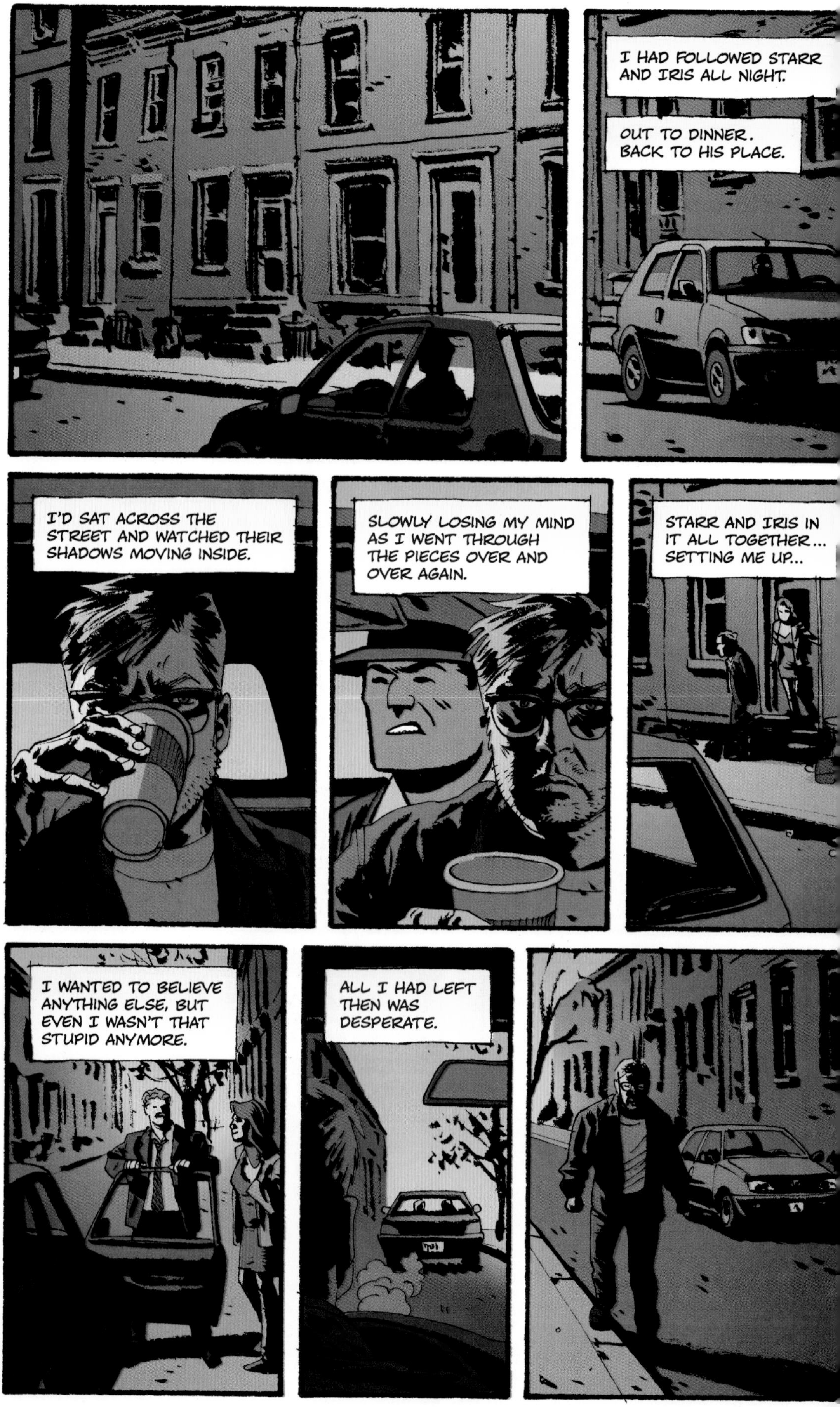
I HAD FOLLOWED STARR AND IRIS ALL NIGHT.
OUT TO DINNER. BACK TO HIS PLACE.
I'D SAT ACROSS THE STREET AND WATCHED THEIR SHADOWS MOVING INSIDE.
SLOWLY LOSING MY MIND AS I WENT THROUGH THE PIECES OVER AND OVER AGAIN.
STARR AND IRIS IN IT ALL TOGETHER... SETTING ME UP...
I WANTED TO BELIEVE ANYTHING ELSE, BUT EVEN I WASN'T THAT STUPID ANYMORE.
ALL I HAD LEFT THEN WAS DESPERATE.

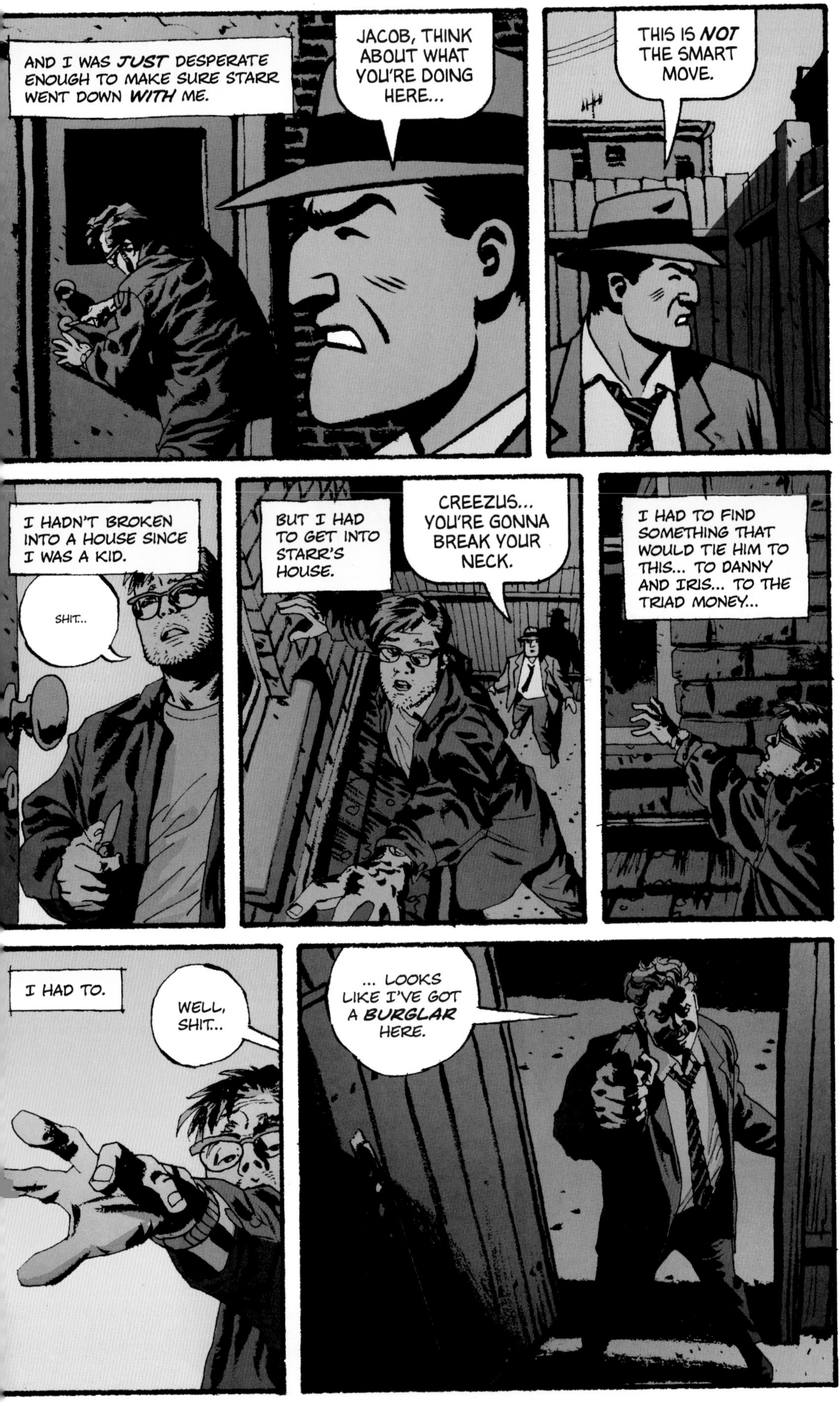
AND I WAS JUST DESPERATE ENOUGH TO MAKE SURE STARR WENT DOWN WITH ME.
JACOB, THINK ABOUT WHAT YOU'RE DOING HERE...
THIS IS NOT THE SMART MOVE.
I HADN'T BROKEN INTO A HOUSE SINCE I WAS A KID.
SHIT...
BUT I HAD TO GET INTO STARR'S HOUSE.
CREEZUS... YOU'RE GONNA BREAK YOUR NECK.
I HAD TO FIND SOMETHING THAT WOULD TIE HIM TO THIS... TO DANNY AND IRIS... TO THE TRIAD MONEY...
I HAD TO.
WELL, SHIT...
... LOOKS LIKE I'VE GOT A BURGLAR HERE.

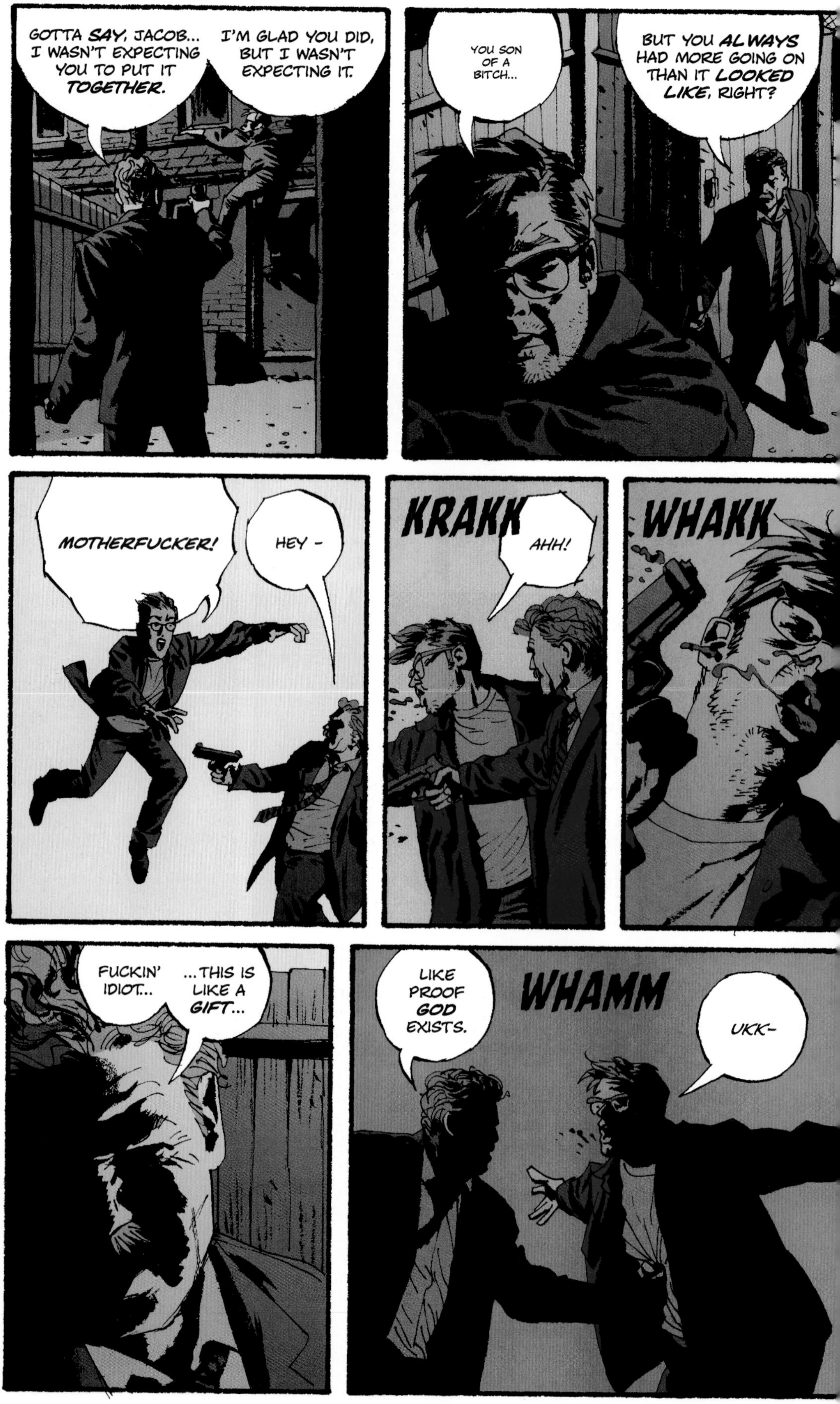
GOTTA SAY, JACOB... I WASN'T EXPECTING YOU TO PUT IT TOGETHER.
I'M GLAD YOU DID, BUT I WASN'T EXPECTING IT.
YOU SON OF A BITCH...
BUT YOU ALWAYS HAD MORE GOING ON THAN IT LOOKED LIKE, RIGHT?
MOTHERFUCKER!
HEY -
KRAKK
AHH!
WHAKK
FUCKIN' IDIOT...
...THIS IS LIKE A GIFT...
LIKE PROOF GOD EXISTS.
WHAMM
UKK-

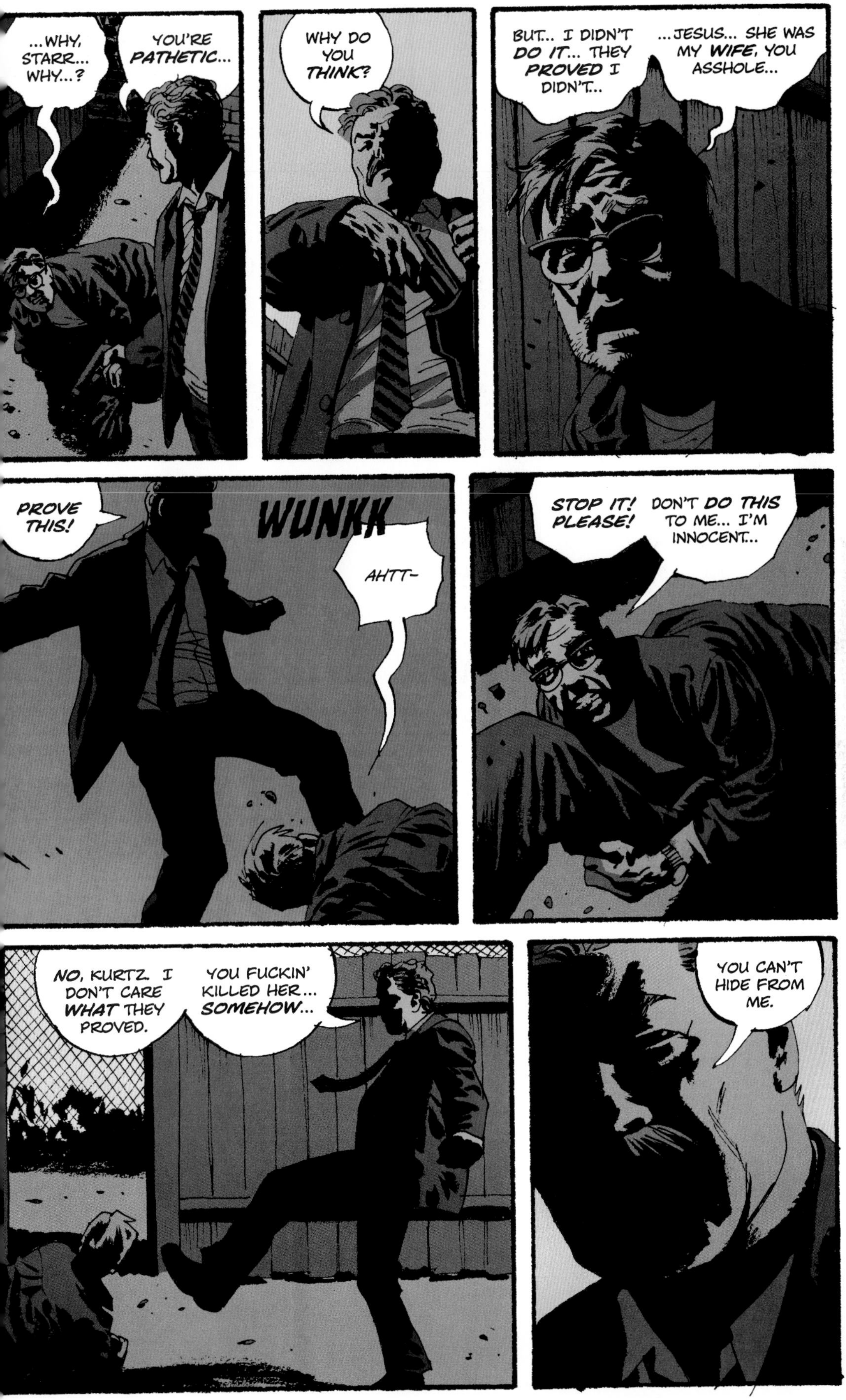
...WHY, STARR... WHY...?
YOU'RE PATHETIC...
WHY DO YOU THINK?
BUT... I DIDN'T DO IT... THEY PROVED I DIDN'T...
...JESUS... SHE WAS MY WIFE, YOU ASSHOLE...
PROVE THIS!
WUNKK
AHTT-
STOP IT! PLEASE!
DON'T DO THIS TO ME... I'M INNOCENT...
NO, KURTZ. I DON'T CARE WHAT THEY PROVED.
YOU FUCKIN' KILLED HER... SOMEHOW...
YOU CAN'T HIDE FROM ME.

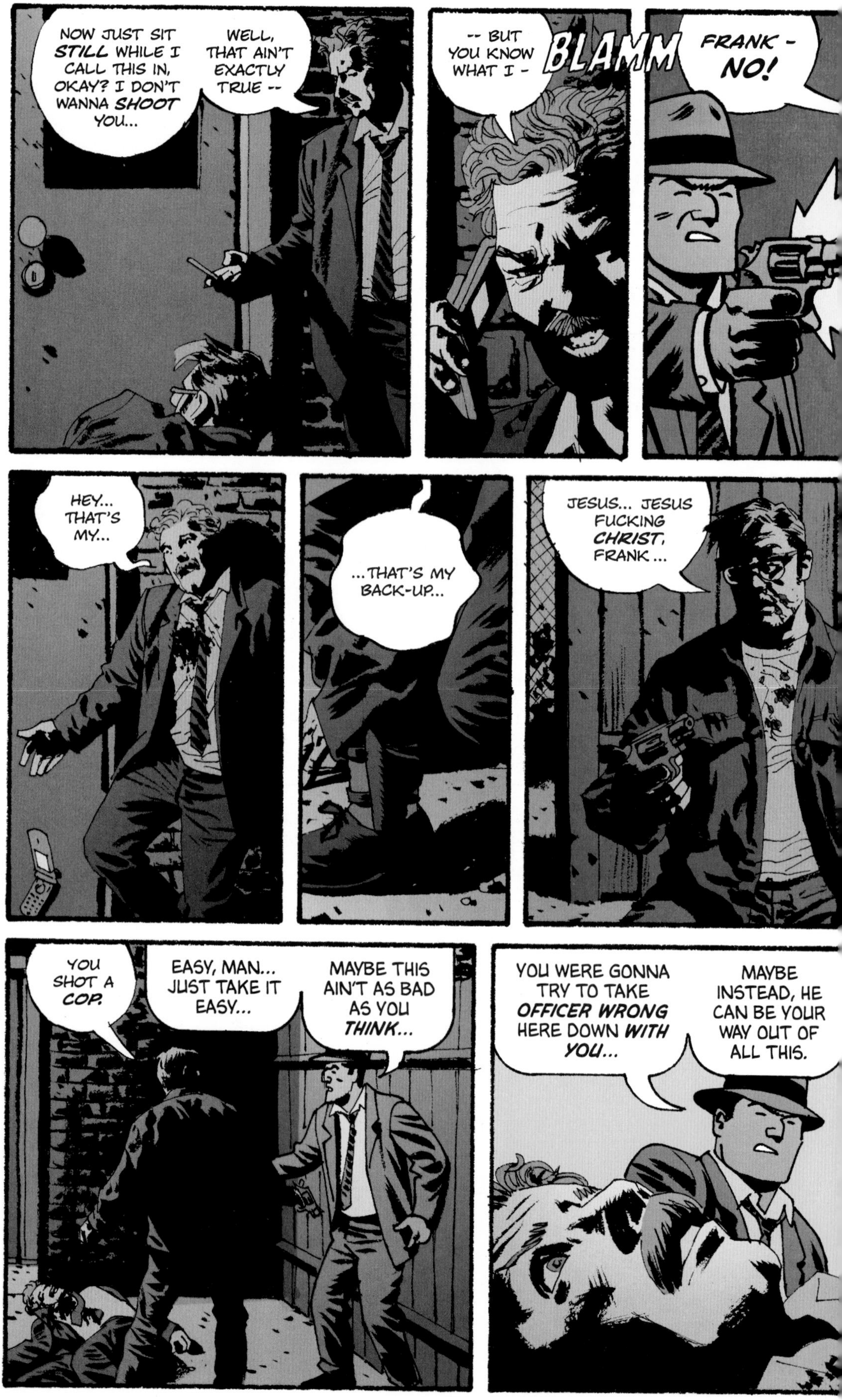
NOW JUST SIT STILL WHILE I CALL THIS IN, OKAY? I DON'T WANNA SHOOT YOU...
WELL, THAT AIN'T EXACTLY TRUE --
-- BUT YOU KNOW WHAT I -
BLAMM
FRANK - NO!
HEY... THAT'S MY...
...THAT'S MY BACK-UP...
JESUS... JESUS FUCKING CHRIST, FRANK...
YOU SHOT A COP.
EASY, MAN... JUST TAKE IT EASY...
MAYBE THIS AIN'T AS BAD AS YOU THINK...
YOU WERE GONNA TRY TO TAKE OFFICER WRONG HERE DOWN WITH YOU...
MAYBE INSTEAD, HE CAN BE YOUR WAY OUT OF ALL THIS.

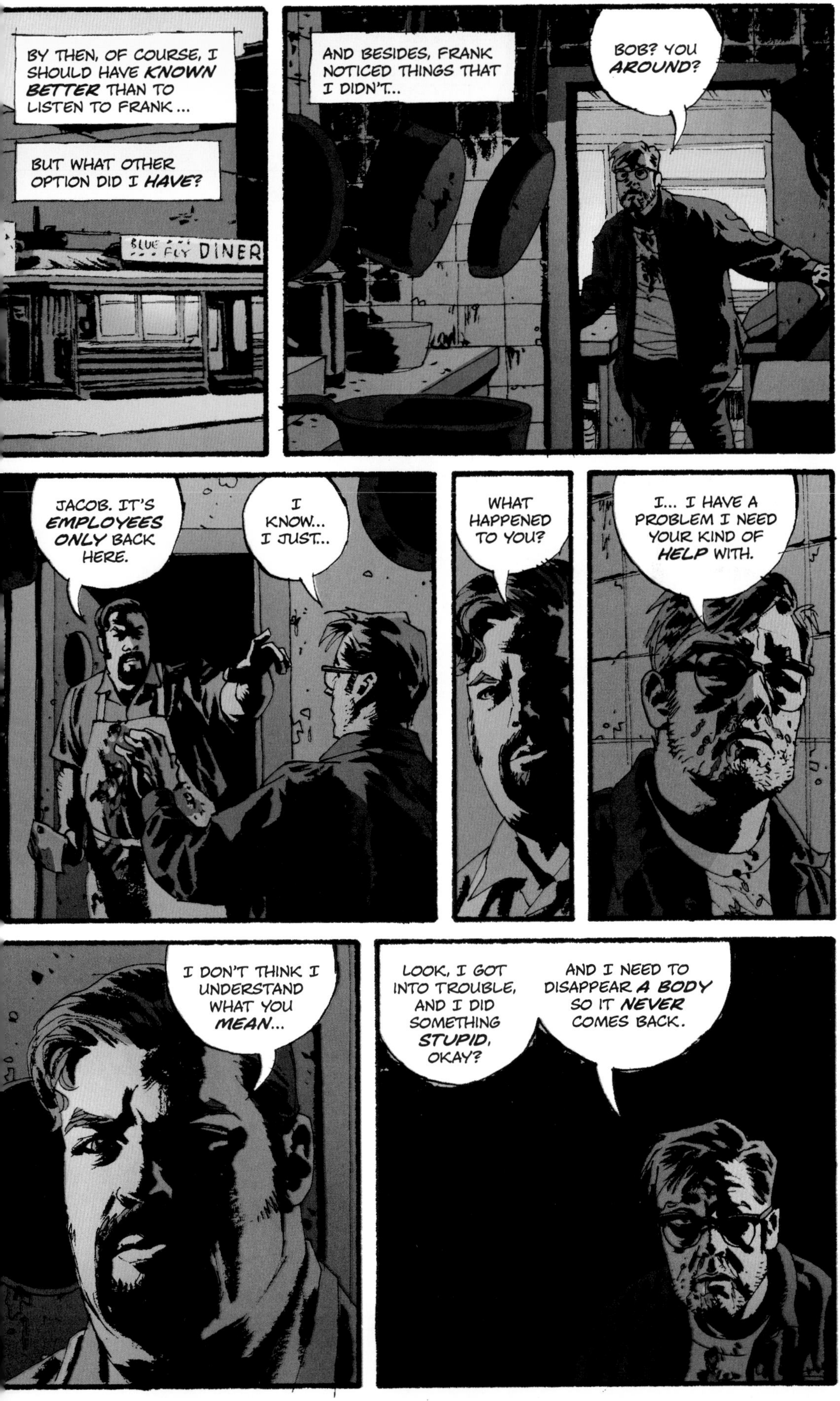
BY THEN, OF COURSE, I SHOULD HAVE KNOWN BETTER THAN TO LISTEN TO FRANK...
BUT WHAT OTHER OPTION DID I HAVE?
BLUE FLY DINER
AND BESIDES, FRANK NOTICED THINGS THAT I DIDN'T...
BOB? YOU AROUND?
JACOB. IT'S EMPLOYEES ONLY BACK HERE.
I KNOW... I JUST...
WHAT HAPPENED TO YOU?
I... I HAVE A PROBLEM I NEED YOUR KIND OF HELP WITH.
I DON'T THINK I UNDERSTAND WHAT YOU MEAN...
LOOK, I GOT INTO TROUBLE, AND I DID SOMETHING STUPID, OKAY?
AND I NEED TO DISAPPEAR A BODY SO IT NEVER COMES BACK.

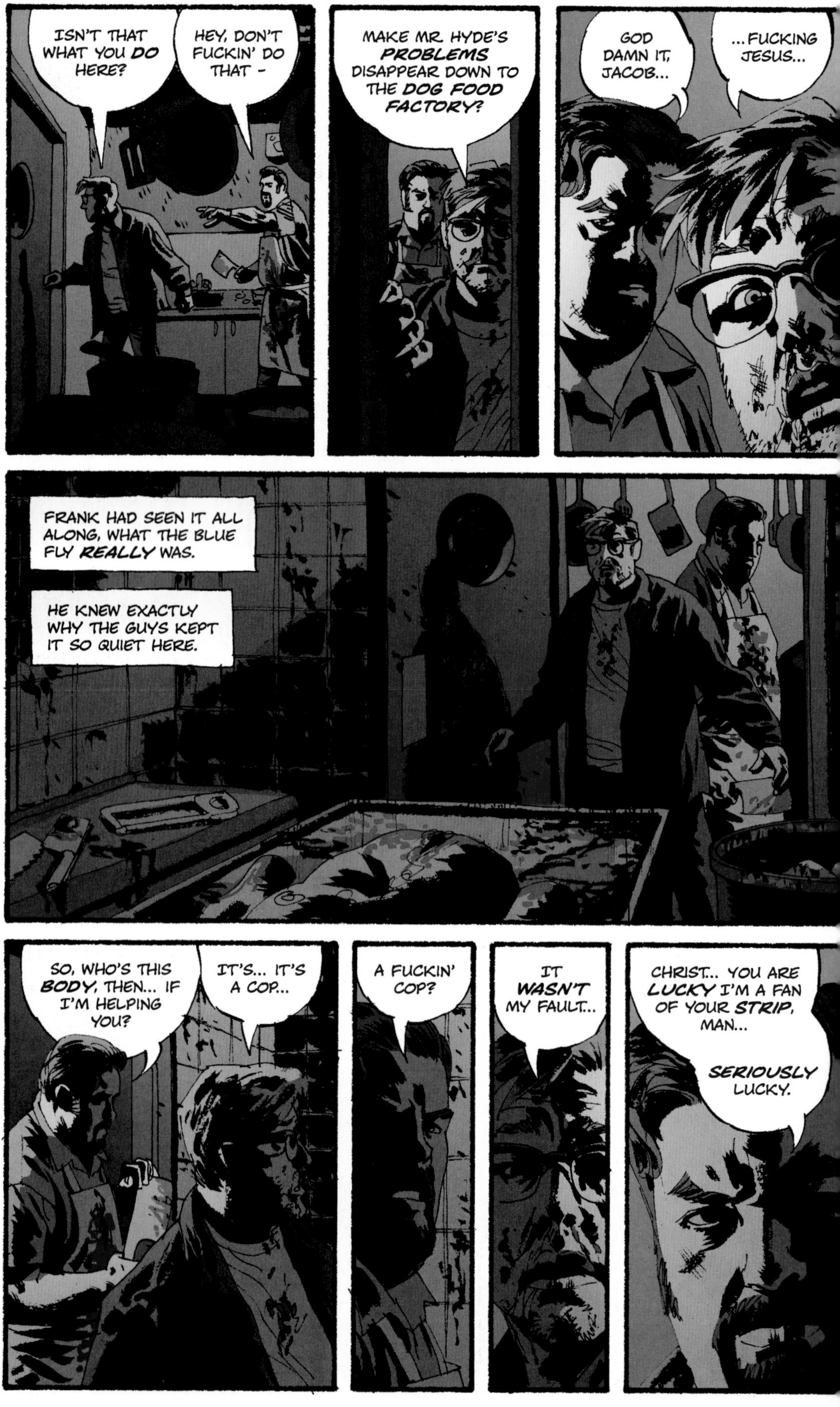
ISN'T THAT WHAT YOU DO HERE?
HEY, DON'T FUCKIN' DO THAT -
MAKE MR. HYDE'S PROBLEMS DISAPPEAR DOWN TO THE DOG FOOD FACTORY?
GOD DAMN IT, JACOB...
...FUCKING JESUS...
FRANK HAD SEEN IT ALL ALONG, WHAT THE BLUE FLY REALLY WAS.
HE KNEW EXACTLY WHY THE GUYS KEPT IT SO QUIET HERE.
SO, WHO'S THIS BODY, THEN... IF I'M HELPING YOU?
IT'S... IT'S A COP...
A FUCKIN' COP?
IT WASN'T MY FAULT...
CHRIST... YOU ARE LUCKY I'M A FAN OF YOUR STRIP, MAN...
SERIOUSLY LUCKY.

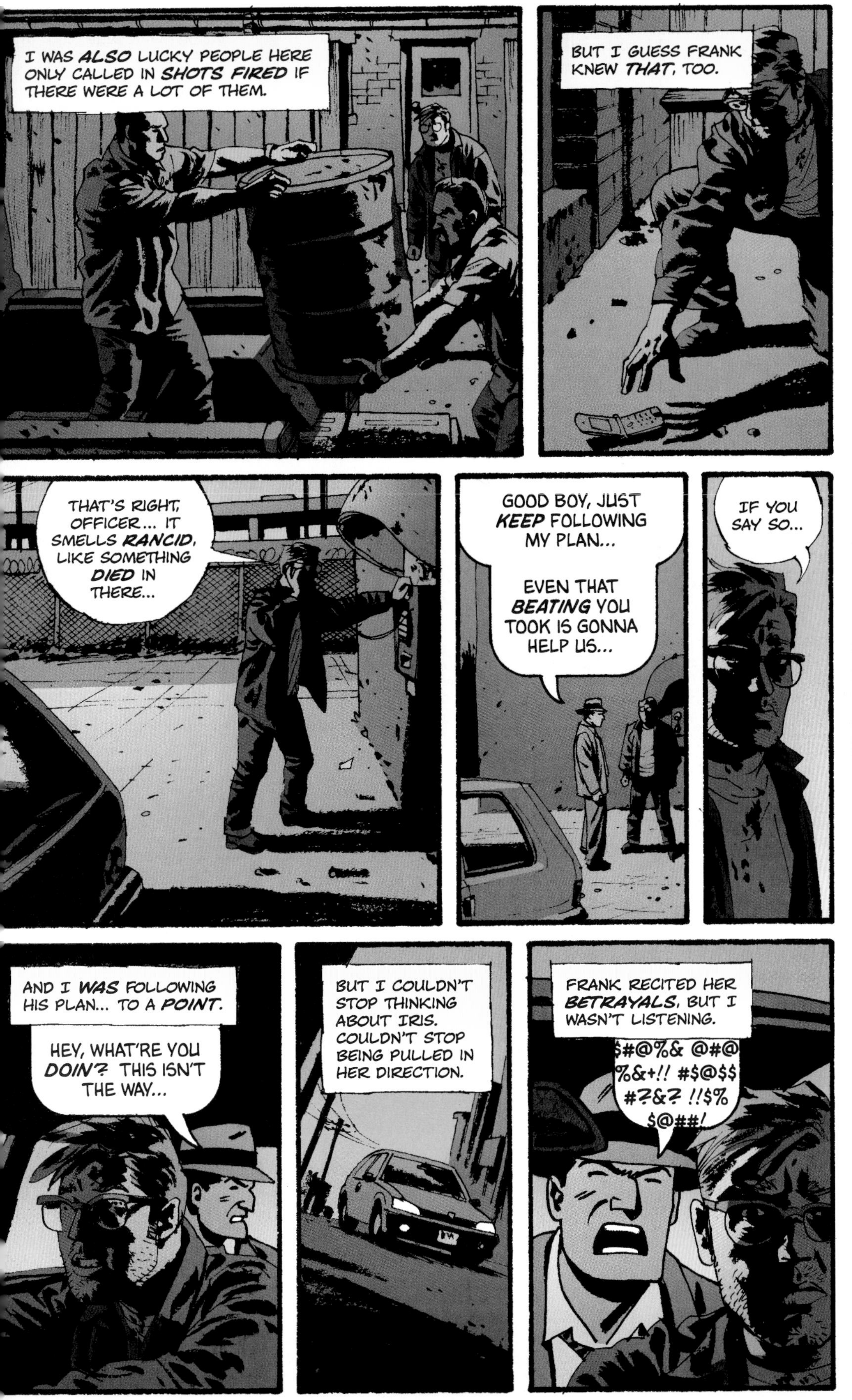
I WAS ALSO LUCKY PEOPLE HERE ONLY CALLED IN SHOTS FIRED IF THERE WERE A LOT OF THEM.
BUT I GUESS FRANK KNEW THAT, TOO.
THAT'S RIGHT, OFFICER... IT SMELLS RANCID, LIKE SOMETHING DIED IN THERE...
GOOD BOY, JUST KEEP FOLLOWING MY PLAN...
EVEN THAT BEATING YOU TOOK IS GONNA HELP US...
IF YOU SAY SO...
AND I WAS FOLLOWING HIS PLAN... TO A POINT.
HEY, WHAT'RE YOU DOIN'? THIS ISN'T THE WAY...
BUT I COULDN'T STOP THINKING ABOUT IRIS. COULDN'T STOP BEING PULLED IN HER DIRECTION.
FRANK RECITED HER BETRAYALS, BUT I WASN'T LISTENING.
$#@%& @#@ %&+!! #$@$$ #?&? !!$% $@##!

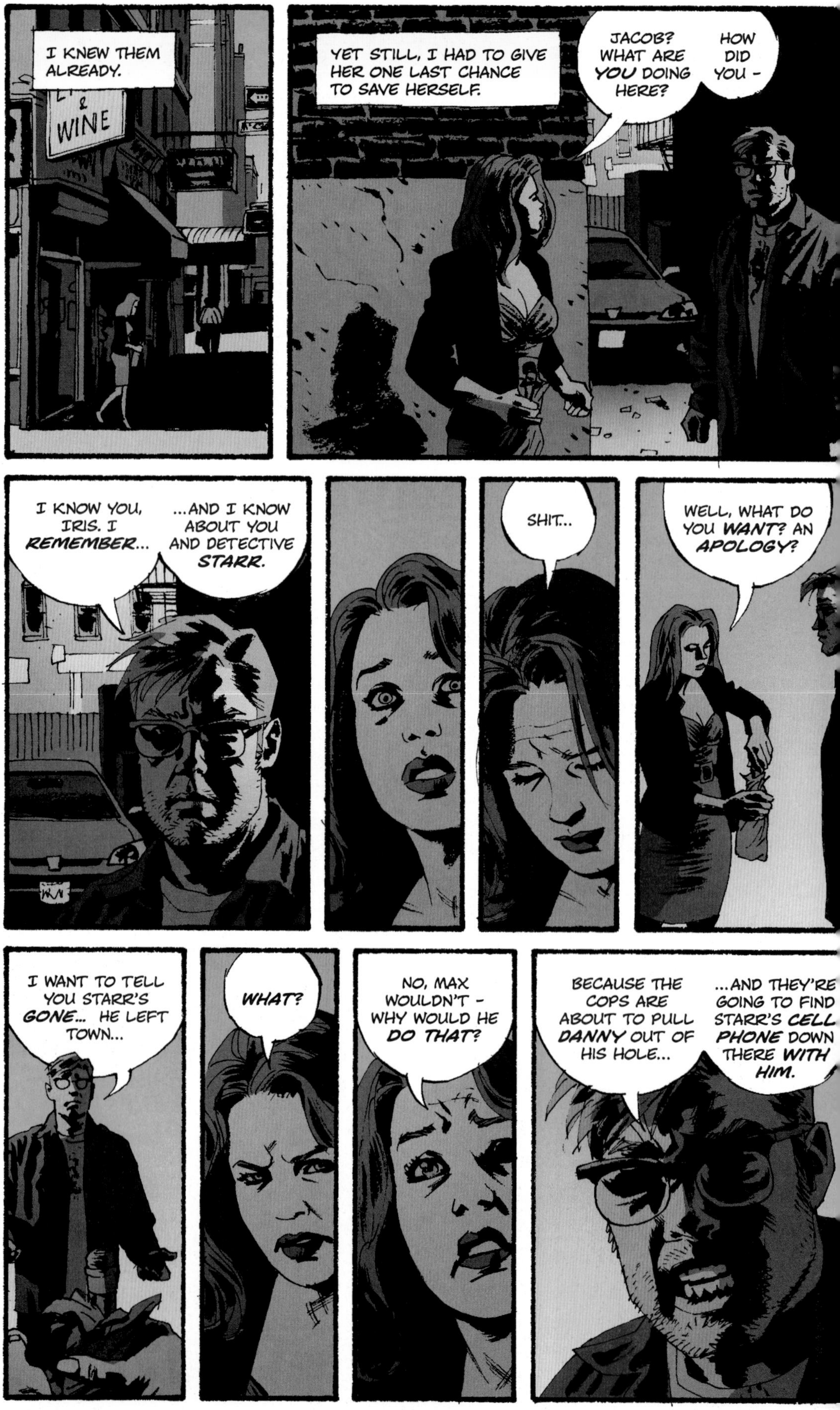
I KNEW THEM ALREADY.
WINE
YET STILL, I HAD TO GIVE HER ONE LAST CHANCE TO SAVE HERSELF.
JACOB? WHAT ARE YOU DOING HERE?
HOW DID YOU -
I KNOW YOU, IRIS. I REMEMBER...
...AND I KNOW ABOUT YOU AND DETECTIVE STARR.
SHIT...
WELL, WHAT DO YOU WANT? AN APOLOGY?
I WANT TO TELL YOU STARR'S GONE... HE LEFT TOWN...
WHAT?
NO, MAX WOULDN'T - WHY WOULD HE DO THAT?
BECAUSE THE COPS ARE ABOUT TO PULL DANNY OUT OF HIS HOLE...
...AND THEY'RE GOING TO FIND STARR'S CELL PHONE DOWN THERE WITH HIM.

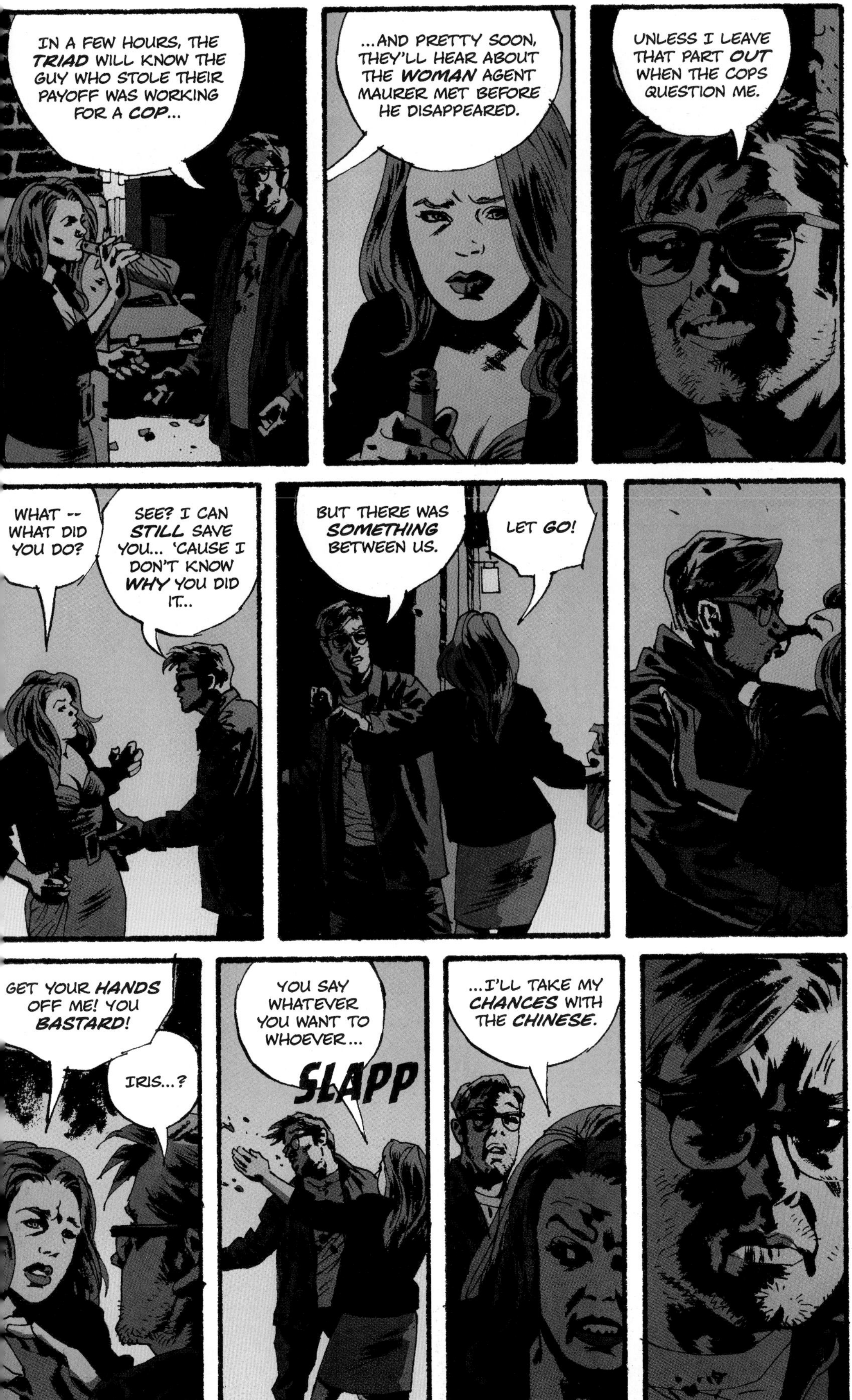
IN A FEW HOURS, THE *TRIAD* WILL KNOW THE GUY WHO STOLE THEIR PAYOFF WAS WORKING FOR A *COP*...
...AND PRETTY SOON, THEY'LL HEAR ABOUT THE *WOMAN* AGENT MAURER MET BEFORE HE DISAPPEARED.
UNLESS I LEAVE THAT PART *OUT* WHEN THE COPS QUESTION ME.
WHAT -- WHAT DID YOU DO?
SEE? I CAN *STILL* SAVE YOU... 'CAUSE I DON'T KNOW *WHY* YOU DID IT...
BUT THERE WAS *SOMETHING* BETWEEN US.
LET *GO*!
GET YOUR *HANDS* OFF ME! YOU *BASTARD*!
IRIS...?
YOU SAY WHATEVER YOU WANT TO WHOEVER...
SLAPP
...I'LL TAKE MY *CHANCES* WITH THE *CHINESE*.

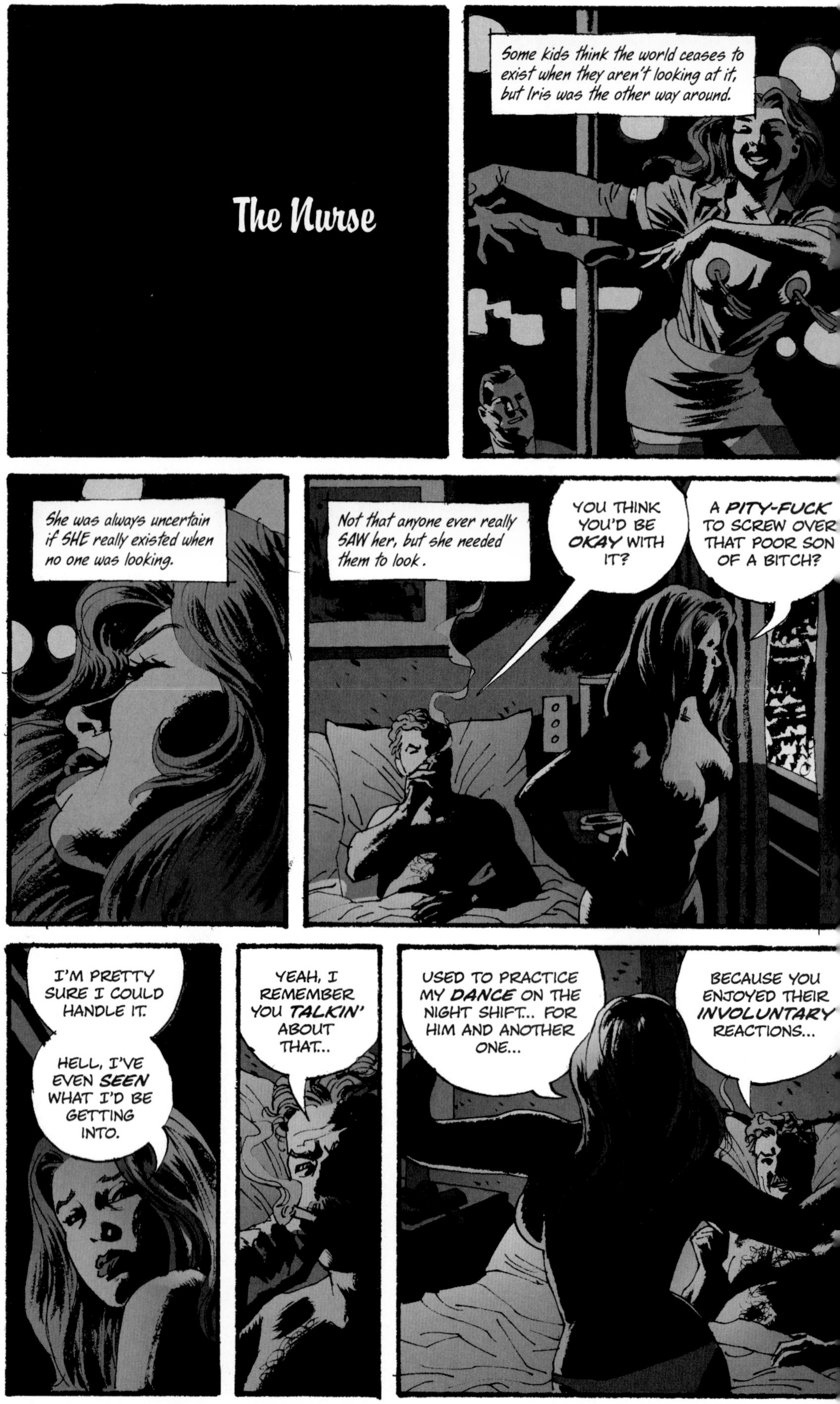
The Nurse
Some kids think the world ceases to exist when they aren't looking at it, but Iris was the other way around.
She was always uncertain if SHE really existed when no one was looking.
Not that anyone ever really SAW her, but she needed them to look.
YOU THINK YOU'D BE OKAY WITH IT?
A PITY-FUCK TO SCREW OVER THAT POOR SON OF A BITCH?
I'M PRETTY SURE I COULD HANDLE IT.
HELL, I'VE EVEN SEEN WHAT I'D BE GETTING INTO.
YEAH, I REMEMBER YOU TALKIN' ABOUT THAT...
USED TO PRACTICE MY DANCE ON THE NIGHT SHIFT... FOR HIM AND ANOTHER ONE...
BECAUSE YOU ENJOYED THEIR INVOLUNTARY REACTIONS...

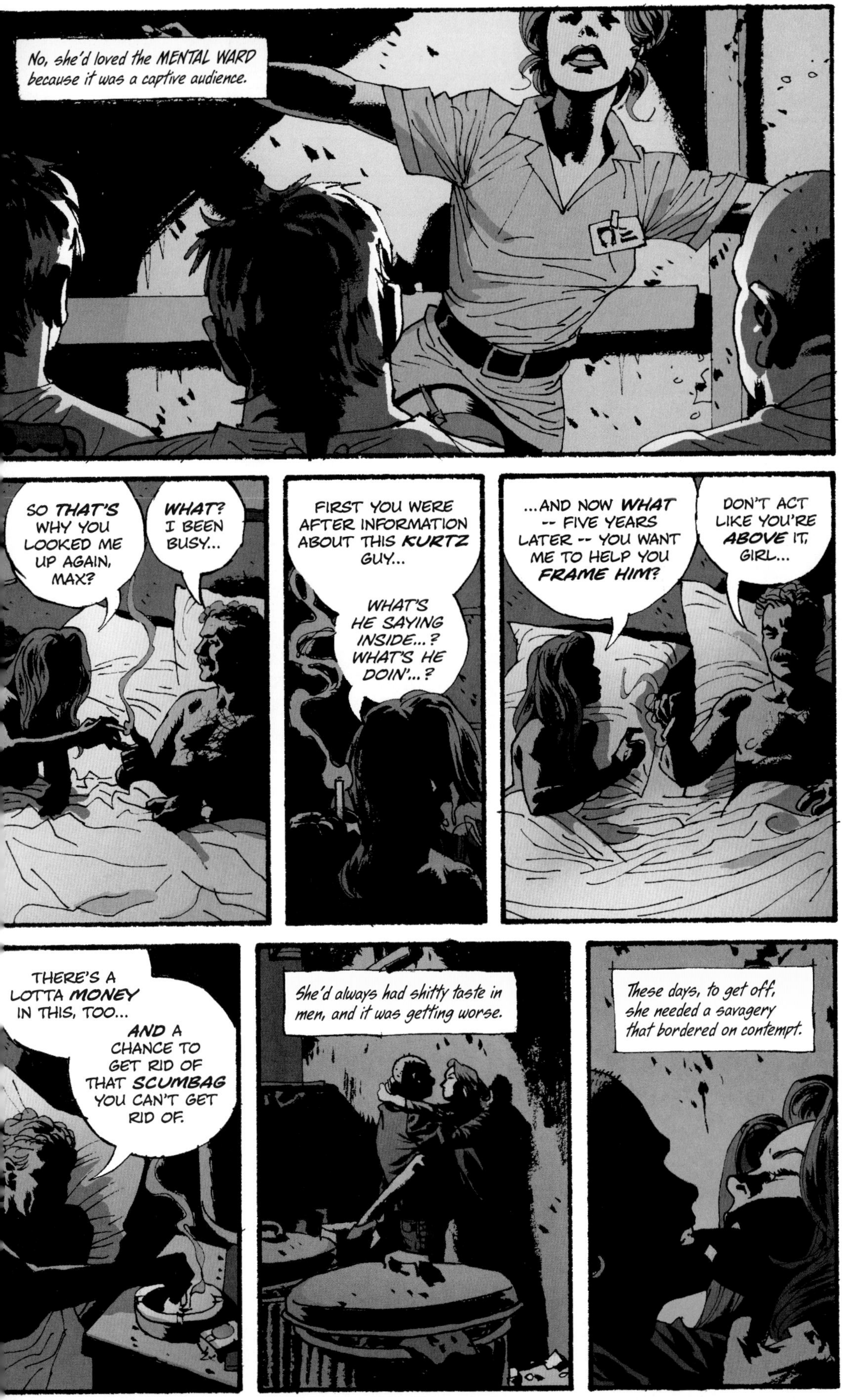
No, she'd loved the MENTAL WARD because it was a captive audience.
SO THAT'S WHY YOU LOOKED ME UP AGAIN, MAX?
WHAT? I BEEN BUSY...
FIRST YOU WERE AFTER INFORMATION ABOUT THIS KURTZ GUY...
WHAT'S HE SAYING INSIDE...? WHAT'S HE DOIN'...?
...AND NOW WHAT -- FIVE YEARS LATER -- YOU WANT ME TO HELP YOU FRAME HIM?
DON'T ACT LIKE YOU'RE ABOVE IT, GIRL...
THERE'S A LOTTA MONEY IN THIS, TOO...
AND A CHANCE TO GET RID OF THAT SCUMBAG YOU CAN'T GET RID OF.
She'd always had shitty taste in men, and it was getting worse.
These days, to get off, she needed a savagery that bordered on contempt.

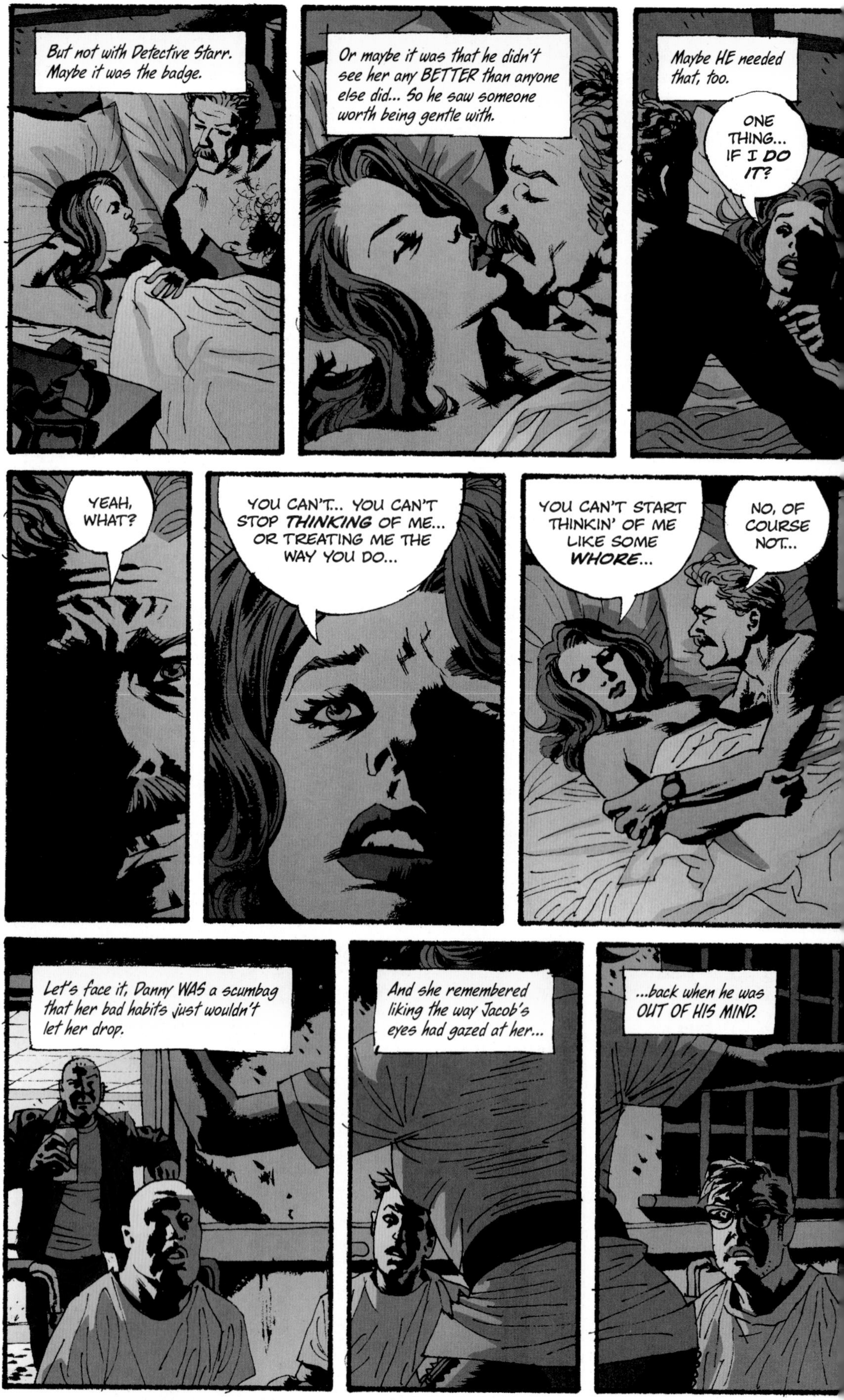

But not with Detective Starr. Maybe it was the badge.
Or maybe it was that he didn't see her any BETTER than anyone else did... So he saw someone worth being gentle with.
Maybe HE needed that, too.
ONE THING... IF I DO IT?
YEAH, WHAT?
YOU CAN'T... YOU CAN'T STOP THINKING OF ME... OR TREATING ME THE WAY YOU DO...
YOU CAN'T START THINKIN' OF ME LIKE SOME WHORE...
NO, OF COURSE NOT...
Let's face it, Danny WAS a scumbag that her bad habits just wouldn't let her drop.
And she remembered liking the way Jacob's eyes had gazed at her...
...back when he was OUT OF HIS MIND.

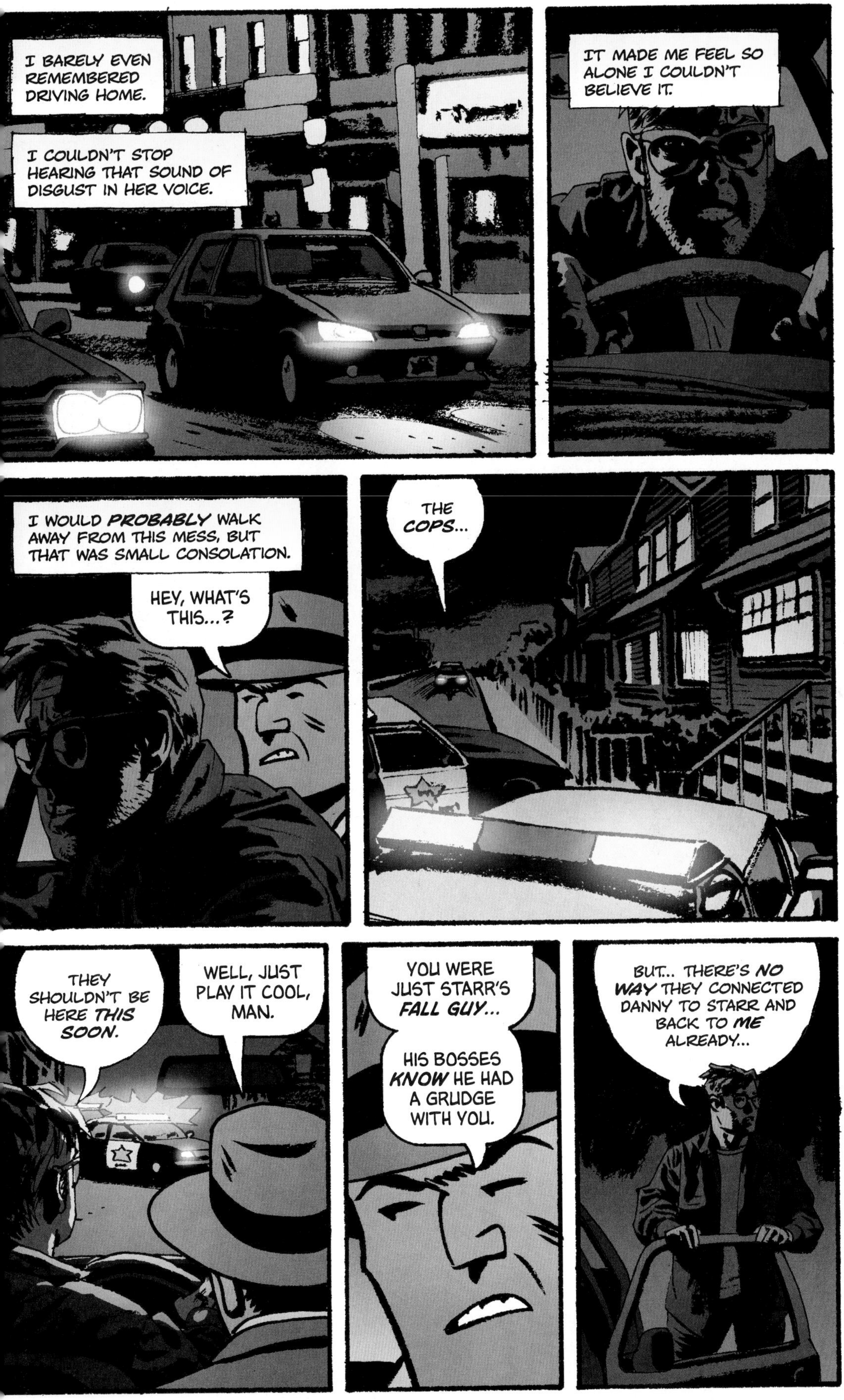
I BARELY EVEN REMEMBERED DRIVING HOME.
I COULDN'T STOP HEARING THAT SOUND OF DISGUST IN HER VOICE.
IT MADE ME FEEL SO ALONE I COULDN'T BELIEVE IT.
I WOULD PROBABLY WALK AWAY FROM THIS MESS, BUT THAT WAS SMALL CONSOLATION.
HEY, WHAT'S THIS...?
THE COPS...
THEY SHOULDN'T BE HERE THIS SOON.
WELL, JUST PLAY IT COOL, MAN.
YOU WERE JUST STARR'S FALL GUY...
HIS BOSSES KNOW HE HAD A GRUDGE WITH YOU.
BUT... THERE'S NO WAY THEY CONNECTED DANNY TO STARR AND BACK TO ME ALREADY...

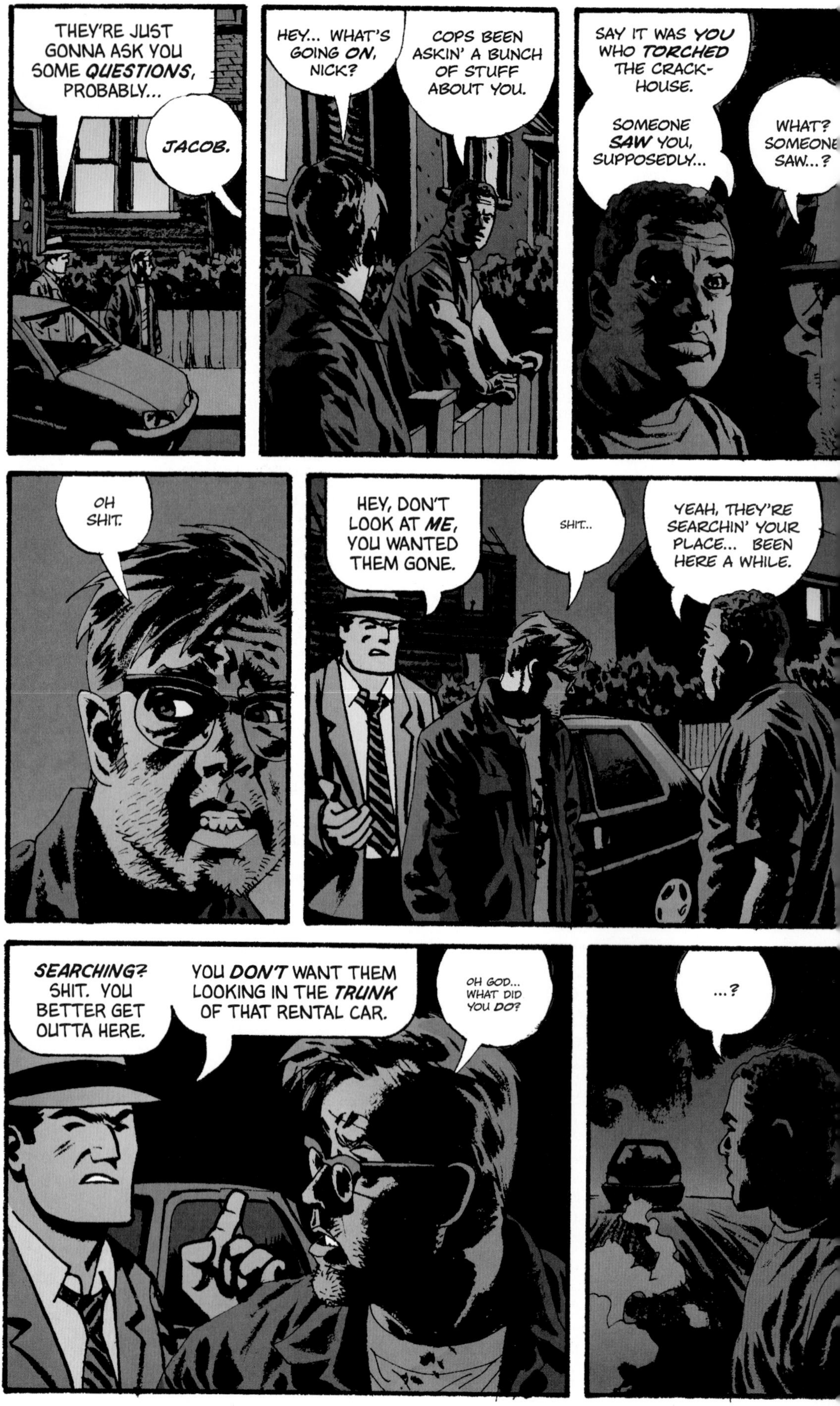
THEY'RE JUST GONNA ASK YOU SOME QUESTIONS, PROBABLY...
JACOB.
HEY... WHAT'S GOING ON, NICK?
COPS BEEN ASKIN' A BUNCH OF STUFF ABOUT YOU.
SAY IT WAS YOU WHO TORCHED THE CRACK-HOUSE.
SOMEONE SAW YOU, SUPPOSEDLY...
WHAT? SOMEONE SAW...?
OH SHIT.
HEY, DON'T LOOK AT ME, YOU WANTED THEM GONE.
SHIT...
YEAH, THEY'RE SEARCHIN' YOUR PLACE... BEEN HERE A WHILE.
SEARCHING? SHIT. YOU BETTER GET OUTTA HERE.
YOU DON'T WANT THEM LOOKING IN THE TRUNK OF THAT RENTAL CAR.
OH GOD... WHAT DID YOU DO?
...?

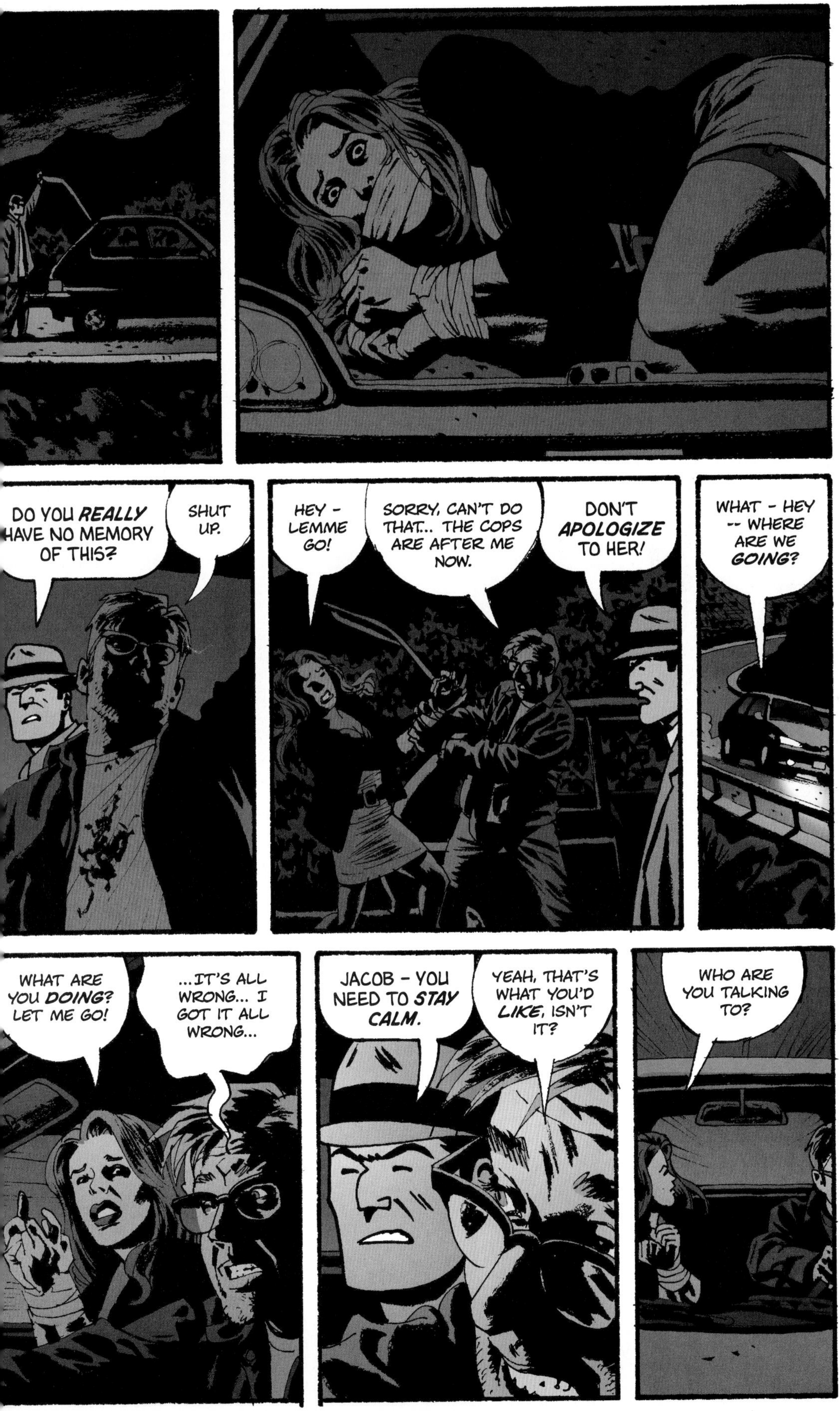
DO YOU REALLY HAVE NO MEMORY OF THIS?
SHUT UP.
HEY - LEMME GO!
SORRY, CAN'T DO THAT... THE COPS ARE AFTER ME NOW.
DON'T APOLOGIZE TO HER!
WHAT - HEY -- WHERE ARE WE GOING?
WHAT ARE YOU DOING? LET ME GO!
...IT'S ALL WRONG... I GOT IT ALL WRONG...
JACOB - YOU NEED TO STAY CALM.
YEAH, THAT'S WHAT YOU'D LIKE, ISN'T IT?
WHO ARE YOU TALKING TO?

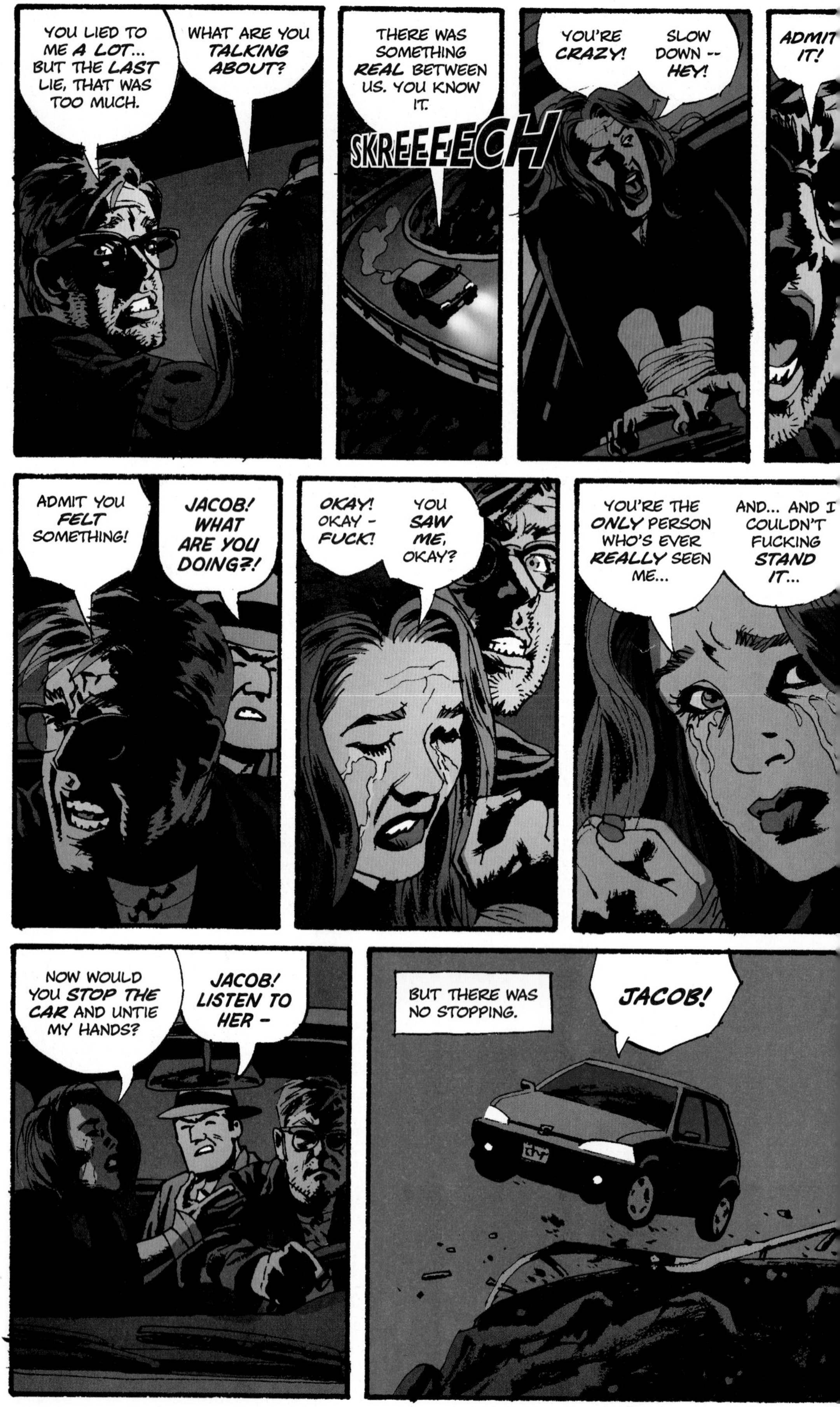

YOU LIED TO ME A LOT... BUT THE LAST LIE, THAT WAS TOO MUCH.
WHAT ARE YOU TALKING ABOUT?
THERE WAS SOMETHING REAL BETWEEN US. YOU KNOW IT.
SKREEEEECH
YOU'RE CRAZY!
SLOW DOWN -- HEY!
ADMIT IT!
ADMIT YOU FELT SOMETHING!
JACOB! WHAT ARE YOU DOING?!
OKAY! OKAY - FUCK!
YOU SAW ME, OKAY?
YOU'RE THE ONLY PERSON WHO'S EVER REALLY SEEN ME...
AND... AND I COULDN'T FUCKING STAND IT...
NOW WOULD YOU STOP THE CAR AND UNTIE MY HANDS?
JACOB! LISTEN TO HER -
BUT THERE WAS NO STOPPING.
JACOB!

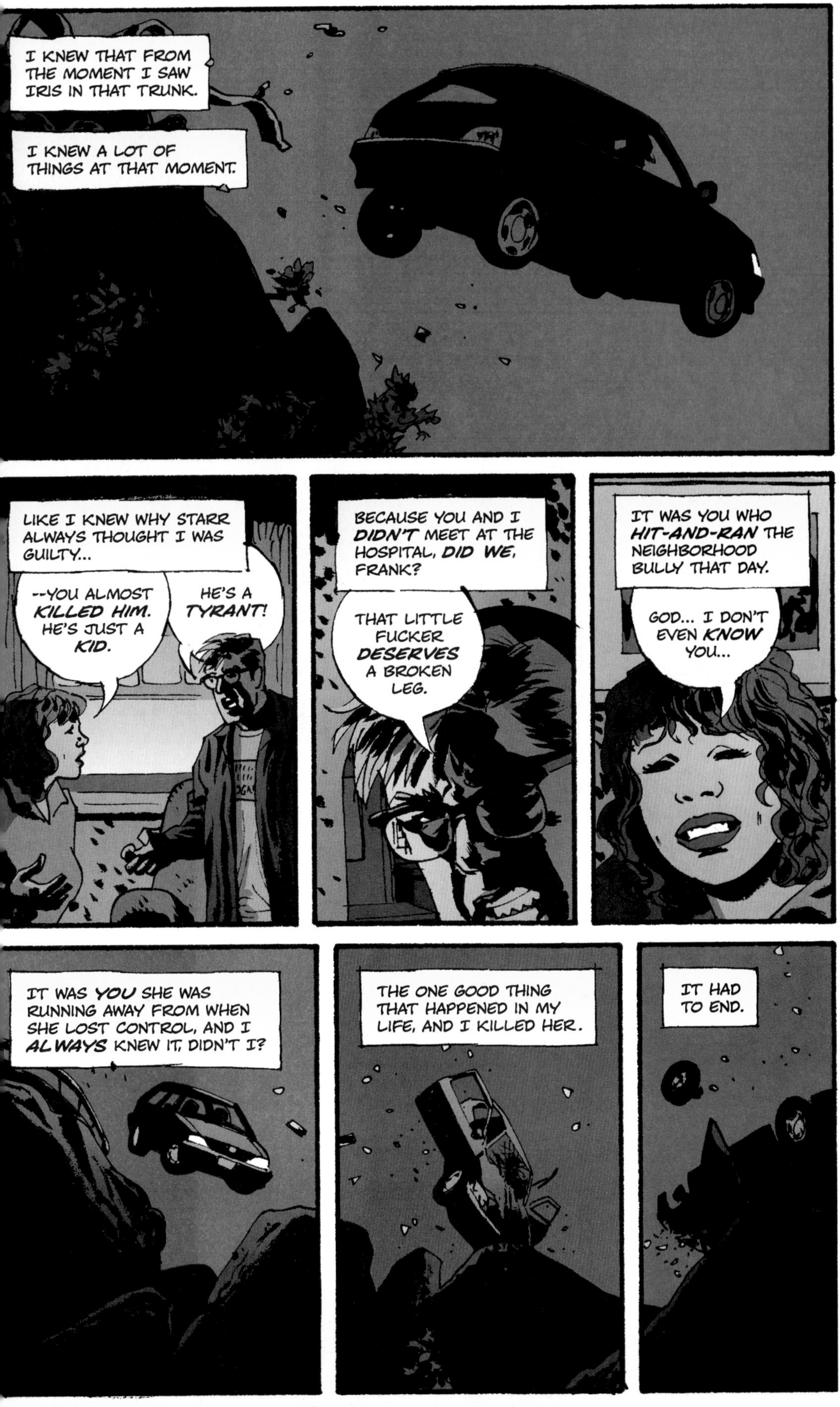
I KNEW THAT FROM THE MOMENT I SAW IRIS IN THAT TRUNK.
I KNEW A LOT OF THINGS AT THAT MOMENT.
LIKE I KNEW WHY STARR ALWAYS THOUGHT I WAS GUILTY...
--YOU ALMOST KILLED HIM. HE'S JUST A KID.
HE'S A TYRANT!
BECAUSE YOU AND I DIDN'T MEET AT THE HOSPITAL, DID WE, FRANK?
THAT LITTLE FUCKER DESERVES A BROKEN LEG.
IT WAS YOU WHO HIT-AND-RAN THE NEIGHBORHOOD BULLY THAT DAY.
GOD... I DON'T EVEN KNOW YOU...
IT WAS YOU SHE WAS RUNNING AWAY FROM WHEN SHE LOST CONTROL, AND I ALWAYS KNEW IT, DIDN'T I?
THE ONE GOOD THING THAT HAPPENED IN MY LIFE, AND I KILLED HER.
IT HAD TO END.

BUT THEN, THAT WOULD BE TOO EASY, WOULDN'T IT?

MISTER KURTZ? CAN HE HEAR ME?

I DON'T KNOW. JACOB, ARE YOU AWAKE?

I *REALLY* WANTED TO TALK TO HIM.

OH, HE CAN HEAR YOU... AND SOMETIMES HE STILL TALKS.

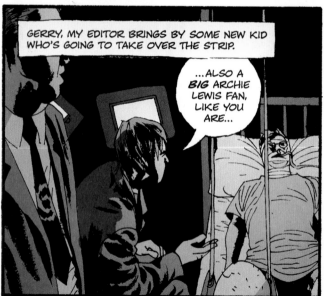

GERRY, MY EDITOR BRINGS BY SOME NEW KID WHO'S GOING TO TAKE OVER THE STRIP.

...ALSO A *BIG* ARCHIE LEWIS FAN, LIKE YOU ARE...

TURNS OUT, *FRANK KAFKA, PRIVATE EYE* IS MORE POPULAR THAN EVER, THANKS TO MY RECENT INFAMY.

... FINISHING YOUR LAST ARC. THE GUY TURNS *INTO* THE SECURITY DOG?

THE AUTHORITIES CAN'T QUITE FIGURE IT ALL OUT, BUT THEY *MOSTLY* BLAME STARR, WHO'S THOUGHT TO BE ON THE RUN.

THE *MISSING* GUY, I MEAN? IS THAT RIGHT?

I WON'T BE CORRECTING THEM ON THAT.

DON'T WORRY ABOUT IT, KEVIN... YOU'LL FIGURE IT OUT.

YOU HIS FRIENDS?

SORT OF.

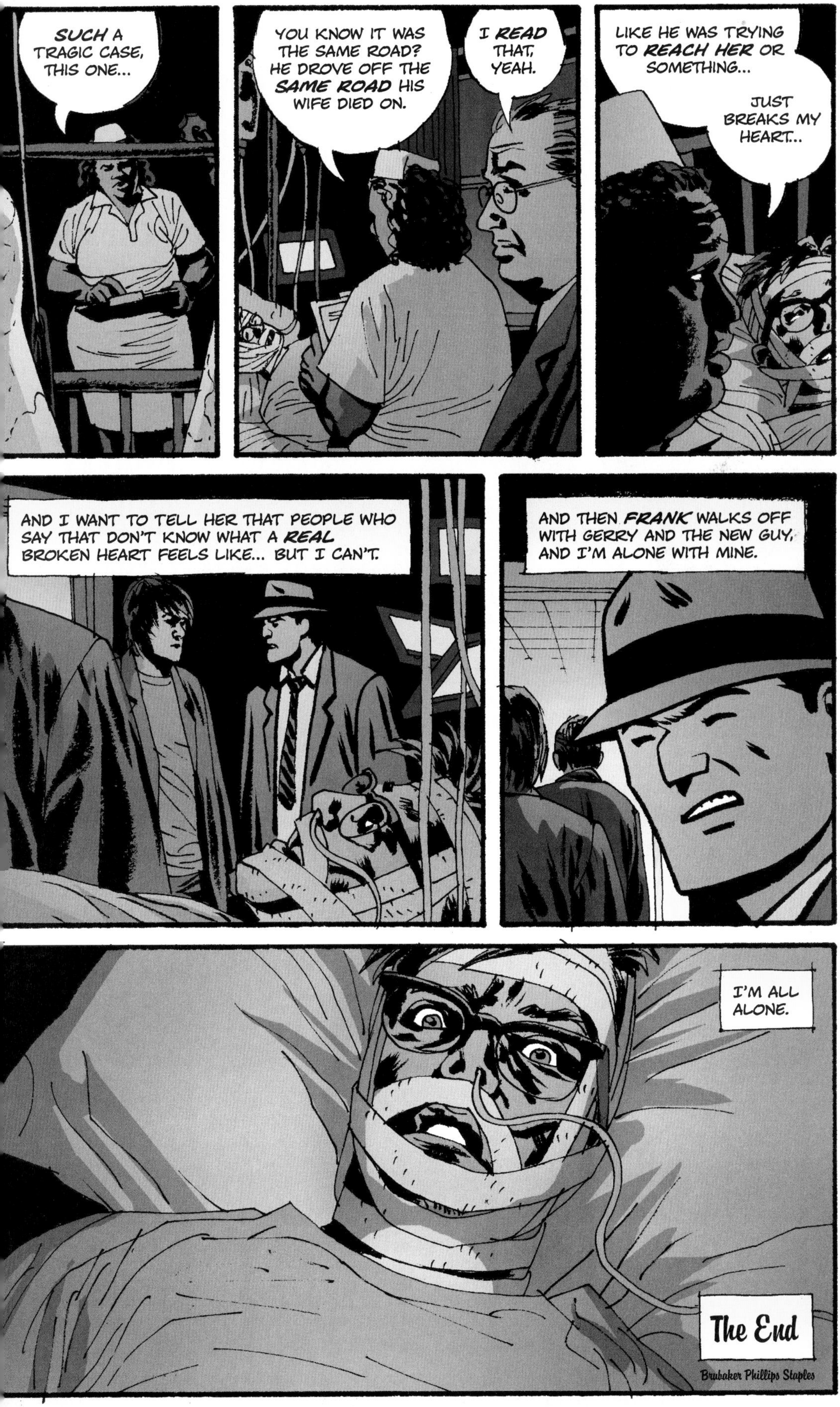
SUCH A TRAGIC CASE, THIS ONE...
YOU KNOW IT WAS THE SAME ROAD? HE DROVE OFF THE SAME ROAD HIS WIFE DIED ON.
I READ THAT, YEAH.
LIKE HE WAS TRYING TO REACH HER OR SOMETHING...
JUST BREAKS MY HEART...
AND I WANT TO TELL HER THAT PEOPLE WHO SAY THAT DON'T KNOW WHAT A REAL BROKEN HEART FEELS LIKE... BUT I CAN'T.
AND THEN FRANK WALKS OFF WITH GERRY AND THE NEW GUY, AND I'M ALONE WITH MINE.
I'M ALL ALONE.
The End
Brubaker Phillips Staples

ritten by ED BRUBAKER and drawn by SEAN PHILLIPS

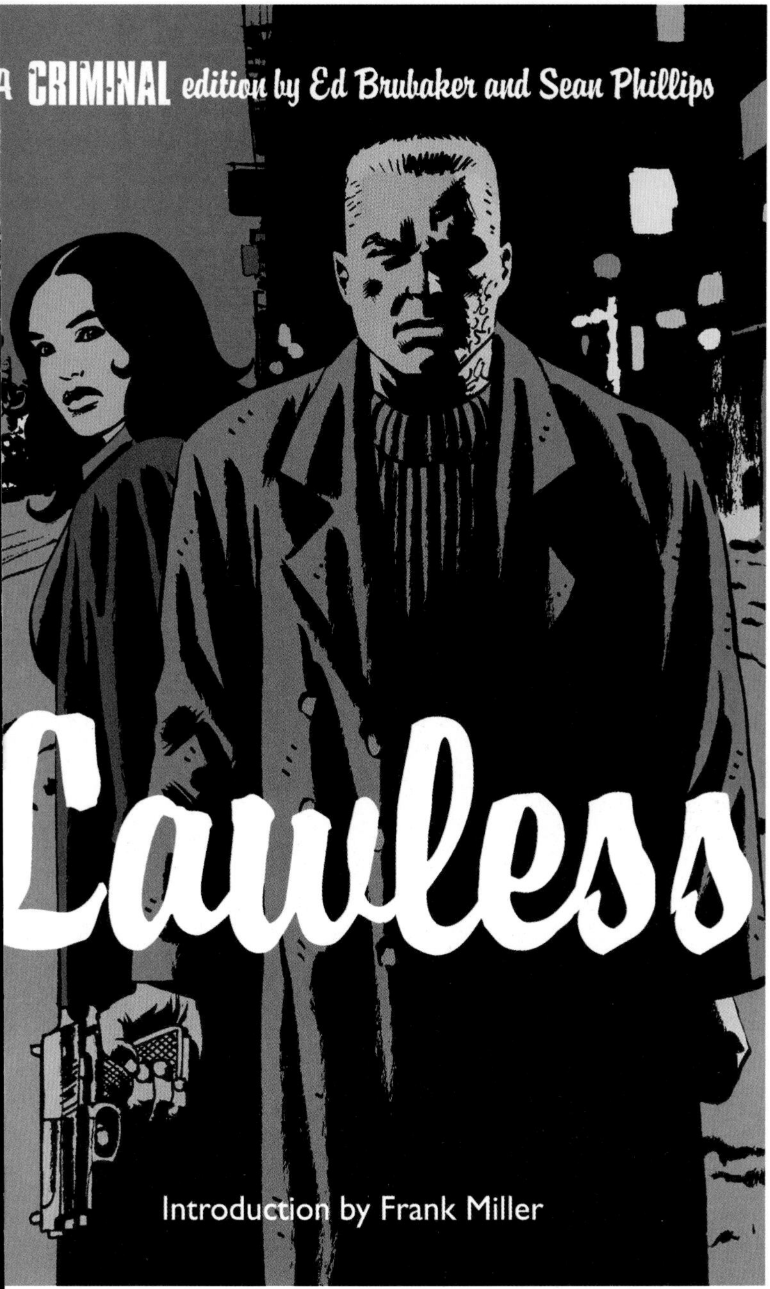

A CRIMINAL edition by Ed Brubaker and Sean Phillips
Lawless
Introduction by Frank Miller

" ...dark and genius..."
David S. Goyer (Batman Begins)

"...spot on, and wonderfully unforgiving."
Frank Miller (Sin City, 300)

"...really f*cking good."
Warren Ellis (Planetary, Fell, Thunderbolts)

"...fine-tuning a well worn genre."
Entertainment Weekly

"...won't find a better crime story than this."
Nashville City Paper

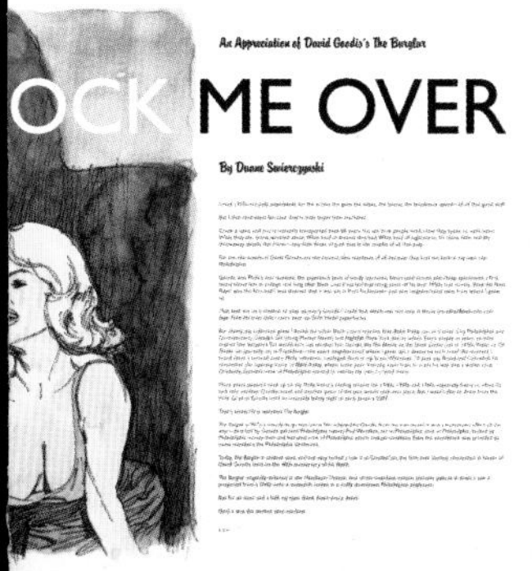

An Appreciation of David Goodis's The Burglar
OCK ME OVER
By Duane Swierczynski

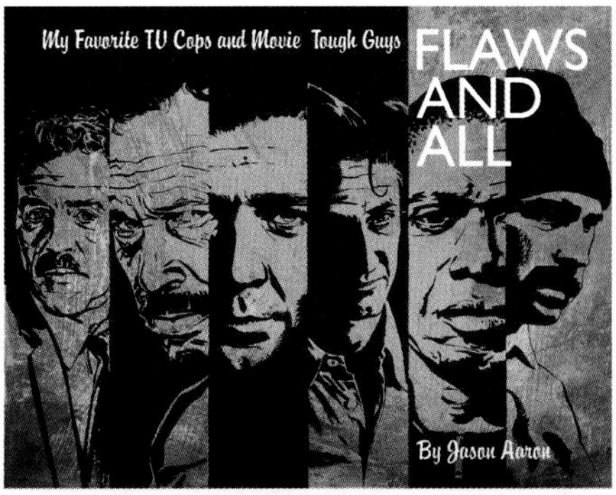

My Favorite TV Cops and Movie Tough Guys
FLAWS AND ALL
By Jason Aaron

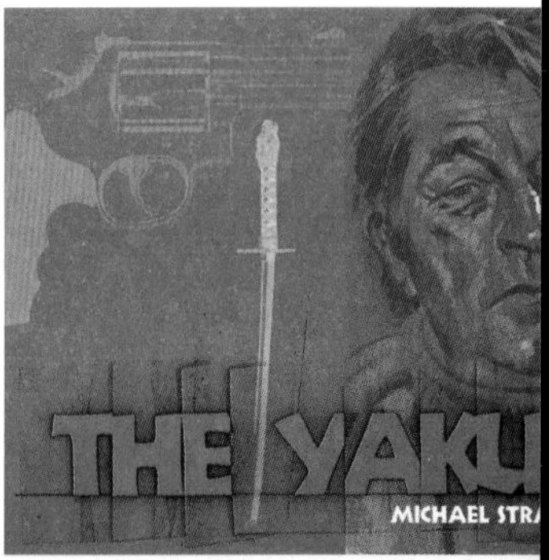

THE YAKU
MICHAEL STR

o Available In Single Issue Form With Additional Material